In the Eye of the Storm

In the Eye of the Storm

A Memoir

Kurt Waldheim

ADLER&ADLER

Published in the United States in 1986 by
Adler & Adler, Publishers, Inc.
4550 Montgomery Avenue
Bethesda, Maryland 20814

Originally published in Great Britain by
George Weidenfeld & Nicolson Limited
91 Clapham High Street
London SW4 7TA

Library of Congress Cataloging in Publication Data

Waldheim, Kurt.
In the eye of the storm.

1. Waldheim, Kurt.   2.   United Nations. Secretary
General—Biography.   3.   Statesmen—Austria—Biography.
4.   World politics—1975–1985.   I. Title
D839.7.W34A34   1986   341.23.'24 [B]   85–14215
ISBN 0–917561–08–2

Printed in the United States of America

First U.S. Edition

Contents

Foreword

This is not a book of memoirs in the ordinary sense, nor is it a comprehensive account of events during my term of office as Secretary General of the United Nations. Had I embarked upon either task, it would have taken me far beyond the confines of this present endeavour.

Instead I have attempted to offer some insight into my background, actions and aspirations. Without dwelling upon the routine and frustrations that are also the hallmarks of any arduous career, I have described those events and episodes which I feel bear some significance for the course of history.

During my forty years of diplomatic service, and in particular during those ten years of close association through the United Nations with the crises and conflicts of the world, I have been granted an unparalleled opportunity to observe – and to some extent influence – the attempts of nations to cope, through collective action, with violence, terror and human suffering. I trust this book will explain why, in certain cases, I acted as I did; what objectives I had in mind; and where I succeeded or failed. If it helps in some small way to achieve that aim, it will have served its purpose.

Acknowledgements

In writing this book, I benefited from the help and advice of many friends and colleagues. Special acknowledgement is due to the sound judgement and unstinting labours of David Popper, who devoted countless days and nights to sorting the wheat from the chaff, staking out the territory to be covered and providing essential detail. I owe special thanks to the literary and editorial contribution of Brian Connell, whose wife, Esme, tirelessly typed initial drafts. His professionalism and expertise made the task so much easier. My sincere thanks also go to Alex MacCormick for her able and stalwart editorial services. Moreover, I am most pleased to acknowledge the extensive help I received from Heinz Nussbaumer, who provided much wise counsel and proved an indispensable intellectual foil.

I wish to place on record my particular thanks to my colleagues in the Secretariat of the United Nations: Raffeuddin Ahmed, Brian Urquhart, Diego Cordovez, George Davidson, George Sherry, James Jonah, André Lewin, Charles Gaulkin, Remy Gorgé, Georg Mautner-Markhof, Rudi Stajduhar and Ferdinand Mayrhofer-Grünbühel. They – and many others in the service of the United Nations –·have contributed to 'the table of my memory', while others, such as Louis Halasz, contributed from the world of journalism. My thanks are also due to my colleagues in the Austrian foreign service, especially Albert Rohan and Anton Prohaska.

Throughout this undertaking I was supported by the dedicated archival research of Christine Ropp, Aurelia Bachmayr, Alain Rouvez and Christopher Hoh at Georgetown University in Washington, DC and the indefatigable enthusiasm of Rosemary Zaleski and Marica Buranich in Vienna.

By no means out of mere convention do I express my sincere gratitude to my wife, Cissy, and my children for the unfailing encouragement and sound advice they have always given as well as the endless patience and understanding they have shown.

ACKNOWLEDGEMENTS

In the course of writing this book I have come to appreciate the frailty of memory. I shall never aspire to the excellence of Mark Twain, whose memory in his youth was reputed to be so good that he could even recall things that never happened. However, with the help of all those named above and many others unnamed, I trust that I have been able to recall the most important things that did happen.

1

Nightmare in Teheran

It was a distinctly forlorn, not to say apprehensive, small group which flew from New York to Paris by Concorde on New Year's Eve 1979 to stay overnight at the airport hotel. I had with me my Pakistani *chef de cabinet*, my young Austrian personal assistant, my French spokesman (of Corsican descent) and a single American United Nations security guard. The gloomy, wintry evening reflected only too well the mood of uncertainty we all felt about this completely unpredictable mission on which we were about to embark. In this sombre atmosphere I was somewhat cheered by a telephone call wishing us well from President Giscard d'Estaing and a courtesy visit from his Foreign Minister, Jean François-Poncet. Shortly before midnight I called my family in New York to wish them a happy New Year and also my daughter, Liselotte, in Geneva. She said I sounded troubled. Indeed I was.

I had undertaken a personal initiative under the auspices of the United Nations to solve the Iranian hostage crisis. On 4 November the revolutionary students had stormed the American embassy in Teheran. This outrage had convulsed the chanceries of every nation and generated feverish activity at the UN, where the Iranians maintained representatives throughout the crisis, their instructions and attitudes contradictory and wavering from day to day. The fundamental problem was to find any centre of power in Iran answerable for the chaotic turmoil in the capital.

There was no doubt as to the glaring illegality of the seizure of the embassy and the holding of its staff as hostages. The duty of a receiving government to guarantee personal immunity and protection to the diplomatic personnel of another state stationed on its territory is one of the most firmly established principles in international law. That duty had been reaffirmed and defined in detail in the Vienna Convention on Diplomatic Relations of 1961. Similar guarantees were contained in the 1955 Treaty of Amity between the United States and Iran. Both governments had agreed to submit disputes arising under these treaties to the International Court of Justice for adjudication.

The Security Council had responded with singular swiftness. By 9 November – only five days after the seizure of the hostages – it had met and called for the release of the fifty-two Americans. Four days later the Iranian Foreign Minister, Abolhassan Bani-Sadr, had responded with a message requesting a meeting of the Council to hear Iran's case and proposing that the United States should agree to an examination of the guilt of the former Shah and return his property and assets. He indicated that he would attend in person to present his government's case.

The Americans would have vetoed any Council meeting based on the Iranian agenda, but they regarded this as an opening, and the very next day Secretary of State Cyrus Vance and Harold Saunders, the Assistant Secretary for Near Eastern affairs, came to New York to consult with me at several secret meetings. To escape detection they even drove up to my residence in an ordinary yellow cab. We worked out the elements of a package solution that we thought might satisfy both sides. It called for the release of the hostages; establishment of a commission of enquiry into allegations of gross violations of human rights in Iran under the Shah's regime; American agreement that Iran could press its claims in American courts for assets allegedly removed illegally; and an undertaking to abide by the provisions of the Vienna Convention on Diplomatic Relations regarding the inviolability of embassy personnel. These were the proposals I was carrying with me as a statement of the American position.

It remained to be seen how the Iranians would react. I had an opportunity to probe for that reaction with Bani-Sadr's personal envoy, Dr Ahmed Salamajian, who had just arrived in New York. Salamajian promised to consider the four-point proposal, but he was quite candid in depicting the situation in his homeland. He told me that his government wanted a solution but was a 'victim of circumstances' in a situation in which the militant revolutionary forces were motivated by their own dynamics. In fact, the request for a Council meeting had been made as much to defuse the situation at home as to allow Iran to present its case.

This frank admission was revealing of the tensions among the main players in Iran: the government, the Revolutionary Council, the militant factions, and the clergy around Khomeini. I sensed that the understandable refusal of the United States through much of November to consider holding a meeting of the Security Council prior to release of the hostages was not helpful. It gave the Iranians a chance to portray the Council as a mere tool of the Americans. Matters were further complicated by Ayatollah Khomeini's repeated statements that there could be no discussion of the hostage problem until the Shah was returned to Iran for trial. Diplomatic immunity, he declared, did not apply to the hostages because they were all spies.

Khomeini's curious views on international law were reflected, albeit in less extreme fashion, in Salamajian's arguments. 'They ask why the Iranians are going after a dying man,' Salamajian said to me, referring to the Shah's terminal cancer. 'He killed thousands and sent more than $30 billion out of the country. Last year alone, 55,000 people were killed. Why should he now live in freedom?

'Iran knows that diplomats should be secure,' he went on, 'but the host country is also entitled to have security from diplomats. If the United States accepts an investigation of the Shah's guilt, the whole matter could be settled in less than an hour.' To my astonishment, he went on to deny that it was correct to refer to the embassy personnel as hostages. 'All that has happened,' he said, 'is that they are not able to do their work.' All I could say in reply was that it hardly seemed to be a normal situation when diplomats were blindfolded, tied up and confined within part of their embassy.

I had several telephone conversations with Bani-Sadr, but found the process exhausting and inconclusive. With the eight-hour time difference, I had to stay up until four o'clock in the morning to make contact with him. The first respondent would talk in Farsi. They would then find somebody to talk French or English and after endless delays I would get through to the minister. His responses were different every day and I was forced to the conclusion that he did not enjoy the confidence of his religious superiors.

Something had to be done to break the impasse, so on 25 November, taking advantage of the jealously husbanded Article 99 of the UN Charter, I wrote to the President of the Security Council in carefully measured terms, drawing attention to the continuing crisis and requesting a further meeting of the Council. On 4 December it met, called again for the release of the hostages and the re-establishment of the principles of diplomatic immunity, and authorized me to 'take all appropriate measures' through my good offices to implement the resolution. The first complication was that Bani-Sadr had been dismissed from office at the end of November and succeeded by Sadegh Ghotbzadeh, so I had to resume my weary round of telephone calls with a new voice, although I did find him somewhat more amenable to reason and rational argument.

Ghotbzadeh was a Western-educated militant nationalist who had participated in the anti-Shah movement ever since his student days. He was no stranger to the United Nations. As I later found out, he had written to me in 1977 urging the creation of a committee to look into human rights violations in Iran and had asked for a meeting with me on the subject. In accordance with the usual practice, his complaint had been routinely

3

despatched to the Human Rights Division of the Secretariat, and he was received by a representative of that body. Though he never mentioned it to me directly, I was told that he used to complain bitterly about my 'refusal' to see him, even though I never knew of his petition. Be that as it may, he certainly suspected me of being a defender of the Shah.

Nevertheless, my first telephone conversation with Ghotbzadeh, on 29 November, was encouraging. Overcoming the doubts of my staff about the propriety of the procedure, I managed to get his telephone number in Teheran and dialled him direct. To my surprise he came on the line, and we had a friendly chat. But he told me that he could not attend the substantive Council meeting scheduled for December in view of the tension in Iran over America's 'anti-Iranian rhetoric'.

It was Donald McHenry, at that time the American Ambassador to the UN, who first suggested that the most positive step would be for me to go to Teheran myself. It was a daunting prospect: the auguries were not good and the information from Teheran was confusing. Christmas was approaching. In an attempt to reach the heart of Khomeini, who was after all a religious leader, I sent him a letter, which was handed to him on 20 December, asking that he release the hostages 'at this season of peace and compassion'. I added that such a gesture 'would be received universally with the deepest appreciation'. In the same letter I offered to visit Teheran to meet him on the subject. I had my reply the next day. Ghotbzadeh, sounding edgy and embarrassed, told me over the telephone that release of the hostages was 'totally out of the question'.

Then Aga Shahi, the Pakistan Foreign Minister, whose government maintained the most direct relationship with the Iranian regime, informed me that I would be received by the Ayatollah Khomeini, but Ghotbzadeh declined to confirm it.

As December advanced, the situation became even more complicated. The Russians had made their first incursion into Afghanistan. The Americans were in the process of proposing their own meeting of the Security Council in order to request the imposition of sanctions against the Iranian regime to bolster their own trade embargo. There was every likelihood that this would be vetoed by the Soviet Union.

The Security Council did meet again during the last three days of the year, but deferred a decision pending the result of my visit. I was not sanguine; indeed I was full of foreboding. The mood in Teheran was clearly hysterical, with unpleasant undertones of ungovernable violence. A UN Secretary General has no gun-boats at his disposal, only his gifts of reasonable persuasion and skill in negotiation, and the moral authority of his office – where it is recognized.

*

Our plane put down at Mehrabad airport near Teheran on New Year's Day. Ghotbzadeh was there to meet us. He seemed depressed and uneasy, shy and almost embarrassed. Of medium height and burly, with a rather square face, he had a not unimpressive personality. He was dressed in a well-cut Western suit, quite the best I saw on anybody during my whole stay, but his shirt was open, without a tie. This appeared to be the fashion in order to demonstrate that everyone supported the revolution.

His conversation in the car during the drive from the airport was disconcerting. He told me that the situation was very unstable and that he could not give me the programme for my visit. 'Of course we invited you to come,' he said, 'but we should avoid the impression that you are here to negotiate the release of the hostages. The important point to stress is that your visit is a fact-finding mission and not a negotiating mission. We shall provide you with evidence of the cruelties of the regime of the Shah, the actions of SAVAK, the security police, and the sufferings of the Iranian people. We have to be very careful.'

I was obliged to conclude that the man was not sure of himself, that he was in trouble, and that although he had invited me on behalf of the Revolutionary Government he himself did not know what was going to happen. He spoke good English and French, had studied at Georgetown University and in Paris, and was regarded by the mullahs and the revolutionaries as a Westerner – he did not enjoy their confidence.

There were mobs of people everywhere. Occasional volleys of gunfire could be heard. When I arrived at the Hilton Hotel, I was surprised at the number of armed guards outside the building and in the lobby. I soon realized why: my presence provided a target of opportunity. The press and media were carrying rumours of assassination plots, frenzied demands for the return of the Shah, outbursts of anger at the United States and contempt for the West in general, and expressions of scorn for the United Nations. The Iranians were being told that I had come to Teheran without even being invited. The militant 'students' announced that they would not let me meet the hostages. Ayatollah Khomeini was reported again as stating that the only solution to the problem would be a 'real trial of America'. There seemed to be an orchestrated campaign to portray the United Nations as a servitor of the Iranian royal family and an institution which chose to ignore the sufferings of the Iranian people.

That evening the Iranian television service showed my arrival at the airport on a split screen. The other half portrayed victims of alleged brutalities by the Shah's secret police. The newscaster said that this 'special' news feature was 'a New Year's gift for the International Court of Justice and the Security Council'. The next morning's newspapers carried photographs of my previous visit in 1978, showing me shaking hands with the Shah and bowing over the hand of his sister, Princess Ashraf, in European fashion. Their radio broadcasts depicted me as a 'stooge of the Great Satan, scheming to get to know Iran's position so as better to protect the interests of his master', the United States.

My formal talks with Ghotbzadeh got nowhere. He launched into the familiar tirade about American exploitation of Iran through the Shah and at one point exclaimed: 'Not a single resolution was passed about that in the United Nations, not a single statement made, and now the United Nations suddenly becomes interested because fifty Americans are involved.' He then reiterated his government's hard-line position: 'Iran demands extradition of the Shah and the return of his wealth in exchange for the freedom of the hostages.'

I put to him the four-point proposal accepted by the Americans: the creation of a commission of enquiry; prior or at least simultaneous release of the hostages; no blocking by the United States of Iranian efforts to recover the Shah's assets through American courts, but no agreement to his extradition; and recognition by Iran of normal diplomatic immunity. Ghotbzadeh at first rejected my proposal out of hand. 'The Americans can't go on acting like spoilt children,' he said, insisting that his government was ready 'to go to the bitter end'. He demanded that the UN General Assembly pass a resolution calling for the Shah's extradition and the surrender of his funds. After Washington had complied with that, the hostages would go free.

At our second session he reported that the Revolutionary Council had rejected the idea of releasing the hostages first. That was out of the question, he said. But he was more accommodating about the international enquiry commission or tribunal. The General Assembly of the United Nations would have to sponsor it, and when the results became known we would be able to talk about the release of the hostages. It was at least an opening, and over the coming months it was to play a determining part in the resolution of the whole affair.

Until then, despite the atmosphere of tension, we had appeared to be engaged in acceptable diplomatic negotiations. Far worse was to come. As placatory gestures, the Iranians had organized two visits for me, one to the Behesht Zahara cemetery to lay a wreath on the graves of the 'revolutionary martyrs' and the other to the former Officers' Club to meet some of the victims of the SAVAK secret police. However, later in the day, Ghotbzadeh rang me up at my hotel to say that he was concerned about rumours of an assassination plot against me by 'foreign agents' and that it would be better not to tempt fate. I insisted that the schedule should go ahead as planned in the hope that the Iranians would accept a gesture of sympathy for the victims of SAVAK on my part and because I did not wish to be forced into continued seclusion. The second morning Ghotbzadeh was on the telephone again to me in a state of some agitation. 'Please do not go to the cemetery,' he said. 'The secret police have found out that they are planning an assassination attempt against your life. Stay at home.'

I protested and told him that I still hoped my visit would help to create a better atmosphere for our negotiations and that I had not come to Teheran to stay in the hotel all the time. He agreed, but said that he could not guarantee my safety. 'You will go in helicopters,' he suggested. I agreed, but then enquired whether it might not be better to arrive earlier than the scheduled time before the crowds gathered. 'No,' he said, 'that is not necessary because we have already announced the cancellation of your visit to the cemetery. We shall keep to the time-table. Nobody will know about it and all will be quiet.' It was a sign of Ghotbzadeh's naivety and lack of influence. Nothing was secret in Teheran. Everything was known to the public. The use of helicopters would invite attention. Nevertheless, I insisted on going.

As our helicopters approached the cemetery, I looked down and could see thousands of people crowding into the grounds awaiting our arrival. As soon as we landed, my *chef de cabinet* Raffeudin Ahmed, my personal assistant Georg Mautner-Markhof, my press spokesman François Giuliani and UN Security Officer John Hrusovsky, together with the Iranian chief of protocol and myself, climbed into cars to take us to the burial site a few hundred yards away. Within seconds the crowds swarmed round the car, jumping on the roof, pounding on it and shouting, their faces twisted in a frenzy of hatred. At first I tried to get out of the car, but my security officer pushed me back so that it could swerve off the road and cut through the rows of graves back to the helicopter, with the frustrated mob in hot pursuit. We got away by the skin of our teeth. Linde Michor, my Austrian secretary, who remained at the hotel watching the whole drama on television, was frightened to death and told me later that for hours she had thought we would never come back.

I was not amused at my next meeting with Ghotbzadeh when his light-hearted reaction to our ordeal was 'Well, you had quite an interesting experience . . .' He had consulted with the Revolutionary Council again, who were intransigent. But I did manage to move him away from his insistence that the proposed commission of enquiry should only 'investigate the Shah's crimes, the theft of state funds and American interference in Iran'. He agreed to Rafee Ahmed's more neutral formula, under which the commission would 'investigate violations of human rights and illegal acts in Iran', a phraseology which could cut both ways.

I thought I was beginning to penetrate the revolutionary façade. Some of Ghotbzadeh's comments indicated that he wanted us to know that he was not free to act. He spoke of the delicacy of the whole situation and of the difficulties facing his government. His own margin of manoeuvre was narrow. Although he was not explicit, his dilemma was clear – how to find a solution that would not expose him to attack by the militants or open the way for his rivals to sabotage his efforts by cutting him off from access to the Imam.

The revolutionaries had ridden to power on a wave of popular hatred of the Shah which had united them. Now that they were in control the various factions and personalities had begun to jockey for influence to prove their loyalty to the Imam while accusing each other of treason.

I realized why Ghotbzadeh had wanted me to cancel my public appearances. He knew he could not prevent the careful orchestration of my 'reception' at the cemetery by those who wished to undermine his position. Even though he shared his rivals' hatred of the Shah and the previous regime, he was trying to find some way to get the hostages released. Unlike the mullahs, he was a man of the world and well aware that the standing and credibility of the Iranian revolution were at stake.

I had some hope that Ghotbzadeh could help me to find a solution to the hostage problem; where I erred was in not appreciating that, like Bani-Sadr before him, he lacked the power to stand up against the more militant elements in and around the government. He could not even arrange a meeting with Khomeini for me, much less a visit to the hostages. But since he did control the foreign ministry, he gave me an opportunity to meet the three American diplomats detained separately there, the Chargé d'Affaires Bruce Laingen, the Political Counsellor Victor Tomseth and the Security Officer Michael Howland. They assured me that they were in reasonably good physical shape, but expressed the fear, rightly as it turned out, that they and the other hostages would remain in custody for some time to come. Laingen also told me that the entire embassy staff had been changed at the beginning of 1979 and that, far from being spies, they had received instructions to establish friendly relations with the new regime.

I was then escorted to the former Officers' Club to meet some of the victims of the Shah's secret police. The large room in which I was to address them was filled to overflowing. As I moved towards the makeshift platform, I noticed that many in the crowd, including children, were crippled, blind or missing arms or legs. They shouted, wept and chanted as if on command as each in turn recounted his sufferings. They approached the platform in wheelchairs, on crutches, waving artificial limbs and stumps, and at one point a man stepped up to the platform and handed me his armless five-year-old boy, claiming that his arms had been cut off by SAVAK agents in order to extract a confession from his older brother, who had been forced to witness the mutilation. It was a shocking and distressing spectacle. But when Ghotbzadeh whispered to me later that the boy was in fact the victim of an accident rather than of SAVAK, I could not help entertaining doubts about other aspects of the demonstration, and about Ghotbzadeh's standing with the revolutionary movement.

We had stayed about an hour, but when we were permitted to leave the corridors had been blocked by a frenzied crowd, screaming and pushing our bodyguards. We were quite badly jostled and lucky to emerge without injury.

Our haunting experience was not yet over. We had one final ordeal to endure. Later that same day, Ghotbzadeh was at last able to arrange a meeting with the Revolutionary Council. I wondered what new, unexpected development would confront me this time.

In the dark of the night our car stopped at the gate of a park somewhere in Teheran. A crowd of rough-looking men, many of them armed with sub-machine-guns, moved in from the shadows. As we stepped out, we were surrounded by them and let through the gates. The path was unlit and the building that loomed ahead was also dark. It looked like an abandoned fortress.

We were carried along by the crowd, some of them forming a hand-clasped circle round us. Our way was lit by flashlights, some of which were shone directly in my eyes. We stumbled forward amid shoving and shouting. Suddenly an old man pushed through the crowd, thrusting the photograph of my meeting with Princess Ashraf into my face. I could not understand a word he said, but his intent was menacing. Finally we were pushed into the building and through a dim lobby into darkened corridors.

I turned to Rafee Ahmed and said: 'Do you think we shall ever get out of here alive?' He nodded uncertainly. Calm and splendid man as he was, he evidently shared my concern. It was an unnerving experience. Here I was, the invited guest of the Revolutionary Government of a member state of the United Nations which appeared not only to be unable to protect me and my delegation against the irresponsible behaviour of its citizens but to be making no apparent attempt to do so. Climbing up the stairs in complete darkness, I wondered whether it was really the duty of a UN Secretary General, representing the world community, to undertake such impossible missions. What risks should one take in helping to prevent a human tragedy fraught with major international consequences? No Charter, no rules provided an answer to this question.

Ahead of us a door opened. I recognized that we were in the old Senate building which I had visited two years earlier. Moving forward, we found ourselves in the presence of the Revolutionary Council of the Islamic Republic of Iran. There were ten members sitting round three sides of a rectangular table, some of them in religious dress, but most in Western suits with open-necked collars, including the deposed Bani-Sadr, whom I thus saw for the first time. The atmosphere resembled that of a court. They wanted us to be the accused pleading our defence.

Chairing the proceeding was Ayatollah Beheshti, later himself the victim of assassination. He was a tall, bearded, good-looking and distinctly impressive figure. He uttered a few words in German for my benefit – he had lived for a time in Germany – and, in a brief reference to my experiences in the city, remarked by way of apology that the demonstrations had not really been directed against me, but against the United States.

He then launched into a tirade, repeating all the familiar arguments. He left us in no doubt that we would be wasting our time if we suggested that the hostages should be released before the creation of a commission of enquiry or simultaneously with it. If I had come to Iran on a fact-finding mission, I could usefully transmit their views to the United States, the United Nations and the media. No matter how strongly outsiders condemned the action of the 'students' in holding the hostages as a violation of international law, they enjoyed the full support of the Iranian people. The problem could not be considered in isolation: the United States had gravely violated international law by its persistent intervention in the internal affairs of Iran and other nations, and the whole pattern of these relationships had to be investigated. That, not the hostage question, was – in Iranian eyes – the basic offence that needed to be dealt with. The extradition of the Shah had to form part of the package.

We were back to square one. I knew that there was not the slightest chance that the Americans would accede to these demands. There was some discussion between Beheshti, Ghotbzadeh and me about the four-point plan I had brought with me, but it remained inconclusive. The others sat listening quietly, not participating. I was by this time thoroughly disheartened, but tried to avoid any show of emotion. I told Beheshti that I would convey the Revolutionary Council's position to the Security Council but that I could not express any personal judgement on it. This clearly displeased him. He seemed to expect me to present the Iranian proposals as my own, or at least with some favourable commentary.

I brought the meeting to a close by asking once more if I could see Ayatollah Khomeini. No, Beheshti said firmly, making it clear that neither the Council nor he personally had any authority to further this request. As we stood up to leave I remarked to Ghotbzadeh that I hoped our exit would be easier than our entry. 'I shall accompany you,' he said in reply. Seconds later, as we left the building, the mob stormed on to the scene once again. Ghotbzadeh was pushed to one side and disappeared from my sight.

A squad of revolutionary guards formed a circle round us and led us out, pushing the demonstrators to one side as they went.

We left the following day, shaken and frustrated. Ghotbzadeh did have the courtesy to pay a farewell visit to our hotel and was clearly very uneasy at the treatment we had received. I returned empty-handed with the slim thread of the commission of enquiry the only material out of which to weave a possible solution.

If there was one experience in all my years at the top of the United Nations which proved the limits and frustrations of this job, it was that trip to Teheran. Carrying the burden of an enormous political and moral responsibility, the Secretary General of the United Nations is faced with one simple truth: he has no executive power. His influence depends on his diplomatic skills and persuasiveness, when he can bring them to bear; but all his efforts, all the chapters of the UN Charter and the principles of international law are of little help if member governments disregard them.

2

Survival Course

It must have helped me to endure an ordeal of that nature to be able to look back on a far from sheltered upbringing. I was born in 1918 into the defeated, ruined, truncated remnant of the former Austro-Hungarian Habsburg Empire. My father was one of the eleven children of a blacksmith in the small village of St Andrä-Wördern, near Vienna. He had bettered himself and become the local schoolmaster and married one of the three daughters of the mayor, a landowner named Petrasch. This might sound like the beginning of a comfortable existence, but Grandfather Petrasch had suffered a heart attack in 1917 and been obliged on medical advice to give up farming and sell his land. He bought a substantial house in the village, where my parents were living, but was ill-advised enough to invest the remaining proceeds in savings accounts. The Austrian crown was devalued to nothing during the post-war period, so that the family lost almost everything and survived in a very poor condition.

If I am to analyse motives, I am convinced that the greatest impetus to my choosing a diplomatic and political career was provided by the circumstances and events of the era in which I grew to manhood. The armistice that marked the end of World War I had been signed a month before I was born. World War II broke out the year I came of age. During the two intervening decades, those twenty youthful years that leave their stamp on a man, my Austria was an infant republic in search of equilibrium, its people groping for identity amid the social disarray brought on by economic and political upheaval. The impact of my country's desperate condition was inescapable during those years. Every Austrian experienced the demoralizing effects of party rivalries and rival power groups, abortive insurrections, the repression of subversive activity, the civil strife of 1934, the murder of Chancellor Dollfuss that same year by Nazi agents and finally the fateful Anschluss.

World War 1 had drained Austria. Set adrift, its mighty parent dismembered, its expectations crushed, the new republic could not sustain itself. Deprived of raw materials and commodities previously available from other regions of the empire, its industries languished and its agricultural output fell to disastrously low levels. Every basic necessity was in short supply.

My father clung to his profession amid the general distress, obtaining rapid, if modest, advancement. Within a year he had been promoted to a school in Neunkirchen, a district capital south of Vienna, near Wiener Neustadt, where my brother Walter was born. After a few years there, he was appointed District School Inspector for Tulln, the provincial capital of my birthplace, where my sister Linde, the youngest of the family, was born.

The little town had no secondary school of its own. The nearest one was some twenty kilometres away in Klosterneuberg. Regardless of the weather, I had to get up at five o'clock every morning, catch the train at six, travel for three-quarters of an hour and then trudge another half-hour to arrive for class. I ate my breakfast on the way, usually a sandwich that my mother made for me from whatever little was available.

Between the station and the school there was a pastry shop. Its window display drew me like a magnet. It became my daily ritual to stop and covet every cake, tart and biscuit behind the glass. I was always hungry. Most Austrians were always hungry. One day, while I was making my imaginary selection, an old friend of my father's greeted me and after the usual exchange of courtesies invited me to choose any sweet I wished. My hesitation was short-lived, but the embarrassment of choice was such that I came away with several. I have remembered that treat all my life.

Otherwise, apart from our straitened circumstances, my early years in secondary school were uneventful. The weeks and months were taken up with trekking back and forth and with lessons, games, parental reprimands and academic exhortations, not to mention the indiscriminate consumption of practically anything digestible, the transient joys and desperation, the chatter, pranks and peccadillos that normally engage the energy and curiosity of boys of that age.

I owed a great deal to my father, both then and later. He regarded nothing as more important than the proper education of his three children and willingly did without to meet our school expenses. My brother Walter, who died in 1974, chose to follow in his footsteps and enjoyed a satisfying career in the teaching profession. My sister Linde proved to have a scientific bent and is the Chief of Radiology at a clinic in Vienna. I hope that in our respective ways we have justified the sacrifices our parents made.

It was not until I was about fifteen that politics assumed any significance. My father was a very open-minded, liberal man, an avowed supporter of Austria's independence and both anti-Nazi and anti-Anschluss with Germany. He attended public meetings, at which he was often the speaker, and enjoyed considerable status in the district because of his involvement in community affairs. Political and social issues had always figured in conversation at the home of my parents and their friends, and I had become sufficiently intrigued by what was said to ask for explanations. I even drew upon this imperfect knowledge to speak with unwarranted authority among my own companions whenever the opportunity arose. But although I was well aware of our country's economic ills, I had not yet awakened to its political afflictions.

In 1933, with the convulsions across our border that led to the advent of Hitler in Germany, the enormity of what was happening suddenly shocked me and my companions out of boyhood. Our adolescent bickering became bitter quarrelling as partisan antagonisms intensified. Friendships broke on political ideologies. As parliamentary order fell apart and government by decree took over, with Mussolini subjecting Chancellor Dollfuss to pressure, it became clear that Austria was being pushed into crisis.

In 1934, civil war broke out between the Christian-Democrat government and the Social Democrats. One day, on my way from Tulln to Vienna, the train was stopped and we all had to get out. Curiosity was too strong, and some of us went to see what had happened. It sickened me to see the extent of human suffering and the enormity of destruction caused by civil strife. I was confused and horrified. I told my father that I could not understand the passions that drove Austrians to kill each other.

The Social Democrats included a radical element espousing what they themselves called Austro-Marxism. I was aware that when they had been in power, just after the First World War, their social programmes had been progressive and of benefit to the working class. The issues on which the parties disagreed did not seem to me to justify such slaughter and destruction. Then, in July 1934, Nazi conspirators assassinated Chancellor Dollfuss.

I still had two years to spend at the *Gymnasium* in Klosterneuberg, but the coming danger was now clear to all. The events which followed, in rapidly accelerating tempo, supported my misgivings. The internal party schism gave the Nazis a clear advantage, and before I was much older Austrian sovereignty had been usurped. The Conservative and Socialist leaders who had opposed annexation were soon to find themselves in the same concentration camps, with time to ponder the futility of their dispute and, in the face of common disillusionment, reconcile their differences of ideology.

In 1936 the Austrian government instituted compulsory military service, and, although I had not quite reached the required age, my family and I thought it best for me to sign up right away so that I might afterwards pursue my studies without interruption. Since I liked horses, I chose the cavalry for my one year's stint. I started as a simple soldier and left with the rank of volunteer corporal, which led automatically to promotion to warrant officer should I ever be recalled to the army.

My father wanted me to study medicine, but I had developed my own firm preference for the law. I wanted to begin my law studies at the university and at the same time register at the Vienna Consular Academy. The admission fees at the Academy were high, but my father, to his eternal credit, agreed to the necessary outlay. His support was all the more selfless and appreciated because I knew that the opportunities in the field I had chosen were far fewer than those in medicine. Unemployment was endemic and the prospects for law graduates were dim. Many young professionals quit the country altogether and went to Germany or, if they could afford the passage, to America.

The Consular Academy was a remarkable institution, founded in the reign of Maria Theresa. It only had about forty students, but it had enjoyed an international reputation for generations and my fellow-students came from every part of the world: America, Britain, most European countries and even a contingent from the Far East.

Influenced by my father's staunch attitudes, I joined the youth movement of the Vaterländische Front in Tulln, which supported Chancellor Schuschnigg, whose government had come to power after the assassination of Dollfuss. We were called das Österreichische Jungvolk – rather a cumbersome title – and we were full of enthusiasm for an independent Austria and had been very active during the period leading up to the Nazi invasion.

Schuschnigg had been summoned to his humiliating meeting with Hitler at Berchtesgaden and on his return had resorted to the desperate measure of holding a referendum, with the Nazi threat ever-present, to determine the extent of the Austrian will for independence. It was a short-lived and hectic period. The Jungvolk were busily engaged in printing and distributing pamphlets encouraging people to resist, and on one of our expeditions the Nazis, who were already roaming the streets, caught us at it. We were quite badly beaten up in the fracas, but we managed to make our way home without anything worse than cuts and bruises. A few days later, it was all over.

On 12 March 1938 the German army marched into Austria. Re-unification with the German Reich was formally proclaimed the following day. On 14 March Hitler arrived in Vienna. Newsreel footage of the occasion appeared to provide evidence of a tumultuous welcome by the Viennese. But no journalist or photographer ventured from the scene of celebration to less conspicuous corners of the capital to film the thousands sitting soberly at home. No camera caught the panic-stricken desperation of those hiding in the city's cellars fearing the persecutions that began almost at once.

My father was arrested a few days after the annexation. I came home one evening from the university to find that the Gestapo had taken him away without a word. Their motives were plain enough, but what they planned to do became a nightmare of anxiety. A Christian Democrat who had openly and publicly defended Austrian independence, he had been denounced by local Nazi sympathizers. Nothing he had said or done justified the punitive attitude of the new authorities, who made him feel the full weight of their intimidation and vindictive tactics. Although he was released on sufferance, they forced him to resign his post immediately and deprived him of all normal means of livelihood.

The family was almost penniless. Walter, Linde and I nevertheless continued with our studies. An aunt and a group of friends pooled whatever they could spare to help us. I gave private lessons in Greek and Latin and managed to continue at the Consular Academy in the morning and at the university in the afternoon and evening. Curiously enough the Nazis did not move in on the Consular Academy immediately. Its international reputation doubtless deterred them, and although they appointed their own director there was no change in the curriculum as long as I was there. I managed to stick it out until I graduated with distinction. I also managed to obtain my Bachelor of Law degree.

I was still getting up at five every morning to make the trip from Tulln to Vienna and was having my own troubles with the police, who made a point of stopping me frequently and challenging my movements. This harass-ment lessened as the threat of European war grew, probably because they knew that I was shortly to be drafted into what was now the German army. There was no way to escape military service. There were some, of course, with bureaucratic influence, sufficient money or relatives abroad, who were able to secure an exit visa by paying the required fees. But even a visa was no guarantee that one would be allowed to leave the country, since all such requests were subject to approval by the Germans. Able-bodied Austrians of military age had little choice.

My brother Walter and I were called up just as the Second World War began. There was, however, one unexpected advantage. A civilian whose politics and activities were under scrutiny was better off as a soldier. The uniform was a protection against the Gestapo and the Nazis. Our family was still under constant police surveillance: my father was detained briefly from time to time and we were always being questioned. We lived in daily apprehension, but in the army there was much less harassment of those known to disapprove of Nazism, and I had no further trouble.

In contrast to the constant threat at home, vigilance was so relaxed that a number of the officers in my unit freely criticized the Nazi system, relatively unconcerned about the risk. Most of the regulars in the German army were not Nazis and many of the Prussian officers did not fall for the Nazi ideology. As I got to know them, I suspected that a few were even engaged in underground activity. It therefore came as no surprise to me in 1944 to learn that army officers had been implicated in the 20 July assassination plot that marked a turning point in Hitler's fortunes.

The fact that there were more anti-Nazis in the army than there were in the civil service probably had a lot to do with the relative permissiveness of the army. Although we always had to exercise discretion, at least our disaffection was allowed more scope. Anti-Nazi literature was circulated clandestinely and I read it all. I found several colleagues who shared my views and our long discussions gave us a chance to air our feelings. Sunday Mass was always well attended. It provided us with a rallying point and a means of manifesting our opposition to the notoriously anti-religious policies of the regime.

I was serving in Reconnaissance Section 45 of the Upper Austrian Division. In the spring of 1941 we were ordered to the eastern front. Serving in the German army was hard to bear, but it was almost a relief to get away from the strains and suspicions that surrounded us at home.

We had a squadron of horse cavalry, a squadron of bicycles, another of motor cycles and some motorized light artillery. Depending on the weather conditions and the terrain, the motorized units went ahead when it was dry, sometimes forty kilometres in front of the infantry regiments. When the rains came and the motorized units got stuck in the mud, the call came for the cavalry. We had to ride ahead and attract the enemy fire in order to pinpoint their positions. It was desperate work, a *Himmelfahrts-kommando* as we called it, a passport to heaven. Every morning I did not know whether I would be alive in the evening.

By December we had reached the area south-west of Orel, where our division was surrounded by Russian forces.

I was wounded in the leg by a grenade splinter. It was not a serious wound, but in the days before other German forces could fight their way through the encirclement to join us it had turned septic. They got me out to a field hospital, where by happy chance I was treated by a Viennese surgeon. '*Mein lieber Freund*,' he said, 'another day and your leg would have gone.'

I was evacuated home, but it took several months in a sanatorium in the mountains before my leg started to heal properly. I walked with a bad limp, and to my undisguised relief was discharged from further service at the front. I made a formal request to be permitted to resume my law studies and take my Master's degree and, rather to my surprise, this was granted. I still had my pay as lieutenant and this helped to see me through.

My father was still at liberty, although the police had picked him up from time to time to enquire into his activities; to escape the harassment he and my mother had moved to Baden, where the pressure was less. I was able to visit them occasionally, but we were never free of the constant security checks.

I gave my father a bad fright one day. I walked straight into the kitchen on one of my visits and found him listening to the BBC news on the radio. This had become a capital offence and two or three people of our acquaintance had been caught and executed. As I opened the door unannounced, my father thought it was the Gestapo. He switched off the radio, visibly relieved to see my face.

It was impossible to leave Austria. The borders had been closed and were heavily patrolled. Even ordinary movements were restricted and the authorities dealt arbitrarily with anyone who did not conform to the regulations. This complicated my studies for a doctorate in law because the university library had been dispersed as a result of the bombing raids and the books and documents I needed had been hidden in obscure and often widely scattered places. I had to dig out the information for my dissertation – on the federalist principles of the German diplomat Konstantin Frantz – in bits and pieces. The physical assembly of the source material proved more exhuasting than the research and the writing;

I finally obtained my degree in 1944.

The lastingly happy event in August of that year was my marriage to Elizabeth Ritschel. She was also studying law and we had met at the university the previous year. Her family had been career officers in the Austro-Hungarian Empire and her father had been seriously wounded during the First World War. When his regiment was finally disbanded, he had become a modestly successful businessman.

Cissy and I had planned to spend our honeymoon in a little mountain village not far from Vienna, but our train had hardly cleared the city when the air raid warning sounded. All the passengers were hustled off and we spent our wedding night in the crowded basement of the local railway station, listening to the bombs falling overhead.

The bombardment of Vienna became relentless during the final year of the war and, with the advance of the Allied armies, Cissy sought refuge in the countryside of Styria to await our first child, Liselotte. She was born the following day, shortly after Austria's liberation by the Allied forces. The parallel with my own birth was poignant, coming on the heels of a terrible war. I prayed that out of this long agony and immediate desolation the world might fashion an abiding peace so that Liselotte and children everywhere might never again suffer such adversity.

Four months later we decided to rejoin my parents at Baden. At least the whole family would be together and somehow we would pool our resources to see us through. The train journey was a fearsome ordeal. We had to travel in a cattle wagon overloaded with produce, poultry, freight of every kind and as many passengers as could be squeezed aboard. Cissy, who was not well, rested on a pile of straw. I perched on a crate of apples. Every now and then she and I exchanged places to keep our limbs from getting cramped. We hardly dared to leave our places next to the baby. We felt like refugees in our own country, and the trip, which normally took three hours, lasted three days.

Controls along the line of demarcation between the Russian and American zones of occupation were scrupulously imposed. We stopped for hours at indeterminate places and innumerable little stations, whose names we could not even read because our cattle car had no windows and we were seldom allowed to leave the train. We were hungry, and above all thirsty. Liselotte never stopped crying.

By the third and final night all the passengers were showing signs of strain. One of them, goaded beyond endurance, threatened to smash our baby's cradle to give himself more room. No wonder I was able to face the ordeals of later life with relative equanimity.

The pleasures of reunion when we finally reached Baden were dimmed by the conditions that awaited us. My parents' house had been bombed and the windows in the part we were due to occupy had all been blown out. We blocked them up as best we could, but we all nearly froze to death that winter. Fuel was hard to come by, and material for repairs non-existent, but the biggest problem was finding enough to eat. The only way we survived was to walk far into the countryside and go from farm to farm asking for any surplus they might have for sale.

3

Khrushchev and the Austrian Treaty

In spite of our difficult circumstances, I had managed to sit the stiff competitive examination for the newly reconstituted Austrian Foreign Service. Of the dozen candidates considered, only four of us were accepted. In November 1945, the Foreign Office offered me an appointment. It was not just a job, it was *the* job – the one I wanted more than any other. It was a very junior post, but it was in the ministry. All my academic preparation, all my interests, all my hopes had been geared to the diplomatic service. After the years of tribulation, I was the happiest man alive.

When I first reported to the ministry in the Ballhausplatz I was twenty-six, a family man and earnestly determined to succeed in my profession. I hoped I had all the formal qualifications that might reasonably be expected of a fledgling diplomat, but in addition I brought with me a long-standing dream, born of experience and sustained by hope. I was still young enough to want to help to create a world in which oppression and injustice and all the corresponding social ills would no longer be tolerated, one in which my country might regain an honourable place and play a useful role again.

The decline of Austria, the collapse of Europe and the wretchedness of war were deeply etched in my consciousness. I knew what hunger and privation were, and what it meant to lose one's national identity and have to submit to foreign masters. At the same time, I recognized that there were rights and conditions to which people everywhere aspired, and I believed wholeheartedly that they could be attained. I was determined to lend whatever talents I possessed to that endeavour.

In order to be in close attendance at the Foreign Office that first year, I boarded in a modest room nearby and went back to Baden and my family only at weekends. The trip was arduous, the means of transportation uncertain; when they broke down, I had a three-hour walk from the outskirts of Vienna. Both Cissy and I found the separation increasingly difficult, so in 1946 we took a small apartment in the city. We have always thought of that as the real beginning of our diplomatic life.

My career had also taken an upward step. After the first few months of the usual humble tasks entrusted to a novice, I was called into the office of the elderly Secretary General of the Foreign Office. He told me that it was intended to appoint me as private secretary to the Foreign Minister, Karl Gruber. He made extensive enquiries into my background and asked whether I felt up to the job. 'This Gruber is a very tough man,' he said. The Minister certainly had that reputation. He had only held the job for a few months, since the general election, which had coincided with my own appointment, and had already gone through two private secretaries. They had both gone in some fear of the Minister and had failed to get along with him. The feeling seemed to be that I would not survive for very long either. I found this invidious and made it pretty clear that I had not survived front-line service in the war in order to be afraid of a Foreign Minister. This seemed to settle the matter and I was duly appointed.

Gruber was an interesting, forceful and highly intelligent man with a very creditable record during the war. He had got out of Vienna after the Anschluss, gone to Berlin and lain low in a job with the German electrical firm of Telefunken. At great risk he had maintained active contact with the Austrian resistance movement, which had clandestine links with Allen Dulles, the long-time head of the CIA. This connection with the American intelligence service had served him in good stead at the end of the war. He was made Governor of the Tyrol, which was in fact in the French zone of occupation, and he established excellent relations with the Americans and the British. When the Christian Democrats, who had re-named themselves the People's Party, won the election in a landslide victory, the Chancellor, Leopold Figl, appointed him Foreign Minister.

Although he had no diplomatic background he quickly gained the necessary expertise and established himself as one of the stronger members of the Cabinet, his position bolstered by the good opinion of the Western Allies. I had no trouble with him. Running his office required discipline, reasonable diligence and a gift for establishing the contacts he needed. I was in no way a protégé of his, but a real friendship developed. It was reported to me that he had said to a colleague: 'If Waldheim tells me we can't do anything about a problem, I believe him. If someone else tells me, I won't believe him. But if Waldheim says it, I know that he would explore every avenue to solve a problem or do something about it. Therefore, if he comes and says it is impossible, I believe him.' That was a great compliment.

The Austrian political parties had learnt the bitter historical lessons of their previous antagonisms and formed a coalition government in spite of the results of the election, giving the Conservatives a clear majority. The early months of the peace had been uncertain. The Russians, who arrived in Vienna first, sought out the venerable Socialist Chancellor of the twenties, Dr Karl Renner, who had represented Austria at the St Germain Peace Conference after the First World War. He was now living in seclusion in Gloggnitz, a small town south of Vienna. He was seventy-five, but still in full vigour, and the Russians asked him to form a provisional government. At first it operated only in their zone of occupation and the Western Allies were wary of it. However, the Austrians have been subtle in their politics for many generations and understand the art of the possible. The western provinces, with Gruber playing an active part, were able to join the provisional government, making it more balanced and effective: the elections had confirmed the unity of the country. Several of the pre-war political figures had survived the Nazi concentration camps, including Leopold Figl, the People's Party Chancellor. Renner, a moderate and a patriot, became President, remaining in that post until he died; he was greatly revered for the part he had played.

Political stability was not the end of our problems, merely the beginning of possible solutions. Austria was still quartered between the occupying powers. The Russians, although with more restraint than in Germany, were exacting reparations from their zone of occupation, and the Cold War that succeeded the Allied victory was complicating all relationships. It is something of a miracle that a start was made in rebuilding our physically ruined country and normalizing its social and economic relationships.

I longed to go abroad, to see at first hand the people and places that I had only read about. Until the year in which I was born, Vienna had been the capital of a large empire comprising many nations. This was reflected in the ethnic diversity of its population. It had been a thriving centre of European power. Despite the depredations of a whole generation, traces of its former cosmopolitan importance were still visible and aroused in me a curiosity to know what lay beyond.

My first foreign assignment came in 1948, when I was posted to our embassy in Paris. This provided useful further training, for we operated on a shoe-string budget and each member of our very limited staff carried a full and varied workload. As First Secretary, I often had to serve as Chargé d'Affaires when the Ambassador was away. I must have earned the ministry's good opinion, because in 1951 I was called back to Vienna as head of its personnel department.

I found the situation already much improved. The Marshall Plan was working wonders in Austria. What remained intractable, expensive and frustrating to the economic recovery of the country as a whole was the continued four-power occupation. Desultory negotiations had been going on for several years to settle the terms for restoring Austrian independence in what we were very careful to call a State Treaty. As far as we were concerned a peace treaty was not appropriate. Austria had not declared war on anyone; it had been a victim of Nazi Germany.

In the summer of 1952, the Austrian government addressed a circular letter to all the countries with which it maintained diplomatic relationships calling for the end of the Allied occupation on agreed terms. The response was indeterminate, but matters were starting to move. In June 1953, Karl Gruber met Pandit Nehru at a secret rendezvous in Switzerland and pleaded with him to intervene on Austria's behalf with the great powers. He also floated as an essential element in the compromises that would have to be made the idea of Austria adopting a posture of military neutrality. It was Gruber's last but most important initiative in office. He had written a book in which he suggested that Leopold Figl had conceded too much to the Communists. Although no firm agreement had been made, the disclosure caused uproar in the People's Party. An enquiry was held, Gruber was dismissed, but appointed as Ambassador to Washington, where he played an essential part in what was to come. A new coalition government was formed with Julius Raab as Chancellor and Leopold Figl as Foreign Minister. The Socialist Party was represented within the government by Vice-Chancellor Adolf Schärf and the Secretary of State for Foreign Affairs, Bruno Kreisky.

Events abroad began to move in Austria's favour. Early in 1954, after several years of freeze, the Foreign Ministers of the four main powers, John Foster Dulles, Georges Bidault, Anthony Eden and Vyacheslav Molotov, once more sat round the same conference table in Berlin. For the first time representatives of the Austrian government, Leopold Figl and his Social-Democrat State Secretary, Bruno Kreisky, participated as equal partners. The Russians had responded to the concept of permanent neutrality for Austria, and agreement on independence was very nearly reached. The sticking point was Molotov's insistence that Allied troops should remain in Austria until such time as the main German issue had been settled; this our government refused to accept.

The year that followed provided the catalyst. NATO had been in existence since 1949; in December 1954 the Federal Republic of Germany was invited to become a member under the provisions of the Treaty of Western European Union. This left its mark on the international situation. In Moscow the Supreme Soviet met in February 1955 to consider the situation in Europe. Foreign Minister Molotov stated: 'The settlement of the Austrian question cannot be considered apart from the German problem – particularly in view of the plan to remilitarize Western Germany – which intensifies the danger of an "Anschluss"; and 'the Soviet

Government considers any further delay in the conclusion of a State Treaty with Austria to be unjustified'. So our Ambassador, Norbert Bischoff, was summoned back to Vienna and within a fortnight Raab, Schärf, Figl and Kreisky had been invited to Moscow to sign the memorandum which provided the basis for the State Treaty.

What followed gave me a fascinating insight into the workings of the Russian mind, which stood me in good stead in the years to come. The prime mover had been Nikita Khrushchev, almost certainly, for all his boorish ways, the most able and imaginative Soviet leader of the post-war period. There were two elements in his attitude. He had formulated the new policy of peaceful co-existence with the West, and this remained his main preoccupation during his term of office. He wanted to establish a better relationship with the Americans in particular but with the Western world in general, and we received interesting indications that he thought that Austria could serve as a showcase for his sincerity, that he really meant what he said by not blocking Austria's way to independence.

The second consideration, since there is no philanthropy in diplomacy, was strategic and military. The Russians had apparently come to the conclusion that by withdrawing Soviet forces from Eastern Austria they would oblige the Western Allies to remove their troops from the remaining two-thirds of the country. With Austria independent and neutral, the NATO powers would lose their lines of communicaiton from Bavaria, through Innsbruck and the Tyrol, to Northern Italy. A neutral barrier would be set up from the Hungarian frontier through Austria and Switzerland to Geneva, and the NATO forces would have to communicate through France.

It was doubtless this argument which enabled Khrushchev to carry the day against the opposition of Molotov and the Soviet army. They would still have their forces along the Hungarian border, so if Austria violated the treaty by joining the Western Alliance, which we had no intention of doing, or if any of the NATO powers violated the treaty, the Russians would be able to intervene.

There are those who assert that Khrushchev's reasoning went further and that he hoped Austria's independence and neutrality would encourage the German Federal Republic to become neutral and break away from the NATO Alliance. I believe that to be naive. Khrushchev was intelligent enough to know that the case of the small republic of Austria was very different to that of West Germany, who were a very important factor in power politics and firmly set on their alliance with the West.

Chancellor Raab and Foreign Mnister Figl provided a fascinating example of how to deal with the Russians. Neither of them were intellectuals or diplomats, but they were direct and patient, and matched the tough Russian negotiators step for step. Raab had been a private businessman, a free-enterprise building contractor in St Pölten, in Lower Austria. He had been active in Austrian politics before the Anschluss as a firm Christian Democrat and member of the Heimwehr. He built up a very good relationship with the Russians and earned their respect. He knew exactly how to deal with them. As the negotiations proceeded and some of his colleagues became impatient he would say: 'Look, you know where I stand. We belong to the Western world, but we should not be provocative. *Es hat keinen Sinn den russischen Bären immer in den Schwanz zu zwicken* – it serves no purpose to go on twisting the Russian bear by the tail.' That was his method, persistent and pleasing, and it worked.

Leopold Figl came from a farmer's family in Rust, a village in Lower Austria, not far from our family home at Tulln. They were not big landowners but well-to-do peasant farmers with a very nice farmhouse. He had that marvellous peasant's instinct and sense of humour. You could give him a dozen files to read and he would just glance at them. He much preferred to be informed orally. He did not speak a word of any foreign language but got on famously with everybody in his country dialect and always arrived at the correct decision.

He was honest and straightforward and always kept his sense of reality. He had his difficulties with each of the four Allied high commissioners in turn, but he always reacted calmly, never lost his nerve, and they all liked him as he was a stabilizing factor in the government and the country. The Russians were under no illusions about his firm roots in Western ideology and Western democracy but they held him in high esteem.

He had an earthy sense of humour, full of little jokes. This was best illustrated in a cartoon which gained world-wide popularity, in which he was depicted, as the negotiations neared their conclusion, as turning to Chancellor Raab and saying: 'Now we have got them softened up, all we have to do is to sing the *Reblaus* and they will give in.' The *Reblaus* is one of those catchy and distinctly popular tunes that the Viennese sing at the time of the wine harvest about the grape-mite who gets drunk to celebrate the new vintage.

The last-minute hitch came, in fact, from the Americans. John Foster Dulles thought there were still one or two clauses in the State Treaty too favourable to the Russians and raised objections. Gruber worked very hard in Washington to bring them round, and he had in fact helped to persuade his American friends to go along with the draft when the Russians climbed down anyway, and all was well.

So we were able to follow the splendid signing ceremony of the State Treaty on 15 May 1955 in the Marble Hall of the beautiful Belvedere Palace, built for Prince Eugene by Lukas von Hildebrandt. Representing the four Allied Powers, Vyacheslav Molotov, Harold Macmillan, John Foster Dulles and Antoine Pinay, together with Austria's Leopold Figl, put their signatures on the document. On 25 October the last soldier of the occupation forces left and the following day the Austrian National Assembly passed the federal law on permanent neutrality.

These events were significant in three ways. In the first place, after years of confrontation East and West had agreed to relinquish their respective zones of occupation. Second, Austrian diplomacy had found a formula that gave the country a universally acceptable role in post-war Europe. Finally, the Soviet policy of *détente* initiated by Khrushchev had created a favourable climate for the realization of the Austrian solution. It was the first substantial thaw in international relationships for ten years.

Khrushchev, whose joviality masked the seriousness of his efforts to achieve *détente*, admired the enormous technological progress of the West and recognized its importance. He considered it in the interest of the Soviet Union to restore trust among the Allies and to bring about peaceful co-existence as a solution to many of the problems existing between states of different ideologies. Possibly he hoped that Austria would serve as an example.

The Austrian example, however, has not been followed, perhaps because, in a large measure, circumstances and geopolitical considerations applicable only to Austria made the solution unique. For Austria, of course, the State Treaty and the status of neutrality were to prove a blessing. It became a healthy country and the reputation it now enjoys clearly demonstrates that a small state can be a constructive factor in the normalization of international relations and the balance of power.

My own career took a similar fortunate turn. During the occupation, Austria had acquired observer status with the United Nations. A few months before our country was admitted as a full member I served as an observer to the world organization. For me it was an unforgettable experience when in December 1955 I led the Austrian delegation, accompanied by the applause of the Assembly membership, to our newly acquired seats in the Assembly Hall. As the day of our admission came as a surprise to my government – nobody was sent over from Vienna – all I could do was to rally my staff to join me in order to make our entry look a little more impressive. Altogether there were three of us. From 1956–60 I became Head of Mission to Canada, with the additional duty of reinforcing our delegation at the UN. Between 1960 and 1964 I served in Vienna, first as head of the Western political department and then as Director General of Political Affairs; I then returned as our Ambassador to the United Nations, where I remained until 1968.

*

Khrushchev deserves a footnote, even at this distance in time. Not only was he the most original and independent-minded Soviet leader of the post-war era, but his initiatives were to have an affect on my own work as Secretary General of the United Nations long after he had been ousted. He paid his first official visit to Austria in 1960, and we thought it proper to give him a warm welcome. Leopold Figl took him down to spend the day at his farm and the two men got on famously. They had much in common. Figl, the true peasant, and Khrushchev, who behaved like one. They both had this natural approach to life, disliked studying the files which the technocrats and bureaucrats forced on them, and preferred to operate by instinct.

At a dinner party in the Imperial Palace at Schönbrunn, he turned to the Austrian Chancellor, who at that time was Dr Gorbach, congratulated him on our sovereign independence, then turned to the corner of the room and pointed. 'Do you know who that man is sitting over there?' he asked. It was Vyacheslav Molotov, ousted by Khrushchev as the Soviet Foreign Minister. In order to maintain his dignity Molotov had been appointed Ambassador to Holland, but the Dutch government refused to give their *agrément.* In 1960 he moved on to Vienna as Soviet representative to the International Atomic Energy Agency, which required no such diplomatic formalities.

'That man,' Khrushchev went on, 'was against your State Treaty. He is not your friend. I had a lot of trouble convincing him and my military people to accept it. If I had not insisted so strongly, the treaty would not have been signed.'

Khrushchev had a formidable natural intelligence and slyness, but he had a genuine concern for contributing to the solution of international problems. Most of all he wanted to establish a close relationship with the United States and to normalize relations with the Western world in general. What has been overlooked is the extent to which he realized that the emergent Third World provided a major bargaining counter in achieving a balance between the two super-power groups.

In a flash of insight he had seen how much political capital could be made from the split between the West and these new nations over the issue of colonialism. During the 1960 General Assembly meeting, with many heads of state and government present, he proposed in a major address the adoption of a declaration concerning the de-colonizing of the remaining dependent territories. It may have sounded like special pleading, but it struck a spark among the representatives of the former colonies.

They were not prepared to accept the Soviet version entirely, as this would have provoked opposition in the West. Nevertheless, by the end of the session they had successfully steered through the Assembly their own text of a Declaration on the Granting of Independence to Colonial Countries and Peoples. The Soviet initiative had earned the gratitude of the entire Third World. A basis had been laid for the proclamation nearly twenty years later by Cuba's Fidel Castro at the 1979 Non-Aligned Conference in Havana of the presumed community of interest between the Communist and developing worlds.

What placed Khrushchev in a different category from all the other Soviet leaders was his independence of mind and action. He did not consult the Politburo in the way he should have done according to their standard practice. That had been good for Austria and for a period was good for the West, because the Politburo was much tougher and more rigid than Khrushchev himself. In his advocacy of peaceful co-existence he went far beyond the normal behaviour of a Soviet leader in order to strengthen the intiative. He exceeded certain limits under the Moscow rules and that was the reason why his colleagues finally threw him out. Even in as dangerous an adventure as the Cuban missile crisis, it was Khrushchev who eventually realized the implications and gave way. He was a strong man and had a forceful personality; his attempts to establish good relationships with the Western world were finally his undoing.

His intervention at the United Nations in favour of decolonization was of lasting effect. With their new agenda and surprisingly firm political discipline, the Third World countries set about changing radically the whole orientation of the world organization. During the 1960s, many westerners came to describe it, depending on their point of view, as an increasingly dangerous or, at best a useless place. Its priorities were not their priorities. It rode rough-shod over their ideas of justice and fairness. Time after time, it put the industrialized nations in the dock. It ground out innumerable resolutions at once castigating the West for its misdemeanours and making constant demands for redress.

It is difficult for a non-participant to realize how striking the changes in tone and substance of the organization have been. I recall a visit to the UN in the sixties by the eminent former Prime Minister of Belgium and former President of the General Assembly, Paul-Henri Spaak. As he observed the proceedings of the Security Council, after an absence of several years, he was thunderstruck. 'My God!' I recall him saying incredulously, 'this is unreal. I no longer recognize the United Nations.'

During these years I saw the role of the diplomat undergo dramatic changes, and foreign policy assume new meanings – in part because of the special problems of the post-war period, but principally because of the development of democratic forms of government and the increasing influence of the media in forming public opinion. The modern diplomat must be prepared to deal publicly, often extemporaneously, with matters far beyond the scope of politics. He is expected to be well informed on a wide variety of economic, social, legal and scientific issues and be ready to set forth his government's view on all of them.

International co-operation frequently requires a diplomat to work on problems that are by no means strictly political. He may find himself obliged to deal with questions of agricultural development, customs procedures, shipping, copyright, space research, ecology or labour legislation. When I served as chairman of the United Nations committee on the Peaceful Uses of Outer Space, I had to do an immense amount of homework on this esoteric subject. Those of us on the committee who were not specialists read scores of books and documents so that we might better understand the problems that concerned us. The same intensive study was required again when I was appointed chairman of the Safeguards Committee of the International Atomic Energy Agency. In these complex times, the diplomat must be a nimble-minded generalist able to turn his intelligence and skills to almost every kind of problem.

As every experienced Foreign Service officer knows, personal feelings have no place in international diplomacy. Just as a government cannot be guided by emotions in protecting its interests, so the diplomat cannot allow his own personal bias to affect his purpose. If he is to be successful, he must base his attitudes on the rational assessment of facts and forces, since concessions normally stem not so much from generosity but from the recognition of their inevitability.

Agreement, after all, is nothing but a balance struck between opposing camps, a compromise between divergent interests. Good personal relations between diplomats can ease the process of negotiation, but the national interest takes precedence over respect or friendship, even over bonds of blood or culture.

Another factor that has become important in recent years is the growth of active public interest in governmental affairs. The diplomat must now take into account the susceptibilities and wishes of the people, for these are given wide dissemination in the media and greatly influence a country's politics. The outcome of diplomatic negotiation often depends as much on the political interplay of internal forces as on external circumstances.

In January 1968 I was giving a lunch at my residence in New York for the members of the UN committee on the Peaceful Uses of Outer Space. As I was delivering a short speech to my guests the butler came from behind and whispered in my ear that the Austrian Chancellor was on the telephone in the library. 'There must be some mistake,' I said. 'I am not expecting any call. Go back and check.'

I knew there was a small political crisis in Vienna. The Chancellor by now was Dr Josef Klaus, a former Governor of Salzburg who had become the leader of the People's Party. After winning the elections a couple of years earlier with an absolute majority he had formed Austria's first one-party government after twenty years of coalition. His Foreign Minister was Dr Lujo Toncic-Sorin, whose father had been Consul-General of Austria in Dalmatia. The two men did not get on together and now Dr Klaus wanted a change. He and I did not know each other at all well, but he was acquainted with my background and I was going through a particularly active period at the United Nations.

It was Dr Klaus on the telephone all right, so I apologized to my guests and went to take the call. As I was leaving the room, I heard the American delegate say to the others: 'Either he is going to be dismissed or be appointed Foreign Minister.' The latter was the case: the Chancellor offered me the portfolio of foreign affairs, which I accepted after a brief discussion with my wife, convinced that I had now reached the peak of my career.

Austria's neutrality is a military one; it does not extend to ideology. The country is committed to Western democratic principles, and for outsiders it is sometimes difficult to reconcile the Austrian type of neutrality with our total freedom of choice in the ideological field, i.e. in our way of life. Soviet intervention in Czechoslovakia in 1968 and the ousting of Dubček brought me face to face with this problem. It occasioned a serious international crisis, which fortunately proved short-lived. Central Europe is an area in which East-West interests clash. I did not expect the Czechoslovak crisis to precipitate a military confrontation, as the super-powers would want to avoid a full-scale conflict. Fortunately, in that assessment I was right.

Nevertheless, these events on the other side of the Austrian border caused a highly critical situation for the government in Vienna. The whole population was, of course, deeply moved by the tragedy of its Czecho-slovak neighbours. A spontaneous wave of goodwill helped the large numbers of refugees to overcome their first misery. Public opinion was vociferously in favour of Dubček and very critical of the Soviet inter-vention. The Austrian media were practically unanimous in condemning the Soviet attitude, and Moscow became very concerned about this reaction. The Austrian government had to tread something of a tightrope in order to explain the existing freedom of expression and information and, on the other hand, to respect its commitment to neutrality. It was not a comfortable time in home politics. The government, under pressure, caught between public expectations and the dictates of political wisdom, formed a small emergency group within the cabinet to handle day-to-day developments.

For about three days the situation became quite ugly. Russian planes violated our air space between the Danube and the Czechoslovak border. On behalf of the government, I instructed our Ambassador in Moscow to lodge a strong protest, but he was not received. I tried repeatedly to contact the Soviet Ambassador in Vienna – to no avail. Then suddenly he called on me and I conveyed to him our protest. He had an answer ready. The weather conditions had been very bad and the planes had regrettably deviated from their normal course.

The reality was much more serious. The Soviets had apparently received wrong reports that NATO forces had entered Austrian territory from Bavaria clandestinely in order to build up a position along the Austro-Czech border, ready for any incursion on the part of the Red Army. We assumed that the flights had been initiated to check this information and when the Soviets had satisifed themselves that it was false, they called off the operation.

I have a small and perhaps inconsequential footnote. I accompanied our President, Franz Jonas, on a state visit to Moscow to mend some fences after the Czechoslovak crisis. My wife and I, together with the President, were put up in the Kremlin and served sumptuous breakfasts on beautiful tableware. Cissy, who normally has coffee and a few biscuits for breakfast, admired the dishes, but commented: 'Whoever told us that the Russians serve caviar at breakfast was wrong. There is no caviar.' The next morning there was a huge tin on the table.

One of my main preoccupations as Foreign Minister concerned the long-drawn-out dispute with Italy over the status of South Tyrol. This had now gone on for more than fifty years, since this predominantly German-speaking territory had been handed over to Italy by the Allied Powers under the Treaty of Saint-Germain of 1919. I will not attempt to summarize the inconclusive negotiations which had continued over the decades, turning around the problem of autonomy for the 250,000 German-speaking South Tyroleans. The problem had been brought before the United Nations by the then Foreign Minister, Bruno Kreisky, in 1960 and, after a lengthy and sometimes acrimonious debate, the General Assembly requested the two sides to resume their bilateral negotiations in order to work out a satisfactory settlement of the dispute. The Austrian government considered this a successful outcome of the debate in the UN as the resolution did, indeed, internationalize the South Tyrolean problem – a result which Austria had always wanted to achieve. Italy, on the other hand, was satisfied with the General Assembly's request that both sides should continue their bilateral negotiations. Following the UN resolution's advice, these negotiations were resumed and some modest progress was made. However, the basic issues remained unresolved for many years. It was in this situation that – when I became Foreign Minister in 1968 – I made a new effort to get out of the existing stalemate. Together with my gifted counterpart Aldo Moro, who was later tragically assassinated by the Red Brigades, we managed to hammer out a long-term agreement providing autonomy for the province of Bolzano. This was to be achieved under a carefully drafted operational calendar, which, despite considerable progress in a number of crucial areas, has still not produced final results. There are still difficulties in connection with the implementation of the agreement. But the heat has been taken out of it and it no longer constitutes a bitter conflict between our two countries.

The Klaus government lost the elections in April 1970 and resigned. A new minority government took over under Bruno Kreisky. At that time I received a telephone call from Dr Kirchschläger who happened to be our envoy in Prague. He is an old friend of mine and we had worked together for many years in the Ministry of Foreign Affairs. He started as legal adviser in the Foreign Office and later became *chef de cabinet* to Foreign Minister Kreisky. We always maintained very close relations, especially since he was very helpful in connection with the working-out of the South Tyrol agreement. I relied heavily on his extensive experience and his excellent legal advice.

Kirchschläger told me that Dr Kreisky had just offered him the post of Foreign Minister, and in view of our long friendship he wanted to keep me informed. I was touched by this thoughtful gesture and told him so, saying that I could not imagine a better successor for my job as Minister of Foreign Affairs of Austria. He has now been President of Austria for eleven years and the friendship which developed in those days still continues.

I was offered two of our senior embassies by the new government; one was London and the other Moscow. However, I was also told that I could return to my previous job in New York. I decided to go back to my former position as Ambassador to the United Nations. I had come to the conclusion that a small country has a better chance to get involved actively in international affairs through the multilateral machinery of the UN than in the bilateral relationships between governments.

A few months later Chancellor Kreisky asked for new elections, and his Social Democrats won an absolute majority.

I was involved in one further foray into our national politics. Presidential elections were due in April 1971 and in the autumn of 1970 the

33

People's Party decided to invite me to present myself as their candidate, in opposition to the incumbent, Franz Jonas, who was ending his first six years in office. I accepted and suffered an honourable defeat, with 47.2% of the votes. I had quite simply taken a period of leave from my duties at the United Nations and, with general agreement, to them I returned.

4

Secretary General

When I returned to New York in May 1971, the second five-year term of U Thant as Secretary General of the United Nations was drawing to a close. He had served the organization faithfully and with great devotion. Weakened by serious illness, he categorically refused to be considered for a third term. A successor would have to be selected. There was no dearth of candidates for the job. The appointment carries high prestige on the world scene and a number of prominent national leaders, with the backing of their countries, were bound to throw their hats into the ring.

The election procedure laid down by the Charter is cumbersome. In order to balance the interests of great and small powers, it provides that the Secretary General shall be appointed by the General Assembly upon recommendation by the Security Council. This means that the real contest occurs in the Security Council, voting by secret ballot. The veto of the permanent members applies, so that a candidate must obtain nine affirmative votes out of a Council of fifteen, including the approval, or at least the abstention, of each of the Big Five (China, France, United Kingdom, USSR and USA).

In the preceding months, quiet but intensive campaigning takes place on behalf of the principal candidates, supported by their governments and sometimes, though not always, by the regional groups to which they belong. Commitments of support are sought, principally from members of the Security Council. Governments weigh candidacies carefully, with an eye to their political consequences. As in all electoral contests in the United Nations, rotation among geographic regions is an important consideration. However, it is far from the only one. Personal competence and reputation, as well as acceptability to the major powers, figure decisively in the final choice.

The day after my arrival I was surprised to see in the *New York Times* an editorial strongly supporting Max Jacobson, the Permanent Representative of Finland, to succeed U Thant as Secretary General. Max was a good friend, so I telephoned him and we arranged to have lunch together two days later in a French restaurant near the Austrian Mission. During our conversation Max said that my name was also mentioned from time to time and he wondered whether I was seriously interested. I told him that some of my friends had informed me that there was talk about me, along with half a dozen others, but that I had not been approached from any quarter in this connection. Obviously, I was interested; for any diplomat in the world, the post of Secretary General of the UN is the utmost aim of a successful career. However, I considered myself at that time a dark horse and nothing more. Having been absent from the United Nations for six months, I was lucky not to have been involved in the pre-election intrigues.

When delegates returned to New York for the 1971 autumn General Assembly session, my name was increasingly mentioned as a possible candidate. I therefore sounded out several ambassadors in a casual fashion, but the result was not at all conclusive. Knowing the danger of being exposed too early, I advised my government not to propose my candidacy publicly but to make confidential inquiries of certain key governments, in their capitals. The result confirmed my own estimate in New York. The race was still wide open and no one could yet say who would emerge as the front runners.

The position of the Western powers could be described as generally friendly to me but non-committal. To help clarify the situation, I arranged a luncheon with the Soviet representative, Jakob Malik. To my surprise, he expressed himself in rather friendly terms about my possible candidacy, although he too did not commit himself. A few days later I received a clue as to the Soviet attitude when I was invited back to a luncheon given by him in the Soviet Mission on 67th Street.

About twenty people were present, mainly ambassadors to the United Nations like myself. Although under the United Nations' special protocol practices I would not normally have expected to sit next to the host, I found myself placed at his left hand. Noting my surprise, Malik turned jovially to me and said: 'You see, I put you nearer to my heart.' It was a typical case of tantalizing indirect Soviet diplomacy.

The Chinese Ambassador, Huang Hua, who later became Foreign Minister of his country, was, as I had expected, very cautious and anything but encouraging. He pointed out that two Europeans had already held the job, but did not indicate that the Chinese had as yet made any decision.

After weeks of diplomatic manoeuvring, the election process finally began in November 1971. The difficult choice to be made between the rival candidates gave promise of an exciting contest. Apart from Max Jacobson and myself, three prominent UN diplomats were waiting in the wings: Argentina's Carlos Ortiz de Rozas, who had been his government's Ambassador in Vienna during my time as Foreign Minister, the High Commissioner for Refugees, Prince Sadruddin Aga Khan, and finally, Terence Sanzé, the Ambassador of Burundi, physically slight but a very ambitious man. George Bush, who was then Ambassador to the United Nations and is now Vice-President of the United States, recalled years later how Sanzé had buttonholed him in one of the lounges of the UN building and had eagerly tried to plead his suitability for the post – and probably to apply a little pressure as well. To no avail: after the second ballot, it was clear that only Jacobson and I had a chance. The other candidates were either vetoed by one of the super-powers or did not obtain enough votes. But still Max was vetoed by the Soviets – and in my case it was the opposition of the Chinese.

At this juncture, the Austrian government once again gave its support to my candidature, both discreetly and effectively, especially in Peking. In his recently published book, Hans Thalberg, then Austrian Ambassador to China, describes how he tried to make delicate allusions to Austrian hopes in his contacts with the Chinese, who tended to be rather sensitive on the subject, but simply found no opportunity to mention my name to Chou En-lai. Thalberg writes that he returned utterly downcast to his hotel and only learned from Chinese politicians after my election as UN Secretary General how impressed Chou En-lai had been at the Austrian's tact and discretion. 'Supposed failure had in fact been success.'

It was China's change of mind that tipped the scales. On 21 December 1971, my fifty-third birthday, the Security Council recommended to the General Assembly that I be elected Secretary General – unanimously, on the proposal of my rival candidate, Carlos Ortiz de Rozas.

At the time, I was far away from the scene of action. Convinced that I could no longer influence the decision, I was taking a stroll through Central Park and learned from an excited young Austrian diplomat after my return to the Austrian Mission that the Security Council had just decided in my favour.

Looking back, I wonder at the calm with which I received the news of the decision. Probably I had inwardly been expecting this result more than I had admitted openly. In strange contrast to the dramatic events that preceded it, it was a prosaic scene that took place a few hours later in a tiny office on the second floor of the UN building – a sparsely furnished room with a spartan desk and without any pictures on the walls. Here I received a few terse words of congratulation from the Ambassador of Sierra Leone, Ismael Kamara, a heavily built man, who was then President of the

Security Council. By some quirk of fate, it was to another Security Council President from Black Africa, the Ugandan Ambassador Otunnu, that I presented my letter of resignation ten years later.

On the day of my election I had barely left the office of the Security Council President when I had the first foretaste of what was to become a routine matter for me in the coming years. Journalists from every country under the sun bustled me into a press room. Their searching questions – immediately followed by the prompt criticism that I had faced the media before my election by the General Assembly – dispelled any illusion I might have had about the pitfalls of my new office. But all worries and doubts were swept away on 22 December, when, in a special session, the General Assembly elected me by acclamation. I was ceremoniously ushered into the crowded Assembly Hall to take the oath of office. My first speech as Secretary General reflected a feeling of confidence and eagerness to get down to my job.

Early on a clear, sunny day in January 1972 I walked into the vertical slab building that houses the headquarters of the United Nations secretariat, ascended silently in a special elevator to the thirty-eighth floor and walked down the carpeted corridor to the suite I was to occupy for the next ten years.

I was no stranger to these premises. As Austria's Permanent Representative to the United Nations and then as Austrian Foreign Minister, I had often enough called on the Secretary General on official business over the previous fifteen years. Now I was arriving not as a representative of my country but as the Chief Executive Officer of an organization that represented the closest approach to a world federation that mankind had yet been able to achieve.

It would have been easy to indulge in exalted romanticism about my new position. After all, I had just become, in a sense, a spokesman for humanity. Statesmen could speak for their countries. Religious leaders could mobilize their believers. But there was hardly anyone else who, year in and year out, could give voice to the aspirations of virtually all the nations and peoples of the world; represent their interests; and, so to speak, evoke the conscience of mankind. Alas! The reality, I knew, was different. The lustre of the United Nations had dimmed in the twenty-five years since it had been established. I had seen enough of its day-to-day operations to know that moments of high drama and events of earth-shaking significance were rare. Instead, seen from the inside, the United Nations in 1972 was buffeted by ideological passions, nationalist rivalries, colonial and racial controversies, and conflicting economic and social demands. Its operations were cumbersome, often ineffectual, sometimes even mind-numbing.

The turbulence and confusions which so often seemed to reign in the United Nations – not to speak of its shortcomings and frustrations – had to be viewed as a reflection of conditions in the world at large. The United Nations was an instrument the nations of the world had fashioned to help them solve their international problems. If they could not or would not use it for that purpose, should one blame the tools or those who wielded them?

I knew that this was far too simple an analysis. The organization was more than a mere conduit. It had a corporate personality of its own. What the member states did collectively at its headquarters depended to some extent on the resourcefulness of the Secretary General and his staff. They could head off confrontation and move contentious matters towards agreement. My most challenging task would be to make the most of my opportunities to do this.

My predecessors had in their time faced unprecedented situations. They had made innovative and even brilliant contributions to the work of the organization. Yet Trygve Lie had left office under strong attack from the Soviets as a result of his actions during the Korean War. His successor, Dag Hammarskjöld, had antagonized them even more seriously over the Congo dispute. Only U Thant had served two full five-year terms without losing the co-operation of a super-power. Yet where Hammarskjöld had stretched the powers of his office with risky dynamism, U Thant had been criticized for excessive passivity. Obviously, the political survivability of a Secretary General was by no means assured.

Vice-President George Bush, then head of the US delegation to the UN, had quipped that I should be offered condolences rather than congratulations on my election. Bush is an engaging, open-minded man. His popularity at the United Nations and during his many foreign missions was based on his absolute integrity, his superior grasp of foreign policy fundamentals and his attractive, low-key manner. He has certainly been a valuable spokesman for his government in dealing with a host of international issues.

He is also blessed with an apt sense of humour. At Christmastime 1972 he sent me a modest gift, which I still treasure. It is a miniature tool-kit in a yellow box bearing my name. When I opened it I found it full of small hand tools, which have helped greatly to mitigate my innate personal clumsiness in performing minor household tasks such as hanging pictures and replacing screws. I wondered why Bush had sent me this particular Yuletide remembrance. On a little card tucked into the box was the legend: 'Merry Christmas and Happy New Year, and I hope this kit of tools will help you to solve the problems of the world.' It was a thoughtful and touching gesture.

In those early days I was, of course, confident that I could manage those problems. It was essentially a matter of using the limited powers of my office under the United Nations Charter to the fullest degree, while maintaining tolerable relations with the member states, whose support was indispensable. If this meant that my public posture had to be cautious and impartial in dealing with disputes, that would have to be accepted. It might be emotionally satisfying to play to the gallery in the world arena, but it was likely to be counter-productive. What was vital was that I should use every ounce of my energy to keep the organization functioning as successfully as it possibly could. I believed deeply – and I still do – that in the long run the world organization offers the best prospect we have of avoiding our own destruction and attaining a more just world order.

I knew from the very beginning that I had to find my way through the jungle of American and international media and to attract them to the political and humanitarian goals of the United Nations – a difficult task, as I found out in one of my first meetings with the American mass media. In a networked programme called *Meet the Press* I was asked: 'You served in the German army; how is that compatible with your new function?' I replied with some asperity that I and my whole family had been anti-Nazi and that the alternative to being called up was execution. That seemed to settle the matter for the time being.

However, I am sorry to say that a similar campaign against me was revived in a later stage of my Secretary-Generalship. Apparently in connection with my outspoken attitude in regard to the Middle East problem and my strong defence of the legitimate rights of the Palestinians – although at the same time I equally championed the right of Israel to exist in recognized and secure boundaries – some circles in the United States attacked me vigorously as having been a Nazi, since I had served in the German army. One of the most outspoken critics was Congressman Stephan Solarz, who represented the Borough of Brooklyn in the American Congress. It was only after a personal, private meeting with him, organized by the Austrian Ambassador, Thomas Klestil, in which I explained my background in detail to the Congressman, that Solarz stopped his attacks and told me frankly: 'Had I known all this, I would never have attacked you.' I appreciated this act of honesty.

Since I was fully acquainted with the working methods of the United Nations, I had no illusions about what was waiting for me. I am basically a pragmatist. I do not belong to that group of intellectuals who feel that everything has to be seen and done through an intellectual approach. I was always deeply convinced that you have a much better chance of succeeding if you approach your problem in a practical, realistic way.

From my long experience in diplomacy and politics in Austria, I was convinced that intense personal contacts were indispensable to success.

But in addition to that purely personal approach, I thought that some changes, some adaptation of the working methods of the General Assembly – and perhaps even of the Security Council – were necessary.

The agenda of the General Assembly was too long and too repetitive. Every year we had more than a hundred items to be debated. One had to weed out the agenda, but I soon found out that it was *auf Granit beissen* – biting stone. Whenever I suggested the deletion of an item on the agenda for the next Assembly, the steering committee started a long discussion and finally one or the other of the interested groups decided to keep it in.

On the other hand, each year we had the same extensive and acrimonious debate on issues such as the Middle East, South Africa and similar problems, without making any progress. This led, of course, to a sense of frustration in the membership. I do not question the good faith of those who sponsor such an approach. I do, however, question their judgement, if they really desire to avoid an unending cycle of conflicts in those regions and achieve constructive solutions. And I fear that, by pressing matters too far, they are weakening the fabric of the United Nations generally.

I learned a salutary lesson from one initiative that ran into the ground. I had attended the Munich Olympics and was shocked and appalled by the assassination of the Israeli athletes. So I determined to do something against the spread of terrorism, even if no member state did. I wanted the Assembly to deal with the matter. But some Arab delegations did not agree, they wanted to eliminate the proposal. Their main argument was: Why are you proposing this? You should know that this kind of political terrorism is the consequence of the fact that the world community is not dealing with the underlying causes. It is the unresolved Palestinian issue which is at the root of the problem, and even under the Charter of the United Nations a people has the right to use force – not terrorism, of course – to get independence.

The main spokesman for the Arabs at the time was the late Saudi Ambassador, Yamil Baroodi, who was a rather bizarre figure, highly intelligent and very outspoken. He had a tendency to make long statements and as a result prolonged every debate. However, he had a sense of humour, and was capable of producing good ideas, which very often led to a compromise. On this occasion he achieved precisely this result: the compromise he suggested solved the procedural problem. The General Assembly decided to include the item on the agenda, although with a rather ambiguous title, namely 'International terrorism and its underlying causes'.

I was disappointed not to get a better response, but I knew we had to make a beginning; this is something the public does not usually understand. The question of terrorism was on the agenda of the United Nations year after year but no concrete action was taken. It was not until 1977, on the proposal of the Federal Republic of Germany, that the General Assembly adopted a resolution against the hijacking of civilian aircraft. In 1983, after the tragic killings of South Korean government officials in Rangoon, the world organization strongly condemned this criminal act and agreed on a number of concrete recommendations to combat international terrorism.

The Secretary General has the public image of a hard-pressed individual perpetually attempting to find solutions for political and diplomatic crises in various parts of the world. No doubt this is the most important part of his job. But his responsibilities extend into many other fields. He must exercise a similar type of leadership through the whole range of economic, social, cultural and humanitarian affairs with which the organization deals. And, as 'the chief administrative officer of the organization', he is responsible for maintaining and directing the staff required to service its activities and carry out its decisions.

In the best of circumstances, this would be a difficult task. The number of people employed in the United Nations Secretariat approaches 14,000. They are drawn from a membership of 159 states, of widely varying cultural, educational and linguistic accomplishments. And they are scattered among scores of regional centres, information offices and operational outposts on every continent.

The headquarters resemble a smoothly functioning machine. Heads of governments, foreign ministers, diplomats and hundreds of other dele-gates bustle about in comfortable meeting-rooms. The tidal wave of oratory rolls on; the endless flow of documents, reports and resolutions pours forth, apparently from nowhere. In the three months of the Assembly meeting, some 140 agenda items will be considered by close to 1,500 representatives and their alternates. An avalanche of statements, proposals, resolutions, amendments and votes will be recorded, as the Assembly does its work through seven standing committees and in six official languages.

The performance may seem effortless, and it is certainly unobtrusive. But supporting its visible symbols – the experts assisting the delegates, the simultaneous interpreters overcoming the barriers of language, the security guards maintaining order – a large staff labours behind the scenes to permit the methodical and expeditious conduct of business. The Secretariat includes professionals in every field of United Nations activity. Many collect and analyse data, prepare reports, conduct investigations and otherwise facilitate the deliberations and decision-making of its principal organs. Others have operational responsibilities: they plan economic development projects, assist refugees, support military observers and peace-keeping forces, or study human rights problems. Without these and other similar services, the organization could not function.

At the apex of this structure stands the Secretary General. He is not chosen because of his administrative ability. If he has it, so much the better; but political stature, skill and acceptability will certainly be the primary criteria governing his selection. In my own case, I was fortunate in having had years of diplomatic experience in the Austrian Foreign Service and, in addition, administrative experience as Director of Personnel in the Foreign Ministry and as Foreign Minister. The transition from leadership of a national service to the post of Secretary General was a less drastic shift for me than it may have been for some of my predecessors.

None the less, the change was a formidable one. Managing the Austrian Foreign Service does not begin to compare with running a multi-million-dollar enterprise like the modern United Nations. When I became Secretary General in 1972, the first budget I presented to the General Assembly was a relatively modest $210 million, with an additional $15–20 million in voluntary or extra-budgetary funds. When I left office at the end of 1981, the Assembly had just approved a budget approaching $750 million annually, with an additional $80 million in extra-budgetary funds. The rate of increase was in large part due to inflation. In dollar terms the regular budget has almost levelled off over the last few years.

It is important to keep these matters in perspective. Arguably, the Secretariat may be overstaffed, and the cost of running the United Nations may be too high. But the work force is a good deal smaller than the uniformed police force of the City of New York (over 22,000) or its sanitation department. For the United States, the largest contributor to the budget at 25% of the total, the direct appropriation for the United Nations is the equivalent, per capita, of about 80 cents per year – less than the price of a packet of cigarettes. The United Nations budget can be compared with what New York spends on its fire department. In relation to the many billions of dollars spent each year by the nations of the world on the destructive weapons of war, the sums devoted to the prevention of war, the maintenance of peace, and the quest for higher living standards and greater freedom for all are small indeed.

The guiding principle and the unique feature of the Secretariat is the concept of an independent and impartial international civil service. The original model runs back to the League of Nations and was largely based on the traditions of integrity and excellence of the British civil service. For the predominantly Western corps of officials who staffed the United Nations in its formative stages, the requirements were easily understood and to a large degree accepted. Their attitudes reflected the high hopes for the United Nations at its inception, and the idealism with which it was energized in its early years.

Over the course of time, however, the independence of the Secretariat has come under increasing pressure. As one state or group of states appeared to press its particular claims, others tended to react in the same way to protect their own positions. Thus the impartiality and the organic unity of the Secretariat were threatened and the ideal of a truly international staff has to some extent faded.

At the level of the Secretary General, who must take action in areas of high political volatility, the maintenance of independence and neutrality poses a vexing dilemma. If the Secretary General takes the initiative to move left or right – acts or refrains from acting – on a particular issue, he will probably please some states and antagonize others. The Secretary General who loses the confidence of a permanent member of the Security Council enjoying the veto is in a most difficult position. His effectiveness is gravely impaired and his usefulness therefore jeopardized. He can work productively only if he maintains harmonious relations with United Nations members of all persuasions.

The public does not always understand this. It expects the Secretary General to speak out forcefully in favour of one or the other cause and, *per contra*, to distance himself from certain resolutions or decisions of the General Assembly. As I have said on many occasions, I had no doubt that, for instance, the resolution, adopted by the General Assembly with an overwhelming majority, equating Zionism and racism did serious damage to the image of the United Nations. At the time I was criticized in some circles, especially in the West, for failing to condemn the resolution publicly. It is still my considered opinion that as the General Assembly, composed of representatives of sovereign states, is one of the main organs of the United Nations, it is not for the Secretary General publicly to criticize its decisions, even if he personally believes that they are wrong. Of course, I did not fail to express to the authors of the resolution and other governments my deep concern at this unfortunate initiative, asking them to avoid future similar actions, which could only harm the prestige of the world organization. At any rate, such action was not repeated during my term of office.

Fortunately, during my long term of office I was able to maintain the confidence of the membership, which during that time grew to 156. That in itself gave me considerable satisfaction. This was even more important as the original East-West confrontations had been overtaken by the massive admission of Third World countries.

I regarded it as a primary responsibility of my position to resist demands by member states for actions I considered prejudicial to United Nations purposes and principles. It was a challenge to my diplomatic dexterity to do so in ways that in the broader sense resulted in the greatest benefit to the organization. Similar forces converge upon the Secretary General in his management of the Secretariat staff, notably in the fields of recruitment and promotion. Here, I regret to say, political pressures have become all too common. To a degree this is understandable. As the influx of so many new states into the organization took place over the last quarter century, it was natural for the new entrants to seek positions for their nationals in the Secretariat. Article 101 of the Charter specifies competence and efficiency as the paramount consideration in employment. It also adds: 'Due regard shall be paid to the importance of recruiting the staff on as wide a geographical basis as possible.'

This would be a difficult process at best. But two factors have made it even more so. First, in proportionate terms, the Secretariat has not grown nearly as quickly as the number of new members. Second, over 75% of the United Nations staff hired during its early years entered as career international civil servants on a permanent tenure basis. Consequently the early members of the United Nations – including not only the Western states but also countries like India, Egypt and the Philippines – still enjoy a relative over-representation among the United Nations employees.

Thus the personnel practices of the United Nations have resulted in creating a test of wills, as it were, between the Secretary General and the representatives of governments. He is concerned with maintaining the quality of staff performance; they are seeking additional positions for their nationals. Frequently he must make difficult choices among competing candidates backed by their own embassies. Some of the smaller delegations concentrate more on personal matters than on issues before the Organization. Obtaining a job for a compatriot can be the major preoccupation of certain diplomats.

There is another aspect of Secretariat personnel policy which has a bearing on how closely it approaches the ideal of an international civil service. Over the course of time, the proportion of staff recruited for limited, fixed terms has grown until it comprises close to half the total of those employed. From the United Nations' earliest days, the Soviet bloc has appointed all its nationals in this category. They are therefore temporary employees and it has to be assumed that they will return home on conclusion of their United Nations service. Other countries now follow the same practice.

Perhaps surprisingly, this procedure has not been as harmful as might have been expected. Indeed, fixed-term employment has one very definite advantage. It is very difficult to remove a full career employee who fails to measure up to his job requirements after some years of service. A fixed-term contract offers at least the possibility for a serious performance review and a decision on whether to extend the contract.

We had recurrent problems on personnel matters with Ambassador Jakob Malik, who for many years headed the Soviet Delegation in New York. I had to deal repeatedly with his complaints and try to do what I properly could to be responsive. Malik was an excitable type. His voice would rise and he would pound the table if he felt aggrieved – or wished to appear so. One day he was particularly irate. 'The Secretary General has failed in this,' he said. 'He has not kept his agreement. In five years he was going to bring the quota of Soviet employees up to the minimum level of the desirable range for our country. Now, after five years have passed, we have not reached it.'

In fact, we were very close to it. But one of my colleagues sitting in the meeting with me could not resist responding with a classic retort. 'You know, Mr Ambassador,' he said, 'this is not the first time that five-year plans have not been achieved.' Malik roared with laughter.

We referred humorously to this exchange during several subsequent personnel discussions. But once, while I was away from New York, Malik wrote me a letter voicing his usual remonstrances. The reply, written by a colleague in my absence, made the same rejoinder. But this time the response was different. I received a stiff communication from Malik, who was obviously furious. It was one thing for us to have our little joke orally, but quite another to record it in files that would get back to Moscow.

The second incident involved a Secretariat official who on his own initiative reassigned a Chinese employee, moving him to a more important position. Within twenty-four hours of his being informed, the Chinese Ambassador visited the official with a protest. His response to the explanation given was blunt: 'Who wants a more important job? We weren't consulted on this. We don't believe in being pushed around. As far as we're concerned he will stay where he is.'

Making allowances for its unique characteristics, I do not believe that the Secretariat needs to apologize for the general standard of its work. Like any large bureaucratic organization, it has its star performers and its drones. Its shortcomings are in large measure duplicated in national bureaucracies. One must guard against a certain Euro-American ethnocentrism here. Westerners too often assume that they are the principal repositories of bureaucratic skills, and that the level of personnel from the developing countries is generally inferior. In a very narrow sense, as applied to certain highly technical or expert fields, this may be true. But in positions where negotiation, inter-personal relations, organizing ability and similar attributes are important – as they so often are – representatives of non-Western cultures are equally capable, if with a different style.

Special considerations apply at the top levels of the Secretariat. These are positions carrying political implications stemming from their distribution among the major powers. It would be foolhardy to try to tamper in any substantial way with the long-established balance prevailing among them. Any change in the nationality of the occupants of one of the major posts at the Under Secretary General level requires compensatory steps to ensure that no country's representation is downgraded. A Soviet national, for example, has always held the post of Under Secretary General for Security Council Affairs. An American has usually held the important political position of Under Secretary General for General Assembly Affairs, although the late Ralph Bunche, a US citizen, was responsible for special political matters, a sort of trouble-shooter, for instance, in the Middle East.

When I took office, I felt there was a need for new blood at this level. By exercising some ingenuity and persuasiveness, I was able to make the necessary adjustments in such a way that no state considered itself to have lost ground, and I like to believe that the Secretariat maintained a strong professional and managerial team at the top.

I do not propose to list all the changes I made over a ten-year period, but two – which I consider of particular importance – deserve special mention. On the death of Ralph Bunche, the outstanding American negotiator of the earlier armistice agreements and peace-keeping arrangements between Israel and the Arab states, I was able to promote Brian Urquhart of the United Kingdom as his successor. Urquhart, a man of immense experience since the earliest days of the United Nations, is considered the foremost authority on the organization and maintenance of its various peace-keeping and observer forces. Second, I co-opted George Davidson of Canada as Under Secretary General for Administration and Management.

Brian Urquhart is a sterling character. He had joined the United Nations as one of its earliest young officers in 1945, after serving as a paratrooper during the landing of the Allies in France. He had been the victim of an appalling accident: his parachute had failed to open properly and although he fell on a pile of rubbish, he broke most of the bones in his body. By a miracle he survived and regained full physical vigour. There was no sign of his injuries. Short, slight, with an attractive, intelligent air to him, he became one of my most trusted colleagues. He had a clear mind and was always blunt and courageous. He never minced his words when we found ourselves in disagreement and I had complete confidence in him.

Over the years, he was my senior executive officer during some of the worst crises with which we had to deal.

I had met George Davidson during my four years as Ambassador in Canada. He had held ministerial posts in Immigration and in the Finance Ministry. He then became President of the Canadian Broadcasting Corporation and was in that post when I approached him to join the Secretariat. A liberal, open-minded man, with a great sense of humour and very competent, he had immense experience in administrative affairs. He did an outstanding job in the United Nations and kept its complex machinery running smoothly in a way that helped me to concentrate on other matters.

I was also fortunate in my successive American colleagues as Under Secretary General for General Assembly Affairs. The first was Bradford Morse, a highly respected former US Congressman who voluntarily resigned to become a staff member of the United Nations. Because of his long experience as a parliamentarian, he was an ideal choice as the top official to deal with General Assembly Affairs. He filled this post with great skill and distinction for many years before I appointed him as Administrator of the United Nations Development Programme (UNDP), one of the most important aid programmes for the Third World, which has a budget bigger than that of the whole United Nations. Since the American government provides a high proportion of the funds, the nomination for this top post lies in their hands.

At the General Assembly Morse was succeeded by William Buffum, who had previously been head of the United Nations desk in the State Department in Washington. I had known him well in that capacity and welcomed his nomination. A well-informed man, very loyal and co-operative, I also made him responsible for the UN Human Rights Division in Geneva, headed by a Dutch civil servant.

Interestingly, the French preferred that their top Secretariat official should supervise the United Nations' economic and social functions. This was quite appropriate; but when economic development became a matter of overriding priority for the new Third World majority in the organization, there was a feeling that this should be reflected in the structure of the Secretariat – and that the top official concerned should come from a less developed country.

The solution was to create the position of Director General for Development and International Economic Cooperation, ranking above the Under Secretaries General. His role is one of co-ordination of the many activities bearing on the development process. As first occupant of this position I appointed Kenneth Dadzie of Ghana, a knowledgeable and experienced diplomat and economist. When I left office, he was replaced by Jean Ripert of France, who had been serving as Under Secretary General for the Department of International Economic and Social Affairs. This move seemed to gainsay the proprietary feeling of the developing countries with regard to the post. But it was rationalized by pointing out that the new Secretary General, Javier Pérez de Cuellar of Peru, was from a developing country, while I was not. Thus, over all, the principle of balance was preserved.

Relationships between Western and Eastern bloc staff members in the Secretariat, especially from the two super-powers, inevitably exhibited a degree of suspicion, due to the Soviet policy of only seconding personnel for limited periods. They sent some perfectly competent people and we had to take their loyalty to the organization on trust. Nevertheless we had various brushes with the FBI, who were always monitoring the activities of these Soviet members of the Secretariat should they appear to be taking advantage of their residence in New York for other purposes.

From time to time we would be asked to collaborate in investigations, but I only remember one occasion when a Russian employee of the UN was caught red-handed and expelled. We did have trouble over another Soviet staff member, Geli Dnjeprovsky, who was appointed head of the Personnel Department in Geneva. The American authorities had built up a substantial dossier about him and his appointment was called into question. He had served perfectly well in New York and, as the accusations were not pressed and no evidence was presented, the affair blew over.

The most remarkable episode involved Arkadiev Shevchenko, the most senior Soviet national in the UN Secretariat, who was the Under Secretary General for Security Council Affairs. He was a very competent official and had once worked as special assistant to Andrey Gromyko. He had always seemed to me a staunch supporter of Soviet interests in the United Nations but he had, as his recently published memoirs make clear, already established contacts with the American CIA over a considerable period of time.

His defection caused a substantial furore and involved the United Nations in considerable complications. I first learnt of his dramatic decision at three o'clock in the morning of 8 April 1978, when I was on an official visit to the United Kingdom and the Republic of Ireland. Ferdinand Mayrhofer-Grünbühel, my personal assistant, had been telephoned by Shevchenko, who only two days previously had spoken of going to Moscow to visit his purportedly sick mother. Now the story had taken a completely different turn. In a tense voice Shevchenko told my assistant: 'Look, I do not want to return to the Soviet Union – never!' He added, 'I would ask you to inform the Secretary General.' At first, my assistant thought that Shevchenko had perhaps drunk a glass too many, as he was known to do on occasion. 'Do you know what you're doing?' Mayrhofer asked anxiously. 'Of course I know,' was the reply. 'I've been thinking about it for a long time.'

Over the next few days it was Mayrhofer whom Shevchenko phoned from a hideout somewhere in the Pocono Mountains in Pennsylvania and requested him to inform his wife Lina. She was a tall, good-looking woman, known to be very outgoing and outspoken on social occasions. On hearing the news, she burst into hysterics and demanded to know where her husband was – until somebody took the receiver out of her hands.

Upon my return to New York, all the necessary negotiations for the termination of Shevchenko's contract with the UN had been initiated with the assistance of the American lawyer Ernest Gross, an attorney with experience of the United Nations. None the less, Arkady Shevchenko expressed the wish to see me once more – in order to offer me some kind of explanation. With the help of the Americans and in order to hoodwink the journalists haunting the building, we had to arrange a rather unusual route to my office. A convoy of CIA limousines brought Arkady Shevchenko to an apartment building close to the UN Headquarters where Under Secretary George Davidson, lived. From that point the Canadian Chief of UN Security, Colonel Trimble, took over and drove him into the garage, and, together with my personal assistant, led Shevchenko through a back door into the freight elevator, which whisked them up to the thirty-eighth floor. When Shevchenko entered my office, I immediately noticed his air of unease, and he remained very subdued. In a soft voice he explained in general terms the reasons for his defection: he could no longer live under the Soviet system, he said, it was a question of survival. He apologized for the inconvenience and diplomatic embarrassment that his defection had caused before he went on to reveal the main reason for his visit. He informed me that his wife had been forced to return to the Soviet Union, where his daughter was, and he sought my co-operation in securing their return. We were, of course, already aware of Lina Shevchenko's departure for Moscow a few days earlier. On being asked by the US Immigration Service at Kennedy Airport whether she was leaving the country of her own free will, Lina Shevchenko had replied in a firm voice, 'Yes.'

After our meeting, Arkady Shevchenko left the UN building in the same surreptitious manner as he had entered it, pausing only to clear up his office, which had been sealed during his absence. I never saw my former Under Secretary again. My interventions with the Soviet authorities on behalf of his wife and daughter met with a sharp rebuff and a demand on the part of Ambassador Troyanovsky that the Americans should return Shevchenko to Moscow immediately. Subsequent endeavours came to an end when we were informed that Lina Shevchenko had committed suicide.

Apart from these incidents, I had no bad experiences with other leading Soviet officials. Because of their established rotation system, they usually stayed only a few years and then returned to Moscow, where they were often given high positions in the Foreign Ministry. One of the most prominent Under Secretaries General was Anatoly Dobrynin, who, for many years now, has served as Ambassador to Washington. During my term of office I had a succession of other high-ranking Soviet officials as Under Secretaries. Besides Arkadiev Shevchenko, there were Wasily Kutakov, Vyacheslav Ustinov and Mikhail D. Sytenko, all rather quiet and co-operative colleagues. I did my best to keep them informed on current matters and in this way was able to maintain good working relations.

Much the most signal event of my first year in office had been the admission of the People's Republic of China. Although the Communists had consolidated their control over the Chinese mainland in 1949, it was not until the end of 1971, just before I became Secretary General, that their delegates took their seats in the United Nations. Previously, with the strong support of the United States, the Nationalist government in Taiwan had clung to its status as the sole representative of the State of China. This had increasingly become a fiction. It strained all credulity for a government exercising authority over a population of 16 million on an island off the Chinese mainland to claim to speak for one billion Chinese, one quarter of the human race. The continual battles over the issue of Chinese representation had wasted much time and energy in the United Nations and perhaps more important, had cast a shadow of unreality over the proceedings.

When the substitution was made, the new Chinese representatives moved slowly and carefully into their role in the organization. It took several years before they started to play an active part. At the beginning, they were very uncertain and very unsure of themselves. They did not attempt to dissimulate and were very open about their problems. 'Do understand that we are new, we do not pretend that we know everything,' they told me. 'On the contrary, we are fully aware that this is a completely new atmosphere for us. We do not normally deal with such matters as are discussed here in the United Nations and now suddenly we are confronted with situations where we have to take up a position on each and every problem in the world. We are not used to this.' I found this beguiling, so I monitored their interventions in the various committees and went out of my way to be of assistance to them.

I paid my first visit to China in August 1972 at the height of the summer heat in Peking, which was matched by the warm hospitality extended to us by our Chinese hosts. The great interest which the Chinese showed in my visit was immediately apparent.

The Chinese leaders I met during those four days in Peking included some very distinctive individuals. The most compatible with Westerners was Chou En-lai, who was Prime Minister at that time. He was an impressive personality, a highly cultured man with a sophisticated approach to world politics. Like all his colleagues, he was a staunch defender of the Chinese Communist Party's orthodoxies but he also seemed to have a real appreciation of the value of the United Nations to the international community.

He recognized that it was in China's interest to support the organization in order to establish and improve the status of China, especially in the Third World, but perhaps equally as a means of undermining the pretensions of the USSR to the 'hegemony' the Chinese so relentlessly attacked in their public statements. Like the other Chinese leaders to whom I spoke over the years, Chou appeared to have a real fear of Soviet imperialism and even of an attack by the Soviet armed forces. There was no question as to whom they regarded as their main enemy.

Chou made an almost unprecedented gesture towards the United Nations. The government of Taiwan had continued to pay its annual assessment while it provided the Chinese representation, but that amount had fallen proportionately as new members were admitted during the sixties. Chou proposed voluntarily to increase the Chinese contribution. He reminded me of the poverty of the country and its very low gross national product. But then he said: 'However, we are a great power and I fully understand that we have a corresponding obligation to give the organization adequate support.' Although the following year China did raise its contribution, it reduced it again after the death of Chou En-lai. This is another example of how much can depend on the personal attitude of political leaders and their influence at home.

I knew the head of the Chinese delegation in New York quite well. Huang Hua had been their Ambassador in Canada while I was there. He was a smiling, extremely polite man, not rigid at all. We established a very pleasant personal relationship. My wife had recurrent problems with her back. So did he, and whenever we met on social occasions they would exchange advice on their medical treatment. At one point he even recommended acupuncture and sent for a parcel of Chinese medicaments from Peking.

For most of the time he kept very strictly to the instructions he received from his government. Their dominating attitude was inflexible criticism of 'Soviet imperialism'. For several years there was more or less a permanent confrontation between Peking and Moscow in the different organs of the United Nations. The Russians were more restrained because they had longer experience of the way things were done. They did not like the Chinese attacks but they took them with remarkably good grace and regarded them as inevitable.

The Chinese still consider the Soviet Union as Public Enemy No. 1, not the Americans. They feel that the United States, and the Western world in general, have much more understanding for Chinese problems, are assisting them actively, and share a common hostility towards the Soviet Union.

To this end, the Chinese are prepared to put up with a great deal. Their complacency in the face of continued American support for Taiwan is quite remarkable in view of their previous altercations over the issue, and only emphasizes how far the Chinese are prepared to go in order to obtain the economic and technical assistance from the West, particularly the United States, they feel they need.

The architect of this policy is without any doubt Deng Xiaoping who is an uncommonly strong but somewhat devious personality. It is easy to understand how he has risen to the head of the Chinese Communist Party and the state structure. In my conversations with him I have never felt that we were talking on the same wavelength. On foreign policy he appears to think in strictly bilateral terms, with little regard for multilateral diplomacy. He cultivates American political leaders and has a good relationship with them but, to a quite extraordinary degree, animosity against the Russians pervades his whole approach to matters of substance.

Some of his insights are unexpected. The last time I saw him in Peking was in the course of an extended tour of the Far East in 1981, which included the two Koreas, in the hope of moderating the deep hostility between them. When I discussed this with Deng, he advised me to urge the North Koreans to agree to direct negotiations with South Korea. This surprised me very much, since it amounted to accepting the procedure the South Koreans wanted but the North Koreans rejected. I did not expect Deng to distance himself from the position of his North Korean fellow-Communists.

It did provide a clue to other Chinese attitudes. There is much talk about the 'domino theory' in Asia, according to which a shift to Communist rule in one country induces a similar change in neighbouring countries. In the case of Kampuchea quite the opposite has happened: the Chinese co-operate closely with the Thais, who have a Western type of government and are ruled by the military. The explanation lies in the dominance of nationalism over ideology. National interest is all important: the Chinese find it intolerable to be faced by a large federation of Vietnam, Laos and Kampuchea on their southern borders. Hence their bitter confrontation and the constant skirmishes on the southern border between China and Vietnam.

The same argument dominates the relationship between China and the Soviet Union. There exists in the West the long-term and not unfounded fear that one day the two main Communist powers will bury their differences and come together. Whether this will happen in the far distant future I cannot predict, but certainly in the near future nationalist fervour in China rules it out completely, and their common ideology plays no part in mitigating their mutual hostility.

5

Sadat's War

I inherited a festering situation in the Middle East, the antagonisms and tribulations of which were to dog my entire term of office. The most direct threat to world peace came with the October War of 1973, involving a direct confrontation between the two super-powers. Strenuous intervention by the United Nations, in close co-operation with Washington and Moscow, averted calamity.

The Six Day War of June 1967, the third major test of strength between the protagonists, had brought stunning Israeli victories. The result merely embittered the conflict between Israel and the Arab states, whose determination to regain their lost territories was only heightened. For their part the Israelis soon demonstrated that they were equally determined to hold on to the areas they now occupied, at least until the Arabs were willing to recognize Israel and make peace.

The 1967 war had involved the United Nations in a serious setback. The United Nations Emergency Force, which had effectively served as a buffer between the contestants since 1956, had been withdrawn by my predecessor, U Thant, shortly before the war started, at the imperative demand of Egypt. Western governments blamed him for this decision, which, in their opinion, opened the door for the outbreak of a new war in the Middle East. U Thant suffered heavily under this criticism, stating that he had no choice but to accede to the clearly expressed wish of Egypt's President Gamal Abdel Nasser. In conversation with my predecessor, I noticed how deeply hurt he felt. I myself, having been UN Secretary General for so many years, and having gone through similar experiences repeatedly, understand only too well the psychological ordeal of this honest and highly sensitive man. He was never able to overcome this traumatic experience and I am inclined to believe that it contributed to his steadily failing health in the last year of his life. Brian Urquhart, in whose judgement I had full confidence, told me that U Thant had made his decision only after most careful consultations with Ralph Bunche, the leading American in the United Nations Secretariat and Nobel Peace Prize winner, who had advised him to withdraw the force – for two reasons: first, that under the existing UN rules any peace-keeping operation needs the consent of the parties in conflict; and second, that the risk of bringing the matter before the Security Council would further complicate the situation due to the expected controversy between the super-powers. When U Thant, shortly before the outbreak of the hostilities on 5 January 1967, made a last desperate effort to save the situation by flying to Cairo, it was too late.

When, six days later, the guns were silenced and the geopolitical and strategic situation in the Middle East had completely changed, the parties concerned looked again to the United Nations. After endless, extremely complicated deliberations, which required skilful diplomacy, the Security Council in November 1967 adopted Resolution 242, laying down general guidelines for a just and lasting peace in the area. It was carefully drafted to balance the requirement of Israeli withdrawal from the occupied territories against the establishment of peaceful Arab-Israeli relations, but its unspecific and ambiguous language merely provided the framework for a continuing and largely sterile controversy between governments and in the United Nations. The reason for the controversy was due to a different interpretation of the passage in the Resolution which refers to the withdrawal of the Israeli forces from 'occupied territories' (in the English version of the Resolution) and from '*the* occupied territories' in the French text. The Israelis interpreted Resolution 242 as asking only for the withdrawal from certain, but not all, occupied territories – the Arabs for full withdrawal.

The Middle East continued in turmoil. Egypt and Israel conducted skirmishes in the Sinai. Jordan, fearful of domination by the armed forces of the Palestine Liberation Organization, drove them from its territory in 1970. Acts of violence continued round Israel's frontiers. With the United States supporting Israel and the Soviet Union the Egyptians, there was always the danger of their direct involvement.

At United Nations headquarters we felt hamstrung. We continued to offer our assistance to the parties concerned in their search for agreement, but they were too far apart. It seemed to me essential to build up the peace-keeping system we had so long maintained, but it was reduced to a rump organization called UNTSO, the United Nations Truce Supervision Organization, with headquarters in Jerusalem – in the old, sumptuous British Government House – and Cairo.

By early 1973 the storm clouds were gathering. In January, the Arab Joint Defence Council met in Cairo and gave Egypt the principal role in co-ordinating the campaign against Israel. They introduced a war budget and then demanded a meeting of the Security Council to debate the Middle East situation. It represented a final attempt to regain occupied territories through United Nations channels. When the Security Council met in July, the discussion proved fruitless, culminating in a United States veto of a resolution calling for an Israeli commitment to withdraw from occupied territories in return for parallel commitments by Egypt, Syria and Jordan to make peace. We were back to square one.

I had been much perturbed by the attitude of the Egyptian Foreign Minister, Mohamed Hassan el-Zayyat. He was a calm, serious man and an experienced diplomat. Tall, heavily built, with a very round face, he was never emotional and lost neither his nerve nor his temper during the many frustrating sessions in the Security Council. He complained bitterly to me that the United Nations and the international community seemed unable to solve the Middle East problem and did not even appear capable of resuming the negotiating process. He told me plainly that if the Council was unable to make a constructive decision, Egypt would have no choice but to take 'other measures'. I was under the strong impression that the Egyptians wanted me to convey this information as a kind of last warning to the Americans and Israelis, which I did. Without success, however, as they were not willing to believe that the Egyptians might be preparing a military intervention.

I was reinforced in my fears by General Encio Siilasvuo, the sterling Finn who was the Commander-in-Chief of the UNTSO forces in the Middle East. He reported that there were substantial Egyptian troop movements along the Suez Canal, but he had been unable to determine whether they were routine or preparation for a military operation. The United Nations had no secret intelligence service of its own and was thus unable to obtain confirmation. I took the information seriously, but when I talked to Henry Kissinger, the American Secretary of State, and his advisers, they tended to dismiss our apprehensions. In view of what followed this was quite extraordinary. The Americans and the Israelis had two of the best intelligence services in the world, relying heavily on each other, but they appeared oblivious to the mounting threat.

The situation had become so disquieting that I decided to visit the Middle East myself late in August 1973 to see if it was possible to improve matters through meetings with the heads of government involved. The results were anything but reassuring. In Damascus I was subjected to the customary tough approach of the Syrian Foreign Minister, Abdel Halim Khaddam, who made a point of haranguing visiting foreign dignitaries before they saw President Hafiz al-Assad. I listened to the usual eloquent, extreme and rather unrealistic statement of the Syrian case, which left absolutely no room for accommodation.

In contrast, the President, although equally tough as to substance, was calm and unrhetorical. I do not wish to judge here his internal problems and the repressive measures taken against his political opponents in Syria and within the Arab world. However, in my negotiations with him he presented himself as a very solid person and a responsible negotiator. He is a very impressive figure, with a big square head, always very much in control of himself. He never gets emotional, is very patient and you never have the feeling that he has other things to do rather than to spend his time with you. I saw him many times over the years, and whether this sharp divergence in tone from his combative Foreign Minister is a conscious psychological device intended to augment the President's stature as a statesman or whether it is meant to soften up the visitor, I have never known. Khaddam usually kept quiet in his President's company.

On substance there was no moving Assad. There could be no peace, he said, without full withdrawal by the Israelis from the Sinai and the Golan Heights. I could obtain no hint at all that he was thinking in terms of a military alternative.

I do not share the opinion of those who think that Assad is a stooge of the Russians. He has little alternative but to turn to Moscow for military help since he does not get it from the Americans, but he retains independence in his policies and is jealously determined to assert Syria's position.

I left Damascus more or less empty-handed. The same was true when I called on President Anwar Sadat in Cairo, with whom I maintained a much warmer relationship over the years. He was unsparing in his criticism of the UN's inability to achieve a comprehensive peace settlement for the Middle East. 'Does it help,' he asked me, 'if the Security Council adopts one resolution after another, and none of them are implemented? If it does not act as is its duty, we shall have to take other measures to restore our legitimate rights.'

Here was confirmation of what his Foreign Minister, el-Zayyat, had been saying to me in New York, but he refused to be drawn on details. I cannot say I really blame him. There was no reason why he should tell even the Secretary General of the United Nations that he was in the process of organizing a surprise military offensive. I began to wonder whether the Americans and the Israelis were perhaps right. The Arabs were always well known for using words to exploit situations without really doing anything about it later.

There was certainly close collaboration and collusion between Assad and Sadat. I was struck, during the Non-Aligned Summit Meeting in Algiers, which I attended on 5 September 1973, after having concluded my Middle East tour, to see them sitting together in a corner of the lounge outside the main conference hall, their heads together in deep conversation for a long time, but of course I was not privy to what they were saying.

My visit to Jerusalem to see Prime Minister Golda Meir was perhaps the most disturbing of all my talks. She was very alert at our meetings, competent and full of confidence. However, I was quite taken aback by her attitude. In my annual report to the United Nations at the beginning of the year, I had drawn attention to the mounting tensions and had used the phrase 'time is not on our side in this highly explosive situation'. Mrs Meir had taken exception to this. 'Dr Waldheim,' she said, in a private discussion over luncheon, 'we know you are always saying the situation in the Middle East is dangerous and explosive, but we don't believe you. The Arabs will get used to our existence and in a few years they will recognize us and we shall have peace. So don't worry, it is a disagreeable situation, but we do not believe that there is real danger for us.'

No one could doubt her firmness of purpose or her sincerity in defending her country's security. But her misjudgement of her Arab adversaries was profound. I told her that I could not accept her views. We knew from our observers and my conversations that the situation was deteriorating. The impatience of the Arab states over their failure to recover any of the territories they had lost was growing. I could not escape the feeling that the Israelis were seriously underrating their opponents.

I returned from my tour early in September 1973 with a sense of foreboding. I do not wish to exaggerate. There had been so many alarms and excursions in Arab-Israeli relations that no one could make firm predictions based solely on diplomatic conversations. I had no crystal ball premonition of what was about to happen. But I am still astonished that the Israelis and the Americans, with all the intelligence resources at their disposal, so completely misjudged the situation – though admittedly it is much more difficult to determine the intentions of the potential belligerent than his capabilities. Experienced observers assumed that because the Arab states could not defeat Israel, they would not take up arms against her. I believe that Sadat's offensive across the Suez Canal had the limited objective of proving to the world, and to the Israelis, that Egypt was still strong enough to defend its interests by force and to overcome the humiliation which they had suffered during the 1967 war. I doubt if it was his intention to occupy more than a few miles of territory east of the Suez Canal, knowing that his army would never be able to defeat the Israelis in an all-out war. The purpose of the operation was more psychological than practical, and was intended to give Sadat the opportunity of resuming negotiations from a position of strength.

President Sadat sent his troops across the Suez Canal on 6 October. It was

Yom Kippur, Israel's holiest holiday, and their guard was down. Surprise was complete; the Israelis suffered heavy casualties and had to withdraw from their positions. At the same time, Syrian troops opened fire along the Golan front. Our first reports of the outbreak of hostilities arrived at about 6.45 am New York time in cables from our military observers on the Suez Canal and on the Golan Heights. A few hours later we lost contact with our forward observation post code-named 'copper' on the banks of the canal. The two UN officers – a Frenchman and an Italian – were dead: once again service in the peace-keeping forces had taken its toll.

Early the same morning Secretary of State Kissinger telephoned me from his suite in the Waldorf-Astoria Hotel, where he was staying during the current General Assembly session. He gave me the information from his own sources and told me of his efforts to halt the fighting. It was still not certain whether it was merely a border skirmish or the beginning of a major offensive. He asked me to call on the Syrians and the Egyptians to exercise restraint, particularly the former, with whom the United States was not at the time in contact. He said he would do the same with the Israelis and the Egyptians, whose Foreign Ministers were in New York. I offered to be helpful in any way possible.

The General Assembly had attracted the usual panoply of heads of government, foreign ministers and senior diplomats. Rumours, speculation and proposals of every variety for reacting to the crisis abounded. There was a general demand for the Security Council to call for a cease-fire. For the belligerents, and those supporting them, the matter was less simple. On these occasions, the side holding the military advantage does not wish to be deterred, however slightly, from pursuing its gains through admonitions from the Security Council. Least of all does it want to be called upon to cease fire in the positions gained and without conditions. The losing side is more likely to seek such action – unless it believes that given time it can reverse the military situation and win victory.

There was no agreement on what should be done. I felt that I could not remain silent. The situation was too grave, not only on the field of battle but also on the international scene. The Americans were backing the Israelis, the Soviets the Egyptians. There was a clear possiblity of escalation to general war. As permanent members of the Security Council, the United States and the Soviet Union had to reach some agreement before the Council could take effective action. As a spokesman for the world community, I considered it my duty to impress upon them as well as on the belligerents the need to reverse the trend towards some incalculable disaster.

On 11 October, I took the unusual step of addressing a statement of my views to the members of the Council. I expressed my distress at the tragedy that was unfolding before us and at the more general threat to international peace and security to which it might lead. I urged the Council to take action and to assert itself in the interests of peace. To supplement this appeal, I addressed personal letters to General Secretary Brezhnev and President Nixon. 'I feel very strongly,' I wrote to them, 'that I, as Secretary General of the United Nations, must take every possible opportunity to be of assistance in avoiding an escalation of the war and in bringing all the parties concerned to the point where a just and lasting settlement may at least be reached. In both of these aims the position of your government is crucial.'

Cynics may say that such exhortatory statements are about as effective as drops of water falling on a stone. It is true that in this, as in countless other cases, there was no immediate response from the parties involved. Nevertheless, it was my belief that in an anarchic world someone in authority must give voice to the yearning of people everywhere for peace. This was such a moment and I was the person to do it. Without this faith, no Secretary General of the United Nations can be entirely true to his trust.

In the initial phase neither the Arabs nor the Israelis were prepared for a simple cease-fire, as Foreign Minister el-Zayyat told me. The Egyptians wanted to make it conditional upon an Israeli commitment to withdraw to the pre-1967 armistice lines – that is, to give up the entire Sinai peninsula – and they wanted that commitment guaranteed by the United States. At the same time, Israeli Foreign Minister Abba Eban advocated linking a Security Council call for a cease-fire to a return of the armed forces to the line existing *before* the Egyptian attack. The Israelis maintained that without that condition a meeting of the Security Council would fail to reach agreement and would only convey the impression of impotence and polemic.

Once they had recovered from the storming of their forward positions, the Israeli counter-attack was ferocious. With the help of the Americans, who organized a massive airlift of military equipment of all sorts, they pressed back across the Suez Canal and moved to cut off and destroy the Egyptian Third Army in the south. The tide of battle had shifted and the Egyptian forces faced disaster. They, and Moscow, wanted the fighting stopped. In a few days of intensive diplomacy in Washington, Moscow and New York, the parties hammered out the terms of Resolution 338, which the Security Council adopted on 22 October. They were simple, and on the face of it clear, calling for a cease-fire within twelve hours, linked to a call for the implementation of the long-standing Resolution 242 and the start of negotiations for a just and durable peace.

Modern war is a juggernaut. Unless one side has overwhelmed the other, it is difficult to bring operations to a quick conclusion. The Israelis were now becoming masters of the battle and, when it became clear that the cease-fire had not taken hold, the diplomats in New York began to explore the possibility of sending neutral military officers as United Nations observers or even to raise substantial forces to act as a buffer between the opposing armies.

On 23 October I called Henry Kissinger on the telephone early in the morning to tell him that the Security Council was to meet again; I suggested that it would be highly desirable for it to arrange to send peace-keeping troops from small countries to the combat areas. He said he would consider the idea. It was conveyed to me by several key governments that the immediate solution lay with the small contingent of UNTSO officers still stationed in the area. They were field grade officers, individually designated by their governments. Inconspicuous, experienced and efficient, they had always been a source of unbiased information. I warned General Siilasvuo to hold his people in readiness.

Later that day, after hectic negotiations, the United States, the Soviet Union, the Egyptians, Israelis and Syrians were induced, each for their own reasons, to call a halt to the fighting. The Security Council adopted a second cease-fire resolution in which I was requested to send out UNTSO observers to supervise the cease-fire. By the next evening a number of patrols had been dispatched to the Egyptian forward positions. Similar arrangements were made for the Israeli-Syrian front.

It immediately became clear that this measure would not be sufficient. The Israelis persisted in drawing a noose round the Egyptian Third Army. On 24 October, as his situation grew desperate, President Sadat appealed for American and Soviet troops to be sent to enforce the cease-fire. Backing Sadat, Brezhnev threatened to intervene unilaterally if the United States did not agree to a joint Soviet-American force. In a communication to President Nixon, he stated bluntly: 'I shall say it straight that if you find it impossible to act jointly with us in this matter, we should be faced with the necessity to consider the question of taking appropriate steps unilaterally'. Relations between the super-powers approached the flash point. American forces were placed on a widely-publicized alert during the night of 24/25 October.

In this crisis the Security Council intervened effectively. Under the leadership of Ambassadors Lazar Mojsov of Yugoslavia and Tino Sen of India, the non-aligned members suggested the re-creation of the United Nations Emergency Force that had been so effective after the 1956 Suez Canal war. After consulting with me and my advisers, they proposed a further resolution that would repeat the demand for a cease-fire and request me to increase the number of military observers on both sides of the fighting lines and re-establish UNEF (United Nations Emergency

Force). On 25 October, the Security Council adopted that resolution (No. 340).

The sabre-rattling between Washington and Moscow had become public knowledge, and the resolution included a provision that the personnel of the emergency force was not to be drawn from permanent members of the Security Council – in other words from the big powers. This took account of Henry Kissinger's concern at the prospect of introducing combat troops into the area of conflict. Not surprisingly this provoked Soviet objections, as well as scepticism from two other permanent members, Britain and France. Since the draft also called for additional military observers, it was eventually agreed that Soviet military personnel would be stationed in the Middle East as members of UNTSO instead. After endless haggling, a figure of thirty-six men from each superpower was accepted, because that equalled the largest single Third World country contingent in UNTSO at the time. Their incorporation proceeded smoothly.

The international crisis seemed to be defused and the danger of a Soviet-American military confrontation averted. More significantly, for the first time since the collapse of the UN peace-keeping operations in Sinai before the start of the Six-Day War, authority had been given for the establishment of a 'blue beret' buffer force. If the cease-fire was to hold, it was going to be necessary to interpose United Nations forces physically between the two armies overnight. They would need to arrive on the scene before it had been possible to establish precise demarcation lines on military maps. That was why I had been given a twenty-four-hour deadline for my first report on the deployment of the UN forces.

It was indeed fortunate that the Security Council had acted as it did. Hostilities continued even after the passage of this third resolution, and the Egyptian Third Army was being threatened with starvation and destruction. As the situation worsened I was being harried mercilessly by Sadat's new Foreign Minister, Ismail Fahmy. Fortunately I knew him well. He had been Egypt's delegate to the United Nations General Assembly during my own earlier years and then Ambassador to Austria when I was Foreign Minister. He rang me repeatedly in the middle of the night to question me about the organization of the peace-keeping force and to insist on its immediate deployment. There was increasing desperation in his voice. The Third Army was in the process of being destroyed. It had no proper food or water supplies and was running out of ammunition with which to counter the Israeli attacks. He urged me to make every effort to assure the rapid arrival of our peace-keeping force.

Some of the exchanges were rather emotional. 'This is a turning point in history,' he said during one call. 'We have an opportunity either to go back to war for twenty-five years or to move forward to a real peace.' If the Israeli forces did not pull back, the Egyptians would have to try to extricate the Third Army by other (unspecified) means and there would be war again. Until the Israelis complied with the Security Council resolution, there could be no question of exchanging prisoners of war, negotiating or any other constructive activity.

He insisted that I present these arguments most urgently to the United States government, so I communicated them to Henry Kissinger. It appeared that President Nixon had received a similar message from Anwar Sadat. Once again there was an atmosphere of crisis. The Soviet Union took up the cudgels in Washington on behalf of Egypt, and Kissinger became tough with the Israelis, threatening to act through the Security Council to ensure that non-military supplies reached the Third Army. The upshot of this frenetic diplomacy was that, on 27 October, Egypt accepted an Israeli proposal for direct military talks, the first since the independence of Israel. They were to take place at the Kilometre 101 route marker on the highway between Cairo and Suez under United Nations supervision. Their purpose was to make detailed cease-fire arrangements. Together with the Red Cross, the United Nations was also to supervise the provision of supplies to the Third Army. The UN was to hold the ring.

By 25 October, the Security Council had done what it could to end the fighting. There remained the crucial task of ensuring a cease-fire, to lessen the prospect that, by accident or design, hostilities might break out once more. That task the Council turned over to me and my colleagues in the Secretariat. I had, of course, realized that some such buffer force might become necessary and had done some thinking about how it might best be established. But one aspect of the organization of peace-keeping forces is their individuality. No two are quite alike in their genesis. Except in the broadest terms, each must be organized in accordance with a specific set of political imperatives. When the call comes for action, there is a premium not only on speed but also on ingenuity, improvisation and diplomatic sensitivity. If there are miscalculations, the parties can be seriously antagonized and support for the projected force, both military and financial, can quickly evaporate.

I had two alternatives. One was to appeal by telephone or cable to those governments which had put peace-keeping contingents at our disposal in the past, such as the smaller European countries, the Africans and the Asians. It usually takes two or three weeks to assemble them, and this was too long a delay. It did not take me long to adopt the second alternative, which was to use our peace-keeping force in Cyprus. The situation there was becoming unstable and emotional, so we were taking a considerable risk. I discussed this with Brian Urquhart and we both came to the conclusion that the best and quickest solution would be to ask the British, with their military bases in Akrotiri in the south of Cyprus, if they could place aircraft at our disposal and fly some of the UN troops quickly over to Cairo. They were extremely co-operative, gave us an immediate yes, and we were able to get our people to Cairo overnight.

By the end of the day of 26 October, I could report that 600 men from the Austrian, Finnish and Swedish contingents in Cyprus had landed in Egypt with their motor vehicles, equipment and food, and the next morning they were deployed in the forward areas. It had taken them less than thirty hours to get there. The remaining units followed shortly afterwards.

The command arrangements presented no problem. We were fortunate in having General Siilasvuo on the spot from the headquarters of UNTSO. He was fully familiar with the geography, politics and military organizations of the area, had an able staff and could work effectively with the top Egyptians and Israeli commanders. I put him in charge of UNEF II and he eventually became co-ordinator of all United Nations military operations in the Middle East.

He was an excellent man, big and tall with a reddish face, blue eyes and thinning blond hair. He looked like a simple Finnish countryman and had a certain peasant slyness to him. He was a man of few words. When I arrived later to inspect the whole area he drove me from Cairo to Suez and I do not think we exchanged more than a dozen sentences. He made himself popular with both sides and reminded me of some of the Austrian leaders after the war, who had dealt so capably with the Russians and the Americans by behaving in a rather low-key way whilst always making it clear what they wanted.

In order to avoid the pitfalls of the past, I had insisted that the force was to operate with the full support of the Security Council as an integrated and efficient military unit. Active command was to be exercised by the UN Security Council, through me. The force had to enjoy freedom of movement and communication and operate at all times separately from the armed forces of the contending parties and with complete impartiality. It was understood that UNEF II could not be withdrawn between renewal dates without the Council's consent – meaning, without the approval of all the permanent members.

The Soviet Union and its allies had always maintained that every significant aspect of the operations of a peace-keeping force should be authorized by the Security Council. Most other members had agreed that force commanders needed sufficient authority to deal with situations in the field and that the Secretary General needed the flexibility to resolve day-to-day problems.

The additional contingents to be provided by governments would be selected in consultation with the Council and the two contestants, 'bearing in mind an adequate geographical representation'. This was essential, given the role of regional groups in the organization. Finally, to emphasize the exclusively peace-keeping character of the force, I stipulated that it would possess only defensive weapons and that it would not use force except in self-defence.

The military arrangements needed to implement the terms of the Israeli-Egyptian disengagement under the cease-fire were agreed on 11 November at Kilometre 101 on the Cairo-Suez road. This marked the approximate limit of Israeli defence force control at the time the fighting stopped. One provision in the agreement laid down that: 'As soon as the United Nations checkpoints are established on the Cairo-Suez road, there will be an exchange of all prisoners of war, including the wounded.'

There were several untoward incidents before order was established. An immediate problem arose over control of the road. The Egyptians expected UNEF to set up check-points before any prisoners were exchanged. The Israelis intended to retain control of the road for themselves, while attaching the greatest importance to the earliest possible return of the Israeli prisoners of war in Egyptian hands.

As soon as efforts were made to put the agreement into effect, these opposing viewpoints clashed. It seemed possible that the agreement might break down. General Siilasvuo sought earnestly to overcome the difficulty through extensive contact with the two sides. When, however, no progress had been made at the end of the meeting of 12 November, he decided to carry out the responsibility devolving on UNEF. He thereupon informed the parties that it was the intention of UNEF to establish two UN check-points, one at Kilometre 101 and another at Kilometre 119.

General Yariv, the Israeli army negotiator, objected strongly. 'Blood will spill,' he said, 'if UNEF should attempt to set up the check-points.' Nevertheless, with General Siilasvuo present, UNEF soldiers set up a hut at Kilometre 101 in the late afternoon of 12 November without incident. It was a different matter at Kilometre 119, where no sooner had the structure been erected than Israeli soldiers moved in to dismantle it.

Siilasvuo reported this to me and I instructed him that the UN check-points must be maintained. In an attempt to settle the problem Siilasvuo went to discuss the matter with the Israeli Defence Minister, Moshe Dayan, in Tel Aviv. Even before they could meet, late on 13 November, the Israelis began to threaten the Finnish contingent at Kilometre 119. In view of the imminent possibility of violence Siilasvuo sought further instructions from me by telephone. I told him again that the

UN checkpoints were not to be removed. The Dayan-Siilasvuo meeting seemed to calm things down but on the morning of 14 November, when UNEF tried to re-build the checkpoint, fist fights broke out between Israeli soldiers and the Finnish contingent, who stood their ground.

The Israelis were evidently impressed by their determination. So were the Egyptians, whom we were able to convince that UNEF meant to carry out its tasks with tenacity. General Yariv was obviously instructed to change his attitude. He apologized for any obstacles he might have placed in UNEF's way, and calm was restored, with our people in position. The list of Israeli prisoners of war was made available by the Egyptians and the implementation of the 11 November agreement proceeded smoothly.

In spite of a number of such altercations, the force was not required to use its weapons. It was not intended to function as an organized fighting unit. It is the special attribute of peace-keeping forces that they attain their objective by persuasion and political support, and not by military force.

I obtained authority from the Security Council to build up UNEF II to a maximum strength of 7,000 men. Starting with a nucleus of three European neutral forces from Cyprus, units in battalion strength were soon drawn from nine countries in different parts of the world, giving a permanent force of 4,000 men. In the light of the delicate East-West arrangements underlying the cease-fire resolutions, it was politically unwise to include either NATO or Warsaw Pact forces among those at the front.

The Council did decide, however, to call upon the allies of the super-powers for logistic services which did not require close and continuing contact with the Egyptian forward area and Israeli forces.

Although the work of the logistical contingents was perhaps less exciting than that in the buffer zones, it was the lifeline of the military operation – as it always is. It had to be put in place as quickly as possible. Canada's large and experienced logistics contingents were a natural choice, and so I approached the Canadians first. Consistent with their traditional support for UN peace-keeping, the Canadians responded positively. We arranged for the immediate deployment of their unit.

I was surprised a few days later when, in a closed-door meeting of the Security Council, the Soviet representative voiced his government's dislike of including troops from a NATO country without similar representation from Eastern Europe. For several hours the Security Council representatives, the ambassadors of the belligerent countries, my advisers and I sought to arrive at a workable compromise. Eventually, all agreed to include a second logistics contingent, to be drawn from Poland. Although the division of responsibility between these two units was the subject of protracted negotiation in New York, in the field their service was excellent.

The Israelis did not want the Poles in territories under Israeli control. Nor did they want forces from any nation which did not have diplomatic relations with Israel to be a part of UNEF. Had I acceded to their wishes in this regard, relatively few Third World countries would have qualified. But it was precisely the non-aligned countries' contingents which were necessary if we were to insulate UNEF's operations from super-power involvement. Out of consideration for Israeli sensibilities we consciously sought to draw units from countries relatively friendly to Israel, such as Kenya and Senegal. Nevertheless, the problem of assuring full freedom of movement for such forces remained with us. I could not yield on this principle; it remained a source of contention. Henry Kissinger advised a pragmatic solution – an agreement to disagree – and that in fact was what occurred.

After the first hectic days of the cease-fire, things gradually sorted themselves out. UNEF had arrived at the war fronts as an interposing force and an observation element. By mid-January 1974 agreement had been reached on all stages of the first disengagement agreement; the Force was substantially in place; and all elements of the required military withdrawals were completed by the beginning of March. A second and final step in the Sinai disengagement was arranged in September 1975

Things moved more slowly on the Syrian front. The Syrians were hard bargainers, and agreement on the cease-fire lines in their sector was not reached until late in May 1974, after gruelling diplomatic-shuttle negotiations by Secretary of State Kissinger. Israel and Syria agreed to the establishment of the United Nations Disengagement Observer Force (UNDOF) to be stationed in the buffer zone between the two armies. The Security Council approved the creation of a peace-keeping force generally modelled on UNEF. The two force contingents – Austrians and Iranians – moved into the Golan Heights area by early June. Once they were in place, skirmishing along the front lines ended. I had arranged to be on hand to greet the new troops as they arrived in the ruins of the former Syrian district capital of Kuneitra. Again I was heartened to see my Austrian compatriots together with their Iranian comrades in the forefront of another peace-keeping operation.

Once on the ground, the two forces supervised the process of redeploying the Arab and Israeli troops to the agreed lines. Thereafter they manned the zones of disengagement and inspected the zones of limited armaments and forces. The work was not without danger. In its first six months UNEF suffered four fatalities and many injuries as a result of mine and other explosions.

UNEF also fulfilled a number of humanitarian functions. In co-operation with the Red Cross it was instrumental in carrying out the exchange of prisoners of war and the transfer of displaced civilians. Its truck convoys carried non-military supplies to the trapped Egyptian Third Army. It supervised convoys of food, water and medicine to the city of Suez. And it used dog teams and other methods to recover the bodies of troops killed in battle so that they might be returned to their national authorities.

Notwithstanding all our efforts, we were confronted by serious problems as the Israeli-Egyptian peace-making process continued. The Soviet Union had been frozen out of the disengagement agreements negotiated by Henry Kissinger in 1974 and 1975. By widening the area of disengagement, the 1975 agreement increased the burden on UNEF. The Soviets refused to contribute their share of the additional cost. And when Egypt and Israel, through the mediation of President Jimmy Carter, moved from the Camp David agreements to the conclusion of a peace treaty in 1979, the USSR made it very clear that it would not permit the Security Council to extend UNEF's mandate. We were permitted to use UNTSO observers to monitor the peace treaty arrangements. But this was hardly an adequate substitute for the UNEF presence. The main burden of supervision had to be taken over by a force organized by the United States. I regret the trend, begun in Egypt and continued in Lebanon, to substitute for United Nations peace-keeping forces other types of multi-national forces organized on the initiative of a great power.

True, such forces are simpler to set up. They are easier to finance and, with national backing, certainly can command greater combat strength. On the other hand, they are more likely to serve purely national purposes than are United Nations forces organized in the more general interest. Rather than helping to ensure the permanence of a political solution, they can more easily become part of the problem. Because they serve in areas of international tension, they increase the risk of great-power military confrontation. I hope and believe that in due course the advantages of United Nations peace-keeping will become apparent to all.

Egypt and Syria had failed to achieve their military objectives, but, by his audacious challenge and his initial crossing of the Suez Canal with heavy Israeli casualties, Sadat had been able to erase much of the Arab sense of humiliation on the battlefield. The war also shook Israel's internal political structure. In the longer term these developments set the stage for the events leading, years later, to an Israeli-Egyptian peace settlement negotiated between equals.

Although the Security Council resolution of 22 October had also called on the parties to start negotiations immediately 'under appropriate auspices' to arrive at a just and durable peace, the United Nations was not the prime mover in organizing or conducting the peace conference, which was eventually convened in Geneva on 21 December 1973. That was the work of the United States and the Soviet Union. But the organization did make an essential contribution. It provided the only framework that all the negotiating parties could accept. I welcomed their agreement that, as proposed in a letter to me dated 18 December from the American and Soviet Foreign Ministers, the conference should meet on 21 December under the auspices of the United Nations; that I should convene it; and that I should preside in its opening phase. Normally, I might have questioned these rather peculiar limitations. But in this instance I recognized that only the two great powers were in a position to bring together the warring parties, and that by serving as co-chairmen they were putting the weight of their influence behind the quest for agreement.

There were, of course, alternative possibilities for dealing with this question. This might have been done in the Security Council, or the Geneva Conference might have included all its permanent members. But when I broached these ideas, we ran into opposition from the Israelis. Thus, in a conversation with me in New York on 10 November 1973, Foreign Minister Abba Eban flatly rejected them and told us why he did so. With the two super-powers running the show, he said, Israel at least had a guarantee that it would be a 50–50 proposition. In the Security Council the majority was bound to be anti-Israeli; and the United Kingdom and France had made it clear that they were too concerned about their oil supply from the Arab states to be impartial. Thus the Conference consisted of the two super-powers; Egypt and Jordan sitting for the Arab side (Syria did not appear); Israel; and myself as Chairman and United Nations representative.

Despite the painstaking preparation, a last-minute hitch of the kind that often subjects diplomacy to ridicule almost prevented the conference from convening: early in the morning of 21 December, a few hours before the Conference was to begin, Joseph Sisco, the dynamic US Assistant Secretary of State for Middle Eastern Affairs, knocked vigorously on my door at the Intercontinental Hotel. In some excitement he told me that prolonged efforts made during the previous night had failed to produce an agreement on seating arrangements at the conference table. Would I, he asked, help to find a solution? The problem was that none of the Arab representatives wanted to sit next to the Israelis. All sorts of arrangements were discussed as the Americans, Russians and other participants put their proposals to me in my capacity as chairman. While this was going on, their delegates were sitting in small rooms around the old League of Nations Council chamber in what is now the European headquarters of the United Nations. From the chamber gallery, the press looked down on the empty hall with growing impatience as the hours passed.

On the previous day, 20 December, Gromyko had suggested that seating at the table should 'reflect the political situation'. This could be done, he suggested, if the Soviet Union sat with Egypt and Syria on my right, while the United States, Israel and Jordan sat to my left. This would have had the effect of isolating Jordan from the other Arab states and placing the Soviet Union ostentatiously on their side. It did not comport with the United Nations practice of seating delegations in alphabetic order.

I told Gromyko, therefore, that his proposal would create difficulties. But the United Nations practice had its own disadvantage. It would result in Egypt (in Geneva we use the French titles: République Arabe d'Egypte) sitting between Israel and the Soviet Union. The Egyptians took a dim view of that.

Eventually I suggested to Gromyko that the Soviets should sit next to the Israelis. No one, I said, could accuse them of conspiring with each other. Gromyko grumbled a bit, but finally replied that he would like to have Henry Kissinger make that request of him personally. I told him that as a result of my contacts with the Americans I had discussed the proposal, and it was acceptable. But Gromyko indicated that this would not do. And so I resumed my mini-shuttle back to the Secretary of State and described the situation to him. He took it good-humouredly. 'Why not?' he remarked. We doubled back to the Soviet delegation room; Kissinger, referring to what I had told him, put the request: 'Well, well . . .,' said Gromyko, 'in the interest of peace, I accept your proposal.' Thus the conference was convened with the United States sitting between Egypt and Jordan on one side of me, while the Soviet Union sat between Israel and the empty Syrian chair on the other.

It was interesting to observe the political manoeuvring of the Arab states in connection with the Geneva conference. Opposing as they did any negotiations whatever with the Israelis, the more intransigent countries sharply criticized Egypt. According to Prime Minister Rifa'i of Jordan, Colonel Muhammad al-Gaddafi, the Libyan leader, had gone so far as to threaten to declare war on Egypt if it made an 'unfavourable' agreement at the peace conference. This could be dismissed as a verbal threat. What was more serious was the reaction of the Syrians. They adamantly refused to attend the conference, although in the end they tacitly permitted an empty chair bearing their name to be placed at the conference table.

Syrian President Assad was bitter in his comments on the Egyptian agreement to a cease-fire in the Sinai. Cairo, he said, had broken all the military commitments it had made with Damascus. He described the site of the Egyptian-Israeli military disengagement negotiations at Kilometre 101 as 'the tent of disgrace'. Nevertheless, President Assad was sufficiently practical to ask King Hussein to have Jordan defend Syrian interests at the conference.

The Jordanians had their own fish to fry at Geneva. If this was a conference on disengagement, they felt, it should include the Israeli-Jordanian frontier as well – even though, in contrast to its action in 1967, Jordan had refrained from committing its armed forces during the October War. Just before the conference opened, Rifa'i proposed to me that his country be allowed to cross the Jordan River and establish positions on the Israeli-occupied West Bank. This, he stated, would undoubtedly entice Syria into participating in the conference. Why this should be so I could not see, except on the very dubious premise that rewarding Jordan with territorial gains for attending the conference might induce the Syrians to take their place at the table in the hope that they too might benefit.

A few weeks later Secretary Kissinger confirmed to me that the Jordanians had indeed sought a military disengagement of the Israeli forces from Jordan. They had proposed that Israeli troops move back from the river to the hills some four kilometres to the west. Aside from what would be done about the city of Jericho, they maintained, this should cause no military problem for the Israelis since their main forces were in any case in the hills and not on the river.

The Syrian proposals for disengagement in their territories were equally impracticable. The Syrians wanted assurances that Israel would return not only all the Syrian territory it had occupied in the October War, but the Golan Heights area it had held since 1967. There was something to be said for the Syrian objective of recovering as much as they could of the lands the Israelis had conquered. But to expect this sort of settlement was highly unrealistic, given their military defeat.

The conference accomplished very little and met only once at Foreign Minister level. Although desultory talks continued between ambassadors it was never re-convened formally. The Arabs were at odds with each other, united only in their insistence on the full participation of the Palestine Liberation Organization, which the Americans and Israelis would not countenance. Insubstantial as the conference must have seemed, it did serve a useful purpose. For the first time, apart from military talks at the checkpoint at Kilometre 101, it permitted Israel to sit down at the same table with Egypt and Jordan in a negotiating forum. It was a small step on the long road to regional peace.

The search for the re-convening of the Geneva peace conference continued its protracted course for the best part of three years. The Arabs tended to insist on full participation by the PLO; the Israelis and the Americans would not countenance a separate and defined PLO representation. The Arabs required some demonstration of intent to create an independent Palestinian state, possibly linked with Jordan; the Israelis rigidly resisted such an idea. The Israelis sought recognition of Israel's existence through the conclusion of treaties of peace; the Arabs were, at best, equivocal on the subject.

Notwithstanding these obstacles, it seemed to me that a conference aimed at a comprehensive settlement still offered more hope for progress than any other procedure. I did not expect a fully fledged settlement to emerge from such a gathering; the problem was too complicated for that. But I felt that if the Americans could serve as a moderating influence on the Israelis, while the Soviets helped to deal with the more radical Syrians and the PLO, a conference might take the first steps toward pacification – as had been the case in 1973.

Throughout this period, I maintained close contact with the Syrians and met President Assad regularly in Damascus. I was required to make periodic visits to discuss the extension of the mandate of the United Nations peace-keeping forces stationed on the Golan Heights to monitor the 1974 cease-fire agreement. Assad would patiently spend hours with me in his office, discussing every detail of our problems.

For the Syrians there was only one permissible response to the situation on the Golan Heights. Under the Charter of the United Nations, they insisted, it was the duty of the world organization to force the Israelis out of the territories they were occupying there and in the Sinai. Only if the Security Council stressed the need for Israeli withdrawal would the Syrians agree to another limited extension of the peace-keeping force mandate. It took constant effort to induce them to accept a more moderate attitude. Through protracted discussions, I was able to avoid any interruption in UNDOF's mandate, without prejudicing future action by the Security Council.

As the first expiration date of the mandate approached in November 1974, the Syrians led me to believe that President Hafiz Assad might consent to its renewal if I visited Damascus to discuss matters with him personally. This seemed a small price to pay for maintaining UNDOF. Moreover, it would be genuinely helpful to probe Assad's thinking on the subject. Accordingly, I accepted the Syrian invitation.

Henry Kissinger, however, was troubled by my decision. On 22 November, I received two letters from him asking me not to go. He informed me that his own talks with the Israelis and the Syrians seemed only hours away from success and suggested that I might want to hold off in order to avoid confusion or delay in the 'resolution of one last detail'. He also expressed concern that developments might require my 'careful handling' in New York.

Dr Kissinger's request, probably made at the insistence of the Israelis, put me in an awkward position. The arrangements for my visit had already been made; a last-minute cancellation would be certain to antagonize Assad. At the same time I had no desire to complicate the efforts of Dr Kissinger.

So I postponed my visit for a day. By 24 November, Dr Kissinger had not reported agreement, and I was convinced that he would not be able to do so before I had met Assad. I had no illusions that I could work some sort of diplomatic magic with the notably tough Syrian President. Rather, I believed his main concern was not to be taken for granted, particularly by the United States. A visit by the Secretary General would give him some of the psychological lift he sought. It would also help to keep the United Nations in the negotiating picture, an objective important to me.

On 24 November, therefore, I informed the Secretary of State that, after delaying my trip in view of his reservations, I would proceed with the visit. While in Syria, I wrote, I would do everything I could to reinforce his efforts rather than complicate them. As to his reference to developments in New York, I assured him that I would return there in time to prepare for the next Security Council meeting – a mild reminder that I knew best how to handle my scheduling responsibilities. I left for Damascus later that day.

When I met Assad, on 25 November 1974, he told me that he had changed his position. Syria would now agree, he said, to extend UNDOF's mandate for six months. Having made every possible effort to gain his ends, Assad yielded with good grace. But there was more than this behind Assad's foot-dragging. What he wanted to do was to use his assent to the extension of the UNDOF mandate to gain support for Israel's withdrawal from the territory it was occupying, and for a revival of the Geneva conference, looking towards a peace settlement.

Interestingly, President Sadat of Egypt then took a leaf out of Assad's book, by refusing a further extension of UNEF on the grounds that it would perpetuate Israel's occupation of Egyptian territory. On 21 July 1975, the Security Council publicly appealed to Sadat to reconsider. He did so; negotiations among the parties continued; and on 1 September 1975, Egypt and Israel initialled an agreement for a much broader disengagement of their forces in the Sinai desert. The agreement expanded the UNEF buffer zone four-fold and gave the force additional responsibilities – for example, in facilitating the transfer of the Sinai oil fields to Egypt. The parties also undertook to renew UNEF's mandate annually, thereby diminishing uncertainty about the future.

At the beginning of 1977 the picture suddenly changed. When President Carter assumed office his administration announced that it would give high priority to the problem of reaching a permanent peace settlement.

There were some signs that moderate elements in the Arab world were looking at the Arab-Israeli conflict somewhat more realistically. Encouraged by the change in atmosphere, I made another extended tour of the whole area a month after President Carter's inauguration, talking at length to all the main participants. On my return, I informed Vance and Gromyko that, although I had the impression that the Arabs wished to start serious peace negotiations, the Israeli position remained unchanged.

Extensive bilateral talks on the details of a resumed Geneva conference went on until the autumn 1977 session of the General Assembly. On 1 October, the United States and the Soviet Union, as co-chairmen of the 1973 Conference, issued a joint statement of principles for a resumption. It seemed possible at that moment that the PLO would accept the right of all states in the area, including Israel, to live in peace and that Israel would accept the establishment of a semi-autonomous Palestinian entity on the West Bank and Gaza under some sort of transitional regime.

But before anything could come of these developments, Anwar Sadat, impatient at the apparently interminable minutiae of diplomacy, made his dramatic trip to Jerusalem in November 1977 and shifted the focus of peace-making to an Egyptian-Israeli framework.

On his return from Jerusalem, Sadat first invited the parties, the PLO and the United Nations, to meet in Cairo in December 1977 to advance the peace process. While Sadat's intentions were commendable, it was not a well prepared or well considered proposal. All the other Arab states, antagonized by Sadat's unilateral approach to the Israelis, refused to attend. Only the Americans and the Israelis accepted the invitation.

In view of this controversial situation, I decided to send General Siilasvuo to attend the meeting as an observer only. In keeping with instructions, he sat back from the conference table and did not participate in the discussions. The conference was brief and unproductive.

The following year, President Carter hammered out an agreement between President Sadat and Prime Minister Begin at Camp David. I welcomed the establishment of peace between Egypt and Israel, as I would have between any two United Nations members. But I had mixed emotions about this new development. It caused a deep split in Arab ranks. Egypt remained isolated from its Arab colleagues until early in 1984; and without Egypt, all prospects of a broader move towards peace in the area were excluded.

Sadat's opponents criticized him for abandoning the Palestinians when he reached agreement on Sinai. In my last conversation with him, on 10 July 1978 at Schloss Fuschl in Austria, he denied he had done so. Under the Camp David agreement, he reminded me, the Palestinians were to negotiate an agreement for autonomy within Israel, for a period of five years, after which they could decide in which direction to move. But this was not a solution satisfactory to the PLO or to the other Arab states, particularly since the Israelis construed the term 'autonomous' in a most restrictive way.

Indeed, I believe it is almost inconceivable that the Palestinians, or the Arab world, would accept autonomy for the Palestinian Arabs, even on a temporary basis. They would fear that, as the old diplomatic maxim goes, 'nothing is more permanent than the provisional'. They will insist on their right to self-determination. In this they enjoy broad support among the members of the United Nations. Even the Western Europeans, in their Venice Declaration of 13 June 1980, have aligned themselves on this side.

Without doubt Anwar El Sadat had a fascinating and scintillating personality, courageous, shrewd and daring. He was the first Arab leader to throw in his lot with the Americans in his efforts for peace in the Middle East. To win the favour of the West he did not shy away from any gesture that he thought might be effective in the United States. He was a past master in cultivating the media and the friendship of leading journalists such as Barbara Walters and Walter Cronkite; he timed many of his major decisions to suit the prime viewing and listening time of American newscasts and emphasized his preference for a Western life-style in his dress when he visited America or Europe.

In the many conversations I had with Anwar Sadat in Egypt and during summer visits to Austria, I was struck as much by his visionary ideas as by the intense way in which he projected his image. Perhaps it was one of the causes of his political and personal tragedy that he relied more and more on himself alone in the course of his presidency and scarcely heeded the advice of his chief counsellors. For instance, as he more or less went it alone in the negotiations with Henry Kissinger, who skilfully exploited his ego, there was often no opportunity for correcting Sadat's spontaneous decisions on vital questions. The United Nations, however, had a clearly defined place in his thinking. He appreciated the Organization as a means of mobilizing world public opinion for the Arab cause and for the dispatch of peace-keeping forces. After the peace with Israel, he expected the United Nations to take on an umbrella function in order to protect his policy against attacks from the Arab camp. I clearly remember how often he stressed the importance of that particular function in his talks with me. The element of surprise was an essential pillar of his policy. 'Thinking the unthinkable' was his motto. In what was probably the most dramatic hour of his political career, his address to the Israeli Knesset, Sadat had made it clear what was not the aim of his initiative – a separate peace. Tragically, however, that was precisely his legacy.

I recognized the Camp David accord as an important step towards the establishment of peace between two nations in the area, but I expressed concern about its implications for efforts to achieve a comprehensive settlement. With Sadat's assassination by Arab fundamentalists, the peace process was effectively stalled, at least for some time. The bitter truth is that, despite his historic move to break down the barriers between Israel and Egypt, his dramatic peace mission had reached the end of the road.

Thus we are left with the continuing deadlock, with all its dangerous consequences for world peace. The Geneva Conference still remains the only foreseeable option for the resumption of comprehensive peace negotiations. I hope it will some day be used.

6

Cyprus—The Orphan Child

Cyprus has been the orphan child of the United Nations for more than twenty years, ever since UNFICYP, the peace-keeping force, was first installed in 1964. The UN has provided the only constant thread of conciliation and negotiation between the embattled Greek and Turkish communities. Their problems and mutual antagonisms took up more of my time and attention during my years in office than any other confrontation.

The British had administered the island from 1878 to 1960; when they agreed to establish an independent republic of Cyprus, with Greece and Turkey as fellow guarantor powers. The treaties of alliance, establishment and guarantee worked out in Zürich and London provided an elaborate and complicated constitutional structure of 199 articles, spelling out in detail a political arrangement under which the Turkish Cypriots shared in the functions of government and were guaranteed important minority and veto rights as well as a measure of communal authority. Archbishop Makarios was installed as President and Dr Fazil Kuchuk, the leader of the Turkish Cypriots, as Vice-President.

The Greeks outnumbered the Turks in the population of 650,000 by about four to one; the mutual hostility between the two communities was endemic. Cyprus, moreover, is situated in a key area of East-West conflict. Greece and Turkey are both members of the North Atlantic Treaty Organization and the Cyprus problem, together with other disputes between them, has often threatened to unhinge the eastern end of the NATO alliance. The Republic of Cyprus itself adhered from its inception to a non-aligned posture, and sought and received diplomatic support from the Third World.

The bad blood between the two communities ran too deep to be contained within the administrative structure which had been organized. The complex checks and balances established in the constitution began to break down almost immediately. By the turn of 1963/4 fighting had broken out between the rival factions and the Turkish Cypriots had withdrawn from the central government and set up their own community organizations.

The Security Council acted with commendable vigour and recommended the creation of UNFICYP, with the mandate: 'In the interests of preserving international peace and security, to use its best efforts to prevent a recurrence of fighting and, as necessary, to contribute to the maintenance and restoration of law and order and a return to normal conditions.'

At the insistence of the Cyprus government, the original force of about 6,500 men was drawn from Western countries. They were positioned to serve as a buffer between the Greek Cypriots and the enclaves into which the Turkish Cypriots had withdrawn. The United Nations presence helped to head off or to settle hundreds of incidents, large and small, but it could not prevent or effectively intervene in the large-scale intercommunal conflict which broke out again in 1967, when the Turkish Cypriots set up a 'transitional administration' with full executive, legislative and judicial organs. Turkey was on the verge of intervening, the Security Council was alerted, the guarantor powers became involved and in the end, because of the implications for Western security, American influence was instrumental in restoring a measure of calm, in which the UN organization exerted its influence to re-animate the peace-making effort.

The first intercommunal talks organized for this purpose, as opposed to efforts by outside powers, began in 1968, when negotiators from the two sides met at the home of the UN Special Representative on the island, Ambassador Osorio Tafall of Mexico. They were an able pair. The principal spokesman for the Greek Cypriots, Glafcos Clerides, President of the Cypriot House of Representatives, was an eloquent London-trained barrister who had been an RAF pilot in the Second World War, then an Eoka guerrilla leader under General Grivas, who had harried the British during the final years of colonial rule. His Turkish Cypriot counterpart, Rauf Denktash, President of the Turkish Cypriot Communal Chamber, was also a British-trained lawyer, a tough-minded activist who eventually supplanted Dr Kuchuk as Vice-President.

This first round of talks continued in a desultory fashion until 1971 and were resumed again at my insistence when I became Secretary General. I sent my Under Secretary, the Argentinian diplomat Roberto Guyer, on two visits to the island and he reported some progress, although it was proving impossible to bridge the gap between the Turkish Cypriot demand for local autonomy and the Greek Cypriot fear of a solution that would lead to partition. In the meantime the internal and international situation was deteriorating seriously as the two guarantor powers, Greece and Turkey, increased their intervention and stiffened their attitudes.

Encouraged by the right-wing military junta that had assumed power in Greece, the Greek Cypriot community had become deeply divided between extremists, pressing again for immediate *Enosis* with the mother-land, even if it had to be attained by violence, and the more pragmatic elements headed by Archbishop Makarios who sought to maintain the integrity of the government of Cyprus. General Grivas, the pre-independence guerrilla leader, had returned secretly to the island and was organizing a new irregular force known as Eoka B. Grivas directed an increasingly open campaign of obstruction and violence against the Makarios government. Like the mainland Greek colonels who were supporting him, he regarded the Archbishop as a treacherous back-slider dangerously close to Communist and Third World elements.

Tensions were heightened in January 1972, just as I assumed office, when it became known that Makarios had received a large shipment of arms from Czechoslovakia. It was not entirely clear to what use he proposed to put them. He had created a small elite presidential guard, virtually the only force he could count on. The other Greek Cypriot forces — the Cyprus National Guard, whose officers were Greek army personnel, a section of the police, as well as the military contingent from Greece stationed on the island under the Zürich agreement — were strong backers of Grivas. The Turkish Cypriots could not be certain which of these forces might be used against them and became correspondingly alarmed.

I offered United Nations assistance and, after long negotiations, it was agreed in March that the heavier arms, not required for the President's guard, would not be distributed, but would be stored in designated depots under a two-key system that amounted to UNFICYP custody. Provision was made for joint inspection of the stored weapons. I visited the island myself in June 1972 and talked to the community leaders on both sides, urging them to approach their task in a spirit of accommodation, but their replies were, at best, ambiguous.

I took the opportunity to visit UNFICYP headquarters and some of its observation posts. I found the 'blue berets' performing their duties efficiently and in good spirits. Lightly armed, limited by their peace-keeping functions only to personal self-defence, they were constantly required to deal with incidents jeopardizing the persons and property of the two communities with objectivity, calmness and ingenuity. Virtually their only leverage was the threat that refusal to accept their advice would result in adverse publicity in and through the United Nations. Their success in resolving disputes along the boundaries between the two communities was impressive.

I was particularly struck by their commander, the Indian General Prem Chand, who was known as 'the Conqueror of Katanga', from the part he had played in the United Nations operation to prevent the secession of Katanga from the Congo in the sixties. He looked like a typical graduate from Sandhurst, very British, with his cavalry moustache, very competent. There were few officers in our peace-keeping operations who were his equal. He was a pleasure to talk to, had excellent judgement, and I could always rely on his suggestions.

The situation continued to deteriorate during 1973. The intercommunal talks bogged down, partly because Archbishop Makarios, under criticism from the *Enosis* extremists of Eoka B, could not afford the political costs of compromise. When the Turkish Prime Minister Bülent Ecevit used a public interview to propose a federal state of Cyprus, Makarios reacted sharply, declaring that the Greek Cypriots would never accept any sort of federalist solution. Despite Denktash's denial that there had been any change in policy, the damage had been done, and the result was suspension of the talks. I visited Cyprus again towards the end of August 1973 during my tour of the Arab states and Israel and called on Makarios again, landing by helicopter in front of the presidential palace. He ushered me into his study, where we had a long private talk about the situation. He did not hide his frustration about developments and complained bitterly about what he described as the most unco-operative attitude of the Turkish community. The heat was stupefying, and after an hour or so he complained about it and asked if I would mind if he took his mitre off. I agreed, and took off my own coat. The change in his appearance was distinctly disconcerting. The dignitary of the Orthodox Church was converted into a rather tired man with a very bald head.

The general reputation he has left behind is that of a shrewd, Byzantine politician. It is true that he was very difficult to deal with but I am inclined to think that he was obsessed by a sort of patriotism and that he wanted to defend his country's independence at all costs. Under the British he had been a supporter of *Enosis*, but in office he had moved away from that position, whether because he really believed in the independence of Cyprus or out of personal ambition it is difficult to say. It was doubtless an element in his thinking, because if he had to subordinate himself to a Greek government he might even disappear from the political scene. His attitude certainly brought him into conflict with the extremists and lay at the root of the dramatic events that were shortly to follow.

As the months passed the turmoil within the Greek Cypriot community grew. There were rumours that a rebellion was brewing. Matters were not improved by the coup in Athens in November 1973, which brought to power a group of military officers even more rightist and anti-Communist than their predecessors. Grivas died of a heart attack in January 1974 but his cohorts carried on with their preparations.

In July 1974 Makarios finally challenged the Greek junta. He accused it of conspiring against his government and having tried three times to assassinate him. He demanded the removal of the 650 officers who controlled the pro-Eoka Greek Cypriot National Guard. A few days later, on 15 July, these officers, led by Nicos Sampson, struck back in a successful revolt against his government. Makarios barely escaped with his life, scrambling down the hill behind the presidential palace as the rebels broke in the front entrance. His troops were no match for the National Guard. The new regime proclaimed Sampson, a notorious Eoka gunman, as President.

I alerted the Security Council and issued an appeal to both Turkey and Greece to exercise restraint. Makarios arrived in New York on 18 July and immediately called on me. He described his escape from Nicosia in dramatic terms. The presidential palace had been burned to the ground and, thinking he was still inside, the assailants had reported that he was dead. He had succeeded in making his way to Paphos, at the extreme western end of the island, where he was contacted by General Prem Chand and offered the protection of the UNFICYP camp.

Learning that rebel armoured cars were approaching Paphos and that a small National Guard warship had already fired on the bishop's residence in the town, Makarios had decided to take further refuge in his native village in the Troodos mountains. However, he realized that he would be immobilized if he went into hiding, and made up his mind to leave Cyprus. UNFICYP arranged for him to be picked up by a British helicopter and taken to the air base at Akrotiri. Thence he had flown to Malta and London, where he saw the Prime Minister, Harold Wilson, and the Foreign Secretary, James Callaghan, who had assured him of their support and their refusal to recognize the Sampson regime.

Makarios looked pale and shaky, understandably even more fragile than when I had previously seen him, but he was composed and in full control of his mental faculties. I was particularly impressed by his refusal to accept his government's defeat as more than temporary and his determination to return to the island.

The drama of that week came to a climax. Early in the morning of 20 July, the Turkish government, invoking the treaty of guarantee of 1960, launched a large-scale military operation by sea and air against the north coast of Cyprus. Within a few days the Turkish forces had occupied a wedge-shaped area comprising the main Turkish Cypriot enclave stretching southwards to Nicosia and contiguous territories. UNFICYP was at once in touch with both sides in an attempt to protect civilians. It sought to arrange a cease-fire between the Turkish forces and the Greek Cypriot National Guard, to have Nicosia declared an open city, and to protect the inhabitants and towns of each community situated behind the lines of the other's forces.

The Turkish invasion changed the focus of the Security Council's deliberations. The previous day it had been discussing the revolt in the Greek Cypriot community. Makarios had called it an invasion by Greece. The Greek government was insisting that it was an internal Cypriot affair and the Turks were asserting that Vice-President Denktash was the only remaining legitimate constitutional authority on the island. A draft resolution was circulated in the Council upholding the independence of the Republic of Cyprus.

The next day all thoughts were directed towards the need to stop the fighting, not only to end the suffering on Cyprus but also to prevent hostilities between Greece and Turkey, with the potential threat of still wider involvement. I told the Council that the situation was appalling and extremely dangerous and appealed to the parties to halt the battle in progress and to co-operate with UNFICYP in protecting the civilian population.

The Security Council called for an immediate cease-fire and for co-operation with the United Nations forces to carry out its mandate. Firing did stop on 22 July, although, as my frequent situation reports stated, the cease-fire could best be described as shaky. UNFICYP was receiving requests for assistance from all sides and the work of supervising the truce promised to be difficult. I urgently requested all the countries contributing troops to UNFICYP to reinforce their contingents, and within a fortnight it had been doubled in size.

The very next day, 23 July, the cease-fire was violated in several areas of the island and the Turkish forces advanced in various sectors. However, there were two important, and hopeful, developments: in Athens the Greek military junta collapsed, and on Cyprus Sampson resigned the presidency he had so recently seized by force. This did something to reduce the tension between Greece and Turkey.

The following day, accompanied by Under Secretary Brian Urquhart, the principal UN adviser on peace-keeping problems, I called on Secretary of State Kissinger in Washington. It was a typically hot summer day, but his spacious air-conditioned office, with its curtained windows and tasteful furniture, created an atmosphere of cool relaxation. I had to admire Dr Kissinger's self-possession. With the Nixon administration approaching its last agonized days, he handled the issues before us with his usual wit and aplomb.

As we talked, a secretary came in and said that there was an urgent telephone call for me from New York. Urquhart picked up the receiver to find that it was George Sherry, our able specialist on Cyprus, on the line. He reported that there had been a confrontation at Nicosia international airport between the United Nations forces and the Turkish army. Repudiating an earlier agreement, the Turkish commander on the spot had warned General Prem Chand that if the UN forces were still at the airport the following morning his men would attack. I instructed Prem Chand to stand his ground.

Time was short. It was already evening in Cyprus and the ultimatum would expire in a few hours. Fortunately there is no better world-wide communications system than that at the disposal of the American Secretary of State. He invited us to make full use of his facilities. In a matter of minutes I was connected with the Turkish Prime Minister, Bulent Ecevit, in Ankara. He was not well informed; indeed he was under the impression that Turkish troops had already occupied the airfield. Tersely, I gave him the facts. By an agreement worked out between UNFICYP, the Greek Cypriot National Guard and the local Turkish commander, the guard had withdrawn from the airport and handed it over to the United Nations forces. Turkish military headquarters had now reversed that decision.

Ecevit seemed genuinely surprised. He had not heard of any agreement with UNFICYP, he told me. I repeated that the National Guard had only relinquished the airport on my assurance that it would not fall into Turkish hands. If it was now attacked, his government would be responsible for the bloodshed. Ecevit stated that he would look into the matter at once and do his best to avoid violence.

On the ground the UN forces were busy. To counter reports that Turkish forces already controlled the airport, the political officer, John Miles, led the local press in a long march round its perimeter so that they could see that the 'blue berets' were still in position. Prem Chand had concentrated the bulk of his forces, including men from each of its eight national contingents, on the spot. The British, who gave UNFICYP logistical support from their sovereign bases on the island, offered assistance. British tanks appeared on the scene, while a squadron of A4 aircraft, stationed at Akrotiri, flew overhead.

At the end of our meeting, Dr Kissinger expressed appreciation for my co-operation, both in Cyprus and in the Middle East in general. The United Nations role was indispensable, he said, since it was the only organization which could arrange a cease-fire and establish peace-keeping machinery on the ground. He even went so far as to add, 'You have made a believer in the United Nations out of me.' Coming from a geopolitical realist like Henry Kissinger this was indeed a tribute.

I hurried back to New York to attend the Security Council meeting scheduled for later in the day. It was evening when I reached my small private office behind the Council chamber, but with the assistance of the Turkish Ambassador, Osman Olcay, I succeeded in talking again to Prime Minister Ecevit. He told me with satisfaction that the incident had been settled. He had given the necessary instructions and UNFICYP would continue to hold the airport.

We were greatly relieved that our efforts had caused the Turks to change their minds. We had no desire to disclose what we had done, certainly not to seek praise for it. It would not do to ruffle Turkish sensitivities. That would only make it harder to restore peace. So we left it to Ambassador Olcay to inform the Security Council of the situation in his own words, and allowed the Turks to take credit for avoiding a clash with the United Nations.

It was at this juncture that the United Nations found itself confirmed, more or less by default, as the custodian of its orphan child. In my discussions with the representatives of Britain, France and the US it became clear to me that they had no intention whatsoever of taking serious action to stop the Turkish offensive. Without their leadership, very little could be done. I was not ready, I told them, to shoulder the whole responsibility for further action. UNFICYP's mandate and its strength were not sufficient to resist the Turkish army. It had been intended only to control relationships between the two Cypriot communities. To ask it to do anything more, I would need a much clearer directive from the Security Council.

That directive was not forthcoming, so I took it upon myself, as cautiously as possible, to extend the very narrow mandate of UNFICYP – to act as a buffer between the Greek and Turkish Cypriot communities – in order to mitigate as far as possible the hardships of a conflict it was unable to prevent. Once a cease-fire had taken hold, UNFICYP might again act as an interposition force, with the consent of the other parties. The time for that had clearly not yet arrived. In the meantime the force was fully occupied in doing what it could to maintain the cease-fire, protect and evacuate civilians from any isolated community that found itself surrounded by the forces of the other side and, with the co-operation of the Red Cross, to furnish food, water and other essentials to civilian groups deprived of them by the fighting.

The Security Council had called upon the three guarantor powers, Britain, Greece and Turkey, to meet without delay in negotiations to restore peace and constitutional government in Cyprus. They met in Geneva under the chairmanship of the British Foreign Secretary, James

Callaghan, and on 30 July issued a declaration requiring the areas under the opposing armies' control not to be extended, and calling on UNFICYP to establish and then patrol buffer zones, to police mixed villages and to protect Turkish Cypriot enclaves. The National Guard was required to evacuate Turkish villages it had occupied and detainees on both sides were to be exchanged under the supervision of the Red Cross.

I joined the Foreign Ministers of Great Britain, Turkey and Greece when they resumed their sessions in Geneva on 8 August to determine how the United Nations might best help. It immediately became clear that Turkey was ready to resort to force in order to achieve its goal: the establishment of two regions, distinct geographically and ethnically, with autonomy for each. Turkish Foreign Minister Gunes made it clear that his government no longer felt bound by the cease-fire agreement, since the evacuation of the Turkish Cypriot enclaves called for under the 30 July declaration had not even begun. He demanded the immediate creation of a Turkish Cypriot area on the northern coast embracing 34% of the island's territory.

Under this threat Mr Callaghan made an extraordinary proposal to me. He suggested that British troops might be used to strengthen UNFICYP and that a number of Phantom aircraft might be flown to Cyprus so that the Turks would know that they would be facing British troops wearing blue helmets if they moved beyond the cease-fire line. I told the British Foreign Secretary that I would consider the idea but that I would have to consult with my colleagues in New York and look into the legal problems involved. These proved to be substantial and I so informed him. However he had himself abandoned the proposal after further consultation with his government, reinforced by United States objections to the plan.

On 14 August the Turkish army resumed its advance and the Geneva conference collapsed. Within a short time the two communities were almost completely segregated north and south of the military demarcation line imposed by the Turkish army. The Turkish Cypriot community remained under the protection of 25,000 Turkish troops garrisoned in the north. It became progressively more dependent on mainland Turkey for its support and its economy remained stagnant. In contrast, the Greek Cypriots, despite the influx of 200,000 refugees, quickly built up a thriving economy. Friction continued along the demarcation line, although, with UNFICYP's participation, major violence was avoided. Cyprus had entered upon a new stage in its political life.

In a strictly military sense, the Turkish operation was a success. But from the standpoint of the United Nations, and the principles of the Charter, it created serious problems. The insistence of the Turkish Cypriots and the Ankara government in holding on to the conquered territory for a decade and more has intensified the bitterness between the separated populations. It has made it much harder to work out any agreement whatever between the two communities. In such an atmosphere, *revanchisme* flourishes and true stability becomes almost unattainable.

In February 1975, the 'Turkish Federated State of Cyprus' was established with executive, legislative and judicial institutions. Denktash was elected its President. The following month the Security Council expressed its regret at this unilateral action and called on me to undertake a new mission of good offices and convene the representatives of the two communities to resume negotiations. Thus I was faced for six years with the most thankless and frustrating task of my term of office.

At first we could not even agree on the location of the talks. Archbishop Makarios, who had resumed his functions, suggested New York, but Denktash disagreed. He argued that the Greek Cypriots would have an advantage since they were the accredited representatives at the United Nations. For similar reasons he excluded Rome, Paris and Geneva. A month elapsed before the two delegations finally settled on Vienna, where the Republic of Cyprus had no diplomatic representative. Clerides and Denktash were again nominated as the principal negotiators.

I took the chair at no less than six separate exhaustive, and exhausting, rounds of negotiations with my two Cypriot interlocutors. It would be wearisome to recount the proceedings in detail because the problems always remained the same. First, there was the question of territorial control. With more than a third of the island's territory occupied by the Turkish armed forces, they held a position of strength. The Turkish Cypriots indicated privately that they would consider reducing their area by approximately 10% as part of an overall settlement. The Greek Cypriots for their part began with the premise that the area to be occupied by the Turkish community should reflect its proportion of the island's population, that is to say 18%. At times they indicated they might consider a figure as high as 25%. That gap was never closed.

Related to the territorial question was the fate of the Famagusta area, now in Turkish hands. Famagusta had been the island's major port. Its modern district, known as Varosha, had been the largest hotel and beach resort in Cyprus. Some 35,000 Greek Cypriots who had lived there were eager to return to it – provided, of course, that they could be assured of favourable living conditions.

During my visit to Nicosia in August 1974 I visited Varosha. The Turkish authorities were co-operative and allowed me to wander through the deserted city. It was an appalling sight. The modern tourist hotels stood empty, neglected and in disrepair. Rats were running around; windows were broken; there was an eerie silence.

I tried then, and often subsequently, to work out an arrangement for restoring the city to the Greek Cypriots, either prior to or as the first stage of a more general settlement. But there has been no agreement on the conditions under which its inhabitants might return. It remains a desolate ghost town — a standing monument to the tragedy and wastefulness of intercommunal warfare.

With a common legal background and many years of pre-independence friendship, Clerides and Denktash, the two negotiators in Vienna, proved worthy adversaries. Their freedom of action was closely circumscribed by their respective communities and they were hard bargainers at the conference table. I sometimes felt that they wanted to agree, but neither had the power to do so. In general, Clerides tried to achieve a reasonable compromise by making concessions, Denktash was more prone to stonewalling. He gave the impression that he would be ready to accept an agreement only on his own terms.

We may have placed too much hope in the close personal rapport between the two men. After one long and particularly contentious day of argument, we were all weary, so I invited Clerides and Denktash to dinner at the Hotel Sacher and reserved a small private room so that we could continue the discussion over a good meal in a more relaxed and informal atmosphere. As the evening progressed, the two men unbent. With a good deal of light banter, they seemed to be edging closer to agreement, so much so that in the post-prandial euphoria I even allowed myself to believe that we might be approaching at least a modest breakthrough in the negotiations.

It seemed to me that only minor aspects of the matters under discussion remained to be pinned down. As I said good night, I expressed the hope that they could clarify these points before we met again the next day. 'We shall do our best,' said Clerides, and the two men went off by themselves, arm in arm, in good humour, to a nearby bar. We learned that they stayed there until three o'clock in the morning, but when the meeting was resumed the following day, nothing had changed. We were again mired in disagreement.

It soon became clear that no decision could be reached on a border between the two communities without agreement on the constitutional arrangements under which Cyprus would be reunited. The Greeks insisted that Cyprus must be an independent, sovereign and unitary state, not a federative system. This would give them the benefit of majority rule. Denktash objected to the use of the term 'unitary', which he said the other side interpreted in a sense different from his. For the Turks it was vital that each community be given the widest powers of self-government: a central government would have to have strictly limited authority. We spent endless hours discussing the particular forms that governmental institutions might take at various levels in a federal or confederal structure. Even when we inched towards agreement on broad generalizations, it was never possible to reduce them to precise agreements.

A related issue concerned the right to freedom of movement and residence of Cypriots throughout the island, as well as the right to hold property. The Greeks argued that all the inhabitants of Cyprus must enjoy the same rights. The Turks countered that this should be considered in the context of arrangements to ensure their own security against the danger that they might be overrun by the numerically superior Greeks.

Where we did make slow and painful progress was with the problems of re-settling the refugees who had fled from their homes during the hostilities, and of members of one community trapped in enclaves behind the lines of the other. Apart from the 200,000 Greeks who had fled south, there were some 30,000 Turkish Cypriots in villages in areas under Greek Cypriot control. The feeding, housing, general care and transportation of all these unfortunate people were a major concern, and here we did achieve considerable success. Over the course of time, and with aid from the UN Commissioner for Refugees and relief funds contributed by other countries, it was possible to assist almost all these people to move to new homes.

It was not until the fifth negotiating round in Vienna that there was some hint of movement. In February 1976, to our surprise, Glafcos Clerides pulled a map out of his file and showed us the settlement areas occupied by the Turkish army which the Greeks wished to have back to accommodate their refugees. Denktash and I were given copies. Clerides was always the more amenable of the two and, knowing Denktash as well as he did and for as long as he had, probably overestimated his opponent's capacity for compromise.

I was briefly elated at what seemed to presage real progress. But Clerides had evidently overstepped the bounds marked out for him by President Makarios. When news of his proposal was leaked, allegedly by the Turks, he was accused of secret dealings with Denktash. He had also given the impression to Makarios and others that he was moving towards the conception of a bi-zonal confederation, an idea that the Archbishop was not yet ready to accept. A couple of months later Clerides resigned and almost certainly forfeited his succession to the presidency. We had to start all over again.

The next hope of movement came a year later and involved the two Presidents. Makarios had stated in an interview published in the London *Times* that he might, under certain conditions, accept a federal solution for Cyprus if it safeguarded the unity of the state. This was a surprising development, and it brought Makarios and Denktash together in Nicosia on United Nations premises in the presence of my representative and newly appointed Under Secretary General, Javier Pérez de Cuellar. It is with pleasure that I can present my eventual successor at this point. He had represented Peru for two years as a non-permanent member in the Security Council. When his turn came to take the chair for a month, I had been impressed by his skill and the thoughtful way in which he handled this difficult body. I was in the process of losing my Argentine colleague, Roberto Guyer, because his government wanted him back to become their Ambassador in Germany. To keep the balance I needed another top-ranking official from Latin America. I approached Pérez de Cuellar. He was very willing, his government agreed, and he was appointed to the Secretariat.

I was engaged in one of my periodic tours of the Middle East and arranged to stop over in Cyprus to attend the second Makarios-Denktash meeting. While both sides wanted me there, they could not agree on where my plane should land. The international airport in Nicosia had remained under UNFICYP control but had not been re-opened to traffic. Each side insisted on receiving me at an airport in its own sector of the country. Since I had fitted in the Cyprus stop-over at the end of a gruelling tour, I was more than a little annoyed at this display of political rivalry.

After a hurried exchange of cables, it was finally agreed that my plane would land at Larnaca airport in the government-controlled zone, where representatives of President Makarios would receive me. I would then fly by helicopter to Nicosia airport to be met by representatives of President Denktash. I was to leave Cyprus on a specially prepared runway at the international airport. The arrangements verged on the ridiculous, but were entirely in keeping with the general contentiousness of the two communities.

Our discussion started at seven o'clock in the evening, and we really seemed to be making substantial progress on the basis of an independent, single, non-aligned federal state. Only Makarios had the necessary authority to depart from what had for years been his government's stated position. It looked like a real breakthrough at last.

The negotiations were prolonged. Dinner had been arranged and there came a point when Denktash shouted that he was hungry. Makarios said no, he wanted to continue with the talks. My own contribution was to order a huge plate of sandwiches and beer, and Denktash wolfed the lot. Makarios had a glass of orange juice. Thus fortified, we even drew up a four-point memorandum that appeared to provide solutions to the constitutional and administrative problems, freedom of movement and the powers and functions of the central government. But soon we realized that even Makarios had gone too far for his hard-line supporters. When the next round of talks was held back in Vienna all I heard was a sterile repetition of all the previous points of contention. It seemed pointless to go on. Then, in August 1977, Makarios died. His successor was his former Foreign Minister, Spyros Kyprianou. Although he lacked the charisma of the Archbishop, he had established his leadership through dedication and hard work. Perhaps because he was less sure of his electoral support, he was inclined to be more unyielding in negotiations. He also failed to establish any true personal relationship with Denktash.

Wearily I resumed my rounds. I visited Athens to talk to Premier Karamanlis and Ankara for talks with Prime Minister Ecevit. I lobbied Kyprianou and Denktash. Gradually we persuaded them to hold what I termed a 'high-level meeting' with me in Nicosia on 18 and 19 May 1979. Somewhat to my surprise, my efforts bore fruit. After hours of exhausting negotiations under my auspices, Denktash and Kyprianou reached a ten-point 'summit agreement' on 19 May 1979. Together with the 1977 guidelines, it was to serve as a benchmark for future negotiations. Its first provision was an agreement to resume the intercommunal talks on 15 June 1979. While they were to cover all territorial and constitutional aspects of the subject, priority was to be given to the settlement of Varosha, and special importance to the promotion of goodwill, mutual confidence and the return to normal conditions. (These were the code words for the lifting of the economic restrictions that were injuring the Turkish Cypriot area.)

Once again, we were back on the negotiating track. The new round of intercommunal meetings was opened by my Special Representative, Pérez de Cuellar, in Nicosia. He read a message from me noting the historic importance of this step, after a two-year hiatus, and urging the negotiators to demonstrate the political will and statesmanship which alone could produce agreement. But in a week the talks had to be recessed because of irreconcilable differences over the meaning of the terms 'bi-zonality' and 'security of the Turkish Cypriot community'. Stripped to its essentials, the issue was always the same: should there be a single state in Cyprus, or a confederation of two substantially independent states?

Another year went by without further discussions. In August 1980, the parties agreed to sit down together once again. The talks dragged on month after month in dilatory fashion, in round after unproductive round. Occasionally, some old wine was poured into new bottles, but the basic differences remained unresolved. Some progress was made on secondary issues such as the plight of the remaining refugees, the whereabouts of missing persons and family visits across the demarcation line. Proposals for a fundamental settlement submitted by the two sides in the autumn of 1981 only confirmed the continuing deadlock.

A good indication of the tension prevailing and of the different personalities of the two leaders was provided at one meeting, which took place at UN headquarters in Nicosia. In a large room across the corridor an impressive number of journalists and media reporters were waiting in order to cover the historic event. I asked Kyprianou and Denktash whether they were ready to meet the press and they agreed. As I was leading them towards the cameras the always ebullient Denktash, walking on my left, said to Kyprianou on my right: 'Spiro, why don't you smile?' The reply of the grim-faced Kyprianou was: 'I smiled already once.'

My last official act in this melancholy process was to present the leaders of the two communities with an 'evaluation' of the state of the negotiations, which had been prepared by Ambassador Hugo Gobbi of Argentina, who had by then become the resident UN Special Representative in Nicosia. It contained some ingenious proposals for new constitutional machinery which, among less passionately committed opponents, might have aroused some interest. It was no more successful than our earlier efforts.

For ten years I laboured for innumerable hours and with all the energy at my command to bring about a Cyprus settlement. I have to admit that it was not much closer when I departed than when I arrived. I was often tempted to throw up my hands in utter frustration. It is not within the power of an international civil servant to apply much more than the voice of reason and persuasion in dealing with antagonists who are unwilling to risk the compromises which alone can lead to settlement. As the servant of the world organization, and despite repeated setbacks, I persisted in my efforts. The United Nations could lead the horses to water. It could not make them drink.

On the other hand, the United Nations record in Cyprus is not one of unmitigated failure. Through UNFICYP it has, year after year, held the lid on intercommunal conflict. The force could not prevent the major crises involving Turkey and Greece. That was never its mission. But without UNFICYP in place, the island would have lived in constant disorder, with the risk that its internal turmoil might have set up a disastrous wider war which would have caused far greater turmoil.

The United Nations was an essential catalyst and participant in the long succession of intercommunal and international negotiations seeking a settlement. Directly, both through my personal contacts and through my diplomatic representatives on the spot, I believe I helped to keep the negotiating process in motion. A vast amount of diplomatic spade work has been done which will help in reaching solutions when the parties concerned are willing to profit by them.

7

African Turmoil

One of the most spectacular incidents in the history of the UN, publicized all over the world, occurred in 1960 when Nikita Khrushchev took off his shoe in the densely packed Assembly Hall and pounded vigorously on the desk in front of his seat. He wanted to force a debate on 'Western imperialism', as he called it, in the context of the decolonization process of the Third World. He got the attention he wanted. Shortly afterwards, he proposed a Soviet resolution strongly supporting the aspirations of the Third World countries. This did not fail to have an enormous impact on developing countries. Nevertheless – and without wishing to minimize the importance of Khrushchev's initiative – the undeniable fact is that the decolonialization process was started long before on a bilateral and multilateral basis, in the latter case mainly through the United Nations.

As always in such circumstances victory has many fathers. Indeed since then, more than a hundred countries have gained their independence. This has fundamentally changed the membership of the United Nations and radically altered the balance of power in the organization.

The Western powers were anything but happy with this development. They argued that Soviet domination in eastern Europe was also a form of colonialism. But this left most of the nations of the south, particularly the Africans, unimpressed. As far as they were concerned, colonialism had a racial connotation – the colonizer was white, the colonized people of colour. To them, oppression, real or imagined, of whites by whites, is not colonialism, reprehensible as it may be on other grounds.

To the West this seemed patently unjust, involving a glaringly inequitable double standard of judgement. The parliamentary democracies often asserted that the Soviet bloc, at home and abroad, brushes aside considerations of individual rights and freedoms and makes a mockery of the United Nations Declaration of Human Rights and the covenants which have been concluded to translate its general provisions into binding obligations. They apply the same criticism to most of the developing countries governed by one-party regimes.

For their part, these groups combine to direct the thrust of the United Nations in the field of human rights towards collective 'rights', such as the right to development or the rights of states to control their own resources.

These are in many ways conflicting approaches to the fundamental problems of freedom and welfare. They spring from different philosophical and political premises. It serves no purpose to ignore them, but until satisfactory ways are found to give due weight to both conceptions of human rights, the United Nations will continue to be seriously split and criticized over the issue.

I was given an early baptism in these conflicting tides. Four weeks after I took office I was in Addis Ababa addressing the first Security Council session ever held in Africa. For the Africans it was an historic occasion. For the Council to meet in the large conference centre at the headquarters of the Organization of African Unity marked a coming of age of their new, post-colonial continent. It also highlighted a set of grave and absorbing problems for the United Nations.

For ten years, with scarcely a day's surcease, I had to live with the African dimension. It had literally forced itself on the organization's attention as the number of African members had grown. In 1945 there were only four. By 1970 the number had risen to forty-two, and during my term of office I witnessed the entry of nine more. Five of these were former Portuguese territories; one, Djibouti, had been French; two, the Comoros and Seychelles, were off-shore island groups emerging from colonial status; and the ninth, Zimbabwe, had a troubled progression from the status of a British dependent territory through a disputed to a recognized independence.

European control of African territory had practically vanished by the 1980s. Economic development was progressing, albeit unevenly and with many setbacks. Only in the southern tip of the continent did two major problems remain, the decolonization of Namibia, the former South-West Africa, and the policy of racial discrimination (apartheid) in South Africa.

The most tumultuous event was the collapse of the 500-year-old Portuguese colonial empire. It could no longer withstand the wave of nationalist sentiment that engulfed the African continent. Its armed forces were consumed and its economy burdened by increasingly violent local wars in the overseas territories. The mounting strain provided the major factor in bringing about the revolution which established democratic government in Portugal in the successful *coup d'état* of April 1974. The ostracism which Portugal had suffered within the United Nations system, cut off from many of the benefits of membership of its specialized agencies, was at an end.

The UN was able to act as midwife in the swift, but fraught, transition of power. The new Portuguese government made it clear that it wished to move as quickly as possible to grant independence to its African possessions. To do so in an orderly fashion was not easy. The new authorities were inexperienced. They had to deal with the legacy of bitter opposition from the liberation movements clamouring to assume power. Portugal lacked the resources to endow the overseas territories with the economic assistance they needed if they were to start life as viable societies. Poverty was endemic and the colonies disorganized as the result of the prolonged violence and guerrilla warfare which had continued for nearly thirteen years. There was an alarming shortage of administrative and professional skills, which grew as the Europeans made for home.

The liberation movements were electrified by the change of government in Portugal. They were still deeply suspicious of Portuguese motives. The enmity of decades could not be expunged overnight. Time was needed to wind down the colonial wars. Five separate areas were involved. Two were large, Mozambique, the size of California with a population of over eight million, and Angola, larger than California and Texas combined with five-and-a-half million inhabitants. The smaller territories were Portuguese Guinea on the West African coast, which was to become Guinea-Bissau, the Cape Verde Islands in the Atlantic, which opted for a separate existence, and the smaller islands of São Tome and Principe in the Gulf of Guinea. East Timor in the South-West Pacific was taken over by Indonesia.

With one exception, the independence fighters had merged into one major movement in each territory. This made negotiations much easier. The exception was Angola, where three separate and mutually antagonistic groups contended for control in different areas of the country. Their rivalries complicated preparations for setting up an indigenous government and were to continue to this day.

In the hectic days after the revolution in Lisbon, the new Portuguese leadership realized that they would need help in disengaging from their overseas territories. They reacted favourably to a statement I issued on 17 May 1974, expressing my firm belief that the relevant United Nations resolutions provided the only basis for a peaceful solution of the colonial wars. In the statement I urged the new government to recognize the right of the peoples in the territories to self-determination and independence and to begin negotiations with the liberation movements without delay so that peace could be restored. I offered to provide any assistance I could with the negotiations and pointed out that the General Assembly had requested me to do so.

My conversations with the Portuguese convinced me that they were sincere in their declared intention to end the hostilities and free the territories. But they also revealed serious domestic problems that had to be overcome. As the new Foreign Minister, Mario Soares, described them to me at a meeting in New York on 22 June 1974, there was a risk that the new authorities might be overthrown in a counter-revolution if these problems were not handled carefully. The government was a temporary creation working with the military. It had no electoral mandate. Its first tasks had to be to consolidate democracy and individual liberties at home, and to end the prevailing economic chaos.

Soares had quickly established relationships with the national liberation movements, but there were dangers in moving ahead too swiftly. The Portuguese military were insisting on the need to hold referenda in some of the colonies before independence was granted. If the new government ignored this issue, it might fall.

I could understand the Foreign Minister's concern. Yet it seemed to me that he underestimated the long-term danger to Portugal if the country permitted the opportunity for peaceful change to lapse. I told him that, from my many conversations with African leaders, I could not understand why Portugal did not at least recognize the immediate independence of Mozambique. The situation was bound to deteriorate further if there were any delay, and the autumn UN General Assembly would react forcefully. It was a serious dilemma for Soares. He thought that the delicate balance in Portugal might be upset if he pressed ahead too quickly, but he understood the importance of breaking out of Portugal's diplomatic isolation.

Within a few weeks the pieces began to fall into place. In July 1974 the Portuguese promulgated new constitutional laws for changing the status of the African territories. General de Spinola, the new President, invited me to visit Lisbon. I took a strong team with me and found the Portuguese eager to receive our advice. They lacked experience in dealing with the Africans on an equal footing and were anxious to avoid errors as they mended their fences with the United Nations agencies. Together we worked out a general plan of action.

This recognized the right of all to self-determination and independence. To allay suspicions and anxieties among the liberation movements, it pledged the government's full support for the unity of each territory and its opposition to any attempt, from any quarter, at secession or dismemberment. It laid down the procedures for handing over power and expressed the hope that Portugal might be permitted to participate fully in the social, economic and technical programmes of the United Nations and its specialized agencies.

Despite the bad blood between the parties in Mozambique, an

agreement was signed in Lusaka on 7 September with the representatives of the freedom organization Frelimo, transferring authority to them the following June, the tenth anniversary of Frelimo's founding.

The President, Samora Machel, conveyed to me his appreciation for my part in these arrangements, through what he termed the 'concessions' I had obtained during my visit to Lisbon. How directly my talks there had affected the outcome in Mozambique I cannot say. Certainly in the dire straits the Portuguese had reached, with their economy ruined and their morale shaken by prolonged combat overseas, they were unusually susceptible to guidance.

In the remaining Portuguese African territory, Angola, the situation was much more difficult. Anti-colonial warfare had broken out there in 1961. During the fighting, three separate liberation movements had emerged, the Popular Movement for the Liberation of Angola (MPLA), the National Front for the Liberation of Angola (FNLA) and the National Union for the Total Independence of Angola (UNITA). There was no single representative organization with which the government of Portugal could negotiate. The Organization of African Unity, to which we looked for guidance, recognized both MPLA and FNLA, but not UNITA.

As the Portuguese forces relaxed their hold, relations between the three liberation movements deteriorated and the home government was in a quandary as to how and to whom to relinquish authority. Most of the African states favoured MPLA, and the Organization of African Unity recognized Agostinho Neto as its leader. Based on Luanda, the capital, it enjoyed the support of the USSR. FNLA, led by Holden Roberto, was strongest in the north and was supported from Zaire, reputedly with Chinese backing. UNITA, under Jonas Savimbi, was strongest in the south, where it was said to enjoy Western support, but particularly that of South Africa. Thus were the seeds of continuing conflict laid.

In January 1975, the Portuguese succeeded in concluding a fragile agreement with the three movements at Alvor, recognizing them as the sole legitimate representatives of the Angolan people, declaring that the territory should be a single, indivisible entity, and providing for transitional government and elections and the withdrawal of the Portuguese armed forces within a year.

Fighting soon broke out between the three liberation movements and continued despite repeated attempts to arrange truces. In August 1975, the Portuguese informed me that the Alvor agreement had ceased to function. They intended to remain neutral in the internal struggle and defend the country against a break-up and possible foreign intervention. The Portuguese High Commissioner was granted emergency powers and only the NFLA continued to be represented in the Angolan administration.

In November, the Portuguese made the dramatic suggestion that the United Nations should take over executive authority. We looked into the legal complications and discovered that this could not be done without Security Council and possibly General Assembly approval. With Angola fast becoming a cockpit of East-West rivalry, we did not think it likely that these organs would approve. It was impossible to avoid comparisons with the United Nations embroilment in the Congo some fifteen years earlier, which had nearly destroyed the organization. There was little reason to suppose that it would fare better in this instance.

The Portuguese High Commissioner, Rear Admiral Leonel Cardoso, proclaimed the independence of Angola and its full sovereignty, 'rooted in the Angolan people, who alone are qualified to decide how it is to be exercised.' MPLA took over the government with the help of Cuban troops and Soviet support. Guerrilla warfare with the other two factions has continued ever since.

In different circumstances it might have been possible to contemplate seriously the use of a United Nations administration to facilitate an orderly transfer of power. For that to have succeeded we would have needed sufficient time to work out an agreement among the major powers and with the Organization of African Unity. A peace-keeping force and a corps of United Nations civilian administrators would certainly have been required. In the current atmosphere of international anarchy, the prospect of making such an arrangement was regrettably very slight. Developments in Angola provide a sad illustration of the inadequacies of the international system today.

In South Africa, the situation remains wholly intractable. Powerful, wealthy and unyielding, it has persisted as the bastion of white minority rule. Its guiding principle of apartheid – institutionalized racial discrimination and segregation – has provoked virtually complete condemnation in the United Nations. The membership finds it utterly abhorrent that, as a matter of government policy, blacks, coloureds, Asians and whites should be segregated and that the black majority should be subjected to unjustifiable restrictions imposed on its right to live, move, work and organize freely. Apartheid is totally incompatible with the ideals of the Charter and the provisions of United Nations human rights treaties and declarations. It has been stigmatized as a crime against humanity, deserving of the strongest counter-action the organization can devise.

It may unfortunately be true that few nations have a perfect record as far as racial discrimination is concerned, but no other country has institutionalized racial discrimination and upheld segregation as an official policy, backed by the full force of law.

By the time I assumed office, the General Assembly and the Security Council had long since adopted a wide range of measures designed to demonstrate their disapproval of South African practices. They had not in any serious way affected the stability of the South African government or brought about the desired changes. One of the limiting factors was the unwillingness of the major Western powers to agree to more direct coercive action. Unlike most of the Third World countries, they had large trade, investment and even strategic interests at stake. They were not convinced that coercive steps against South Africa would accomplish the intended purpose. It might even strengthen the South African siege mentality. They also argued that economic isolation would most hurt the working black population of the country without achieving the desired results.

It proved an almost impossible problem to handle. South Africa was governed by a largely committed white community, unprepared to overturn the entire basis of its society and economy – in their view an invitation to commit suicide. It would not do so voluntarily and the United Nations could not force it to, at least not in the short run. It still remained unthinkable for the rest of the world to come to terms with apartheid as a system of political and social management.

The only proper course seemed to me to persist in the kind of measures the organization had already adopted: to step up pressure on Pretoria; patiently to carry on the educational process world-wide; and to win further support from the Western countries in overcoming the apartheid system.

Some part of this was accomplished. Year by year the organization increased the scope of its anti-apartheid measures. In early 1973 the General Assembly adopted an international convention on the suppression and punishment of the crime of apartheid, which came into force in 1976. In 1974 the Assembly took the drastic step of barring South Africa from its sessions and admitting South African national liberation movements recognized by the Organization of African Unity as observers.

This was a procedural device of questionable legality and I had reservations about it. The suspension or expulsion of member countries required action by both the Security Council and the General Assembly. Since such action in the case of South Africa would presumably be vetoed by one or more of the permanent members of the Council, it was very unlikely to be tabled.

The credentials of delegates to the UN are attestations of the fact that they represent the governments for whom they are authorized to speak, and nothing more. To deny their validity on the ground that the government concerned follows a particular policy, however reprehensible, or that it is not representative of the people, is legally not acceptable.

In my judgement it is not helpful to silence the voice of any UN member in the organization's councils. However indefensible a member country's conduct, it should be present at the discussion of the charges against it and given the opportunity to make a considered reply. Not only is this intrinsically fair: in the long run it probably offers more hope for the initiation of a useful dialogue aimed at eliminating apartheid than does a policy of parliamentary ostracism. The United Nations has nothing to gain by the creation of a class of pariah states.

In 1976 the General Assembly adopted a comprehensive programme of action intended to isolate the South African government further from the world community. The following year it sponsored a world conference against apartheid and the Security Council agreed, without veto by the Western powers, to make mandatory the arms embargo against South Africa. Finally, at the end of my term of office in 1981, the General Assembly proclaimed 1982 as The International Year of Mobilization for Sanctions against South Africa.

None of these actions, it is true, produced dramatic or immediate results. Some of the methods employed to conduct the campaign against apartheid may have been ineffective. Nevertheless I believe that the cumulative effect of all that the United Nations has done has been useful, as it has strongly increased international awareness of the problem.

My own contacts with the South African government were frosty, relatively infrequent and inconclusive, although I was at times closely involved with the problem of Namibia (South-West Africa), which the South Africans have continued to occupy in spite of the General Assembly resolution of 1966 terminating their mandate. I did visit Capetown in March 1972 as a result of the Security Council decision inviting me 'to initiate as soon as possible contacts with all the parties concerned'. This was still in the days of John Vorster as Prime Minister and Hilgard Muller as his Foreign Minister. Vorster's speech in the House of Assembly set the tone:

If the Secretary General of the United Nations wishes to come to South Africa to discuss . . . self-determination of non-white peoples with the government, among others, he will . . . find us to be willing partners in the discussions since it is our policy to lead our peoples to self-determination. But if he wishes to come to South Africa to act as a mouthpiece for the extremists of the OAU and others, and decisions taken in that connection, he will nevertheless be welcome and still be very courteously received by us, but I can tell him in advance that he will be wasting his time.

This was the phraseology that had determined South African attitudes over the years, and the talks proved fruitless.

I had insisted that I should visit Namibia, and my hosts fulfilled that commitment in minimum fashion. I was flown to the northern province of the territory, adjacent to the border with Angola, where I met representatives of the Ovambo, the largest single tribal grouping. They complained of frequent incidents involving South African troops, to which the government rejoinder was that its military operations were necessary because of the terrorist activities of SWAPO, the South-West Africa People's Organization. I found the atmosphere extremely tense. Both sides were clearly uneasy about the future.

The authorities were reluctant to take me to Windhoek, the capital of the territory, because, as my other contacts told me, they feared that local groups would stage demonstrations against the government and its policies. I insisted that I could not return to New York without interviewing their representatives. The facilities provided were minimal. My visit was not announced in advance and I was put up in a small, almost unknown hotel. Meetings were arranged with the local groups in a room at the airport shortly before my departure.

I was far from happy about such treatment, but it did give me an opportunity to meet some twenty organized groups and talk to them without the presence of the South African authorities. Many had travelled from distant parts of the territory to see me. In the limited time available I could do little more than listen. I was sufficiently encouraged to recommend on my return the appointment of a United Nations representative to Namibia to explore the possibilities of a peaceful solution. The Security Council agreed. At the end of July 1972 it authorized me to continue with my contacts and to appoint a representative to assist in carrying out its mandate. Finding a suitable representative acceptable to the South African government turned out to be slow going. The South Africans turned down one suggestion after another. Finally they agreed to the appointment of Ambassador Alfred Martin Escher of Switzerland. He had been the Swiss Ambassador in Vienna when I was Austrian Foreign Minister and was an able and experienced diplomat. But he had no knowledge of African problems, nor had he ever worked in the United Nations.

As a result he fell into a South African trap. In October 1972 he spent seventeen days in Namibia, interviewing a wide cross-section of the population. When he returned to Pretoria he informed Prime Minister Vorster of his impression that the majority of the non-white people of the territory supported the establishment of a united, independent Namibia to be established with United Nations assistance.

As was to be expected, the South Africans disagreed with Ambassador Escher's conclusions and his support for the United Nations objectives for Namibia. They induced him to initial a document recording his talks with

South African leaders, in which he appeared to accept much of the South African point of view. Specifically, he approved the idea that the inhabitants of Namibia should gain experience in self-government, on a regional basis, before self-determination could be exercised – the thin end of the wedge for introducing the 'homelands' policy – while retaining restrictive legislation, particularly on freedom of movement, in order to check the infiltration of SWAPO personnel from neighbouring Angola. There would be an advisory council of regional authorities, but the South African Prime Minister would assume responsibility for the territory as a whole.

Escher's action was construed as nothing less than a United Nations endorsement of the policy of 'separate development' – that is, apartheid. Only those who understand the intensity of Third World feeling on Southern African problems will comprehend the outrage with which Escher's report was received: a report, moreover, that I would never have agreed to a representative of mine accepting.

A career diplomat of the old school, Escher had conceived of his mission in terms of an effort to reach agreement with his interlocutors on a basis of mutual accommodation. To the Security Council, where passions ran high, this was not an acceptable framework for negotiations. Its members rejected the report. And there were tragic consequences. Keenly aware of Escher's lack of background knowledge, I had sent with him, as his principal adviser, Mr M. E. Chacko, an able and competent Indian in the Secretariat. But Escher failed to take Chacko with him to his final decisive meeting with Prime Minister Vorster and Foreign Minister Muller, at which agreement was reached on the ill-fated memorandum of understanding. So Chacko was not consulted. As a conscientious international civil servant, he was deeply chagrined by the failure of the mission. Shortly afterwards Chacko died of a heart attack. I am afraid that it may have been brought on by the shock of what had happened.

Not surprisingly, I had a difficult time with the Security Council. I had long talks with African delegates and used all the influence I could to persuade the Council to allow me to continue the talks with South Africa. Eventually it did so. Months of fruitless discussions in Geneva and New York followed. But the damage had been done. Asserting that the United Nations had acted like a 'toothless bulldog', the Organization of African Unity called for termination of the discussions.

In the following years, the lines remained sharply drawn. The South African government moved to provide Namibia with a definitive status satisfactory to it by convening a constitutional conference in 1975, in the Turnhalle, a gymnasium in Windhoek used by the pre-First-World-War German army. From this there developed the Democratic Turnhalle

Alliance (DTA), an aggregation of white and non-white elements favouring a settlement in accordance with South African objectives. Eventually a National Assembly dominated by the DTA was set up, while by the end of 1977 South Africa had created three tribal 'homelands' – semi-independent black enclaves – and was in the process of organizing several more.

Despite the failure of the Escher mission and the subsequent discussions, we in the United Nations continued our search for ways to achieve independence for Namibia. The basis for settlement was laid in Security Council Resolution 385 of 30 January 1976. After strongly condemning South Africa's conduct, the resolution called for free elections under United Nations supervision, South African withdrawal and the transfer of power, with United Nations assistance, to an independent government of the Namibian people. During the year, Secretary of State Henry Kissinger sought vainly to bring South Africa and SWAPO to the conference table in an attempt to reach agreement.

Early in 1977, in the first months of the administration of President Jimmy Carter in the United States, the situation took an encouraging new turn. The five Western members of the Security Council in that year (Canada, France, the Federal Republic of Germany, the United Kingdom and the United States) formed what became known as the Contact Group to work with the government of South Africa, SWAPO and the United Nations for a peaceful settlement of the Namibian problem based on the terms of Resolution 385. By April 1977 the Group had worked out a basic negotiating position. The influence and leadership of the Contact Group gave the negotiating process a new dynamism.

The man who symbolized this dynamism was Andrew Young, whom Carter had appointed as his new Ambassador to the United Nations.

With Andy Young, a completely new type of American diplomat came to head the US Mission to the United Nations. A former Congressman, a close friend of Carter and a symbol of the equal rights campaign of the coloured US population, he performed his duties in New York completely oblivious of the dictates of protocol – successfully, in a sense. For the first time in years, the Third World states again felt that they were understood in Washington. In the end, Andy Young fell a victim to his own imprudence. His public statements, which were occasionally in flagrant contradiction to official Washington policy, and his lack of caution, such as his meeting with the PLO representative in New York, Labib Terzi, forced Carter to recall him from New York.

Whatever one may think of Andy Young, it is certainly no exaggeration to say that he set the ball rolling for the resumption of negotiations on Namibia. Despite some initial reluctance, the Western team managed to gain the qualified support of the so-called front-line African states: Angola,

Botswana, Mozambique, Tanzania, Zambia and Nigeria, the continent's most populous country. This unusual combination often took the lead in political negotiations with the South Africans. In 1977 it seemed to be obtaining a broad measure of agreement from both South Africa and SWAPO on a Western plan.

On behalf of the Foreign Ministers of the Contact Group, Secretary of State Vance urged me in a personal letter of July 1977 to develop a plan for the United Nations machinery needed to put a settlement into effect. 'We recognize,' said the American Secretary, 'that the development by you of such an outline, in advance of a formal mandate, could give rise to some difficulties. Nevertheless, we are convinced that now is the time when your initiative could make a decisive contribution. From the standpoint of stature, expertise and objectivity, an indication from you of the United Nations machinery which might be necessary for this purpose stands the best chance of being persuasive.'

This was flattering, but since SWAPO and the front-line states wanted to move much more quickly and decisively to eliminate the South African presence from Namibia than the Western Group had contemplated, I saw no way to move through the minefield of differing views without a mandate from the Security Council. The Five could and did argue that their approach was more practical and more likely to obtain results than the United Nations' extreme and to them legalistic position. But it would have been worse than useless for me to have generated plans that would put me at odds with the Council. The most I could do was to agree that the Secretariat might provide 'information' requested by the Five.

For a few weeks this procedural problem held us up. The Contact Group continued to seek a lead from me. It was on 19 August 1977 when, on a visit to the British Prime Minister, James Callaghan, I had a surprise visit from the American chargé d'affaires, who delivered a personal letter to me from President Jimmy Carter. He wanted to inform me that progress had been made towards an internationally acceptable solution for Namibia. My contribution at this point, he wrote, would appear especially important. Further, he informed me, SWAPO had indicated that it would have no objection to the Secretariat initiating contingency planning for the role the United Nations should play during the transition to Namibian independence.

To some extent this was true. Sam Nujoma, the President of SWAPO, told me a few days later, in Lagos, that he had no objection to the United Nations contingency planning (a peace-keeping force, interim civil administration, control mechanism for the elections, etc.), provided it was for internal use only and had no official standing. And by this time we had begun work in the Secretariat. Our first study covered plans for United

Nations supervision and control of free elections in Namibia. But peace-keeping operations were a more delicate matter. They fell under the particular prerogative of the Security Council. A clear-cut decision would have to come from it before a concrete plan could be drawn up and broadly discussed.

In 1977 and 1978, the Contact Group worked vigorously to obtain agreement on proposals involving elections supervised by the United Nations, and a United Nations peace-keeping role. Obstacles arose continually, most of them coming from the South Africans. Finally, on 10 April 1978 the Contact Group sent to the President of the Security Council a detailed proposal which in its view was most likely to prove acceptable to the parties and to bring about Namibian independence during the year 1978.

The key to an internationally acceptable transition to independence, the Group stated, was free elections for the whole of Namibia as one political entity. For this to occur, it continued, the Security Council would have to authorize me to appoint a United Nations Special Representative to ensure the holding of free and fair elections.

It was an ambitious proposal, and for a time its prospects seemed bright. The South Africans appeared to accept it, with some conditions, while by mid-July the Contact Group had induced swapo and the front-line states to agree to submit it to the Security Council for implementation. By 27 July 1978 the Security Council had requested me to appoint a Special Representative. I designated Mr Martti Ahtisaari of Finland, who had been the United Nations Commissioner for Namibia under earlier arrangements, to fill this post. We worked out a scheme for a UN Transition Assistance Group (UNTAG) consisting of a civilian component of 360 police and 1,500 professional and support personnel, and a military component of seven battalions and support elements, totalling 7,500 men. These components were to supervise the cessation of hostilities between swapo and the South African forces, the withdrawal or demobilization of armed forces, the elections, and the political process leading to independence.

On 29 September 1978, the Security Council approved our proposals, in a resolution setting up UNTAG, welcoming swapo's willingness to co-operate, and calling upon South Africa to do likewise. Under the proposals, elections for a constituent assembly were to be held in seven months. However, this did not materialize. Hopes were frequently raised and subsequently dashed. Each of the parties was driven by its own interests. swapo pressed for an early implementation of our proposals. The South Africans, on the other hand, found one expedient after another for preventing any real progress towards independence for Namibia. The Contact Group sought persistently to overcome South African objections.

The front-line states strongly backed SWAPO and supported the United Nations plan. We in the United Nations took every constructive step we could to move the negotiations towards a successful conclusion.

Endless difficulties arose over the composition of UNTAG, particularly its military components, the establishment of a demilitarized zone extending on both sides of Namibia's borders with Angola and Zambia, and the bases in which the troops of the two sides would be temporarily held. The South African government further complicated matters by using what it termed the United Nations' lack of impartiality as justification for further delays.

Although I had no illusions about the basic attitude of South Africa, in an effort to cut through the obstacles I sent a mission, headed by Under Secretary General Brian Urquhart to Pretoria. After discussions with top South African officials, he reached the conclusion that internal political difficulties in South Africa were a major barrier to progress. This led to a suggestion that it might be helpful to involve others in the responsibility for future developments. For this purpose we proposed a 'pre-implementation meeting under United Nations auspices' in which both South Africa and the other parties concerned in the implementation process would be included. We hoped that in this way trust and confidence might be restored and the United Nations plan salvaged. It was not easy to work out the organization of the conference to the satisfaction of all the parties, but in the end we were able to do so.

The conference was finally convened in Geneva on 7 January 1981. Its organization was, to say the least, unusual. It consisted of two delegations, one headed by the South African Administrator General of Namibia, Mr Danie Hough, and the other by Sam Nujoma, the President of SWAPO. All others were present as observers: the OAU, the front-line African states and Nigeria, and the Western Contact Group.

As I took the chair for the opening session, the Turnhalle Alliance representatives were seated on one side of me, SWAPO delegates on the other. The former consisted of spokesmen for some twenty different factions, loosely grouped under the same umbrella. When I called on the Turnhalle Alliance at the outset of the proceedings, each individual arose and was introduced by Mr Hough – obviously as a means of conferring status on the groups concerned. When their turn came, the SWAPO representatives reacted quite differently. Stating that they were one united group, and that some members of the delegation were imprisoned in Africa, they objected to individual presentations. Instead, they stood up in a body, raising their clenched fists as a sign of their Marxist orientation. Nothing could have done more to set the South Africans' teeth on edge.

When the stage was set for a final agreement, the South Africans suddenly declared that the United Nations had disqualified itself as an impartial supervisor by recognizing SWAPO as the representative of the Namibian people. Until the United Nations demonstrated its impartiality, the South Africans said that no definite date could be agreed upon for Namibia's independence.

Frustrated and angry, I left Geneva, as I saw no reason why I should chair the meeting any longer. Brian Urquhart, who had taken over from me, did his best to improve the rapport among the participants through informal receptions and a special train journey through the magnificent Swiss countryside. However, there was no substantial change and the conference got nowhere.

Why do I relate the story of Namibia at such great length? Because, to my mind, it is a typical example of three basic truths: first the depth and directness of United Nations involvement in the thorny problem of decolonization; second, the limits to which a Secretary General can go in making use of his authority to decide on crucial matters of peace-keeping without having a clear mandate from the Security Council, a dilemma which Dag Hammerskjöld faced during the Congo crisis, with tragic consequences; third, how the work of the world organization depends on the overall international political environment. Whereas the Western Contact Group was an offspring of the Carter era, characterized by a new approach to black Africa, the election of Ronald Reagan was unquestionably one factor in the intransigence of the South Africans.

The new US Administration undertook a 'policy of constructive engagement' with South Africa – based on the thesis that more could be obtained by friendly persuasion than by threats or efforts to apply political pressure. Further, it created a new pre-condition to a Namibia settlement: a requirement that Cuban troops must first withdraw from Angola.

As my term of office drew to a close, the Western Contact Group plan had been modified and an overlap of new considerations had diminished the earlier emphasis on a UN-sponsored solution in Namibia.

In the same way, South Africa was able to block any solution for the independence of Namibia: it was, and is, expertly stonewalling on its apartheid policy. The representatives of the Third World are often driven to condemn the Western powers as the parties responsible for the failure of the UN to produce results. They contend that if the Security Council were to apply, and actually enforce, comprehensive sanctions against South Africa, the evil of apartheid could be eliminated. They are particularly critical of the United States government. It has the resources, they say, to bring the South Africans round if it wishes to do so.

Although the Western powers agree with the Third World in condemning apartheid, some of them do not share the view that, in itself, it constitutes a threat to international peace and security. This line of argument is received with disdain by African and other Third World countries. I have consistently made it clear that I believe they are right to keep the problem very much alive. What is regrettable is that failure to produce results diminishes United Nations credibility, while acrimony over this burning issue inhibits sensible co-operation for agreed purposes.

It therefore gives me particular satisfaction to record the transition of Rhodesia/Zimbabwe to independence. The UN was not directly involved in the prolonged negotiations but it played a significant part in setting the stage. Sanctions were imposed in 1966 on the minority regime of Ian Smith and, although weakened by widespread evasion, they injured the Rhodesian economy appreciably and thus contributed to political change. I can add a peripheral footnote.

During the events which led up to the attainment of independence for Zimbabwe I had a vivid example of Tanzanian assertiveness in African affairs. President Nyerere was passionately involved in the efforts of the African states to destroy the colonial and racist structure of southern Africa and, as a first step, to bring independence to an African-ruled Rhodesia. After the negotiations at Lancaster House in London in the autumn of 1979 which led to the establishment of the new state of Zimbabwe, he cabled me accusing the British government and its representative in Salisbury, Sir Christopher Soames, of double-crossing Mugabe and favouring his rival Bishop Muzorewa.

He requested me to fly immediately to Salisbury, the capital of Rhodesia, to check on the situation and counter the British mischief.

This was, of course, quite preposterous. The negotiations were bilateral. The United Nations was not involved and I had no right of access. I called the Tanzanian Foreign Minister, Salim Ahmed Salim, a skilful and vociferous anti-colonialist spokesman, and even he was embarrassed. As a long-time Ambassador to the UN he was sufficiently conversant with the United Nations machinery to realize that I had no means of intervention. To pacify his President, I told him that I would take soundings.

Fortunately, the British UN Ambassador at that time, Sir Anthony Parsons, was one of the best people London had ever sent. I filled him in and he offered to lay the matter before his government, who were sufficiently broad-minded to agree that I could send a special envoy. I immediately selected Pérez de Cuellar; he flew to Salisbury and came back with a report that the British were acting very correctly and that there was no question of any mishandling of the situation by Sir Christopher Soames or anyone else. All this I reported duly to President Nyerere, and I never heard from him on the subject again.

The Soviet Union doubtless hoped that its support of the aspirations of the liberated colonial peoples would result in a full alliance with the Third World. These hopes have not been realized, and in my judgement the West is unduly alarmed about the threat of Soviet hegemony in Africa. Many of the new leaders were Marxist in their political outlook and are ruling one-party states, but their appalling economic chaos and their traditional tribal structure do not allow them to import either classical Marxism or Westminster-type democracy. Religious influence is strong, pre-dominantly Moslem, with many Christians, but, even if they are still Animists, they are not imbued with Marxism. Mugabe was an interesting case in point. Jesuit-trained and a Marxist, he gave immediate accreditation to the British and American Ambassadors, but kept Moscow waiting before he permitted it to establish a diplomatic mission. He needed Western economic aid and realized that the Russians had no equivalent counterpart to offer. There was ample precedent. Most of the Arab countries in North Africa – Somalia with its predominantly Moslem population, the countries in the central belt like the Ivory Coast and Senegal – have all turned to the West for help.

The same is true in Angola. They have Cuban troops, but that does not solve their economic problems. I spent several days there in July 1979 as the guest of President Agostinho Neto and was appalled by the poverty of the country. We were put up in a guest villa, probably owned by a former Portuguese administrator, and it was so run down that nothing worked. 'We have no spare parts,' they said. 'We have nothing. We are trying to solve our problems with a minimum of help.' They had made every attempt to open up contacts with the Western world. By the time Neto became ill and went to Moscow for treatment, where he died, it was said that his relationship with the Soviet leaders had become strained.

He had also lost faith in the ability of the United Nations to assist him. I found out that, while I was engaged in tortuous negotiations about Namibia, the Angolans had been secretly engaged in direct talks with South Africa. The realities of power speak their own language.

We have seen much more recently the diplomatic *rapprochement* between President Samora Machel of Mozambique and the South African Prime Minister P. W. Botha. The two countries have been engaged in guerrilla warfare for a decade. Machel's economy is in ruins and Moscow apparently is unable to support him. So he turns to his arch-enemy for economic aid.

Despite the improvement of relations between South Africa and its black neighbours, which is based on economic necessity, and despite some cosmetic changes in their apartheid policy, South Africa remains the major crisis area of the continent. I have no doubt that their policy of racial discrimination will one day collapse. The white man has long realized, despite his fear of annihilation, that he cannot do away with his black compatriots. The black population has long been aware that the white man is not a colonialist in South Africa but has the right to live there. A genuine dialogue is crucial, and both sides must recognize that they need each other. I hope it is not too late for the necessary revolution of the spirit.

8

The New Majority

During the whole of the seventies, when I was Secretary General, world attention focused mainly on wars, conflicts and international crises and on how these were dealt with by the United Nations. Unfortunately this led to a misconception about the work of the world organization. Since the attitudes of the member governments very often did not permit the UN to discharge its duties as foreseen in the Charter, the image of the United Nations deteriorated. Although I fully recognize the importance of the political role of the organization, during my term of office I was faced with a new challenge, the handling of a new phenomenon, namely the growing gap between the rich countries in the North and the poor countries in the South of the globe.

In a world which had not really taken note of the historic dimension of this dramatic awakening in the Third World, the United Nations was the one single place where these forces could express themselves and mobilize the community of nations to draw attention to their plight.

The influx of newly independent countries radically altered the entire character of the United Nations. This massive group of Third World nations was not beholden to the West; it was encouraged, but not controlled, by the Soviet bloc. Its leaders proved highly adept at establishing operational groupings within the organization. In addition to continental and regional groups, they formed two over-arching organizations that included the vast majority of United Nations membership. In the political sphere, the Non-Aligned Movement was designed to function as a third force which could remain aloof from East-West alliances and manoeuvres. Their founding fathers were Tito, Nehru and Nasser, together with the Indonesian President Sukarno. A parallel organization, the 'Group of 77' (actually, now over 125 states), was set up in order to advance the economic and social development of its membership. Each of these groups met periodically to concert strategy and tactics. Their cohesion has remained remarkable, in spite of the fact that they include a number of oil-rich developing countries. This has failed to disturb their common front.

These overlapping coalitions now include virtually all the non-white, non-Western states in Asia and Africa, the bulk of the countries in South America and even a few Soviet allies such as Cuba, Vietnam and the Mongolian People's Republic. They have transformed the parliamentary structure of the United Nations. Bloc politics tends to dominate decision-making. The new majority of the Third World overwhelms the out-numbered West. East-West rivalries, while still predominant in global terms, have become relatively less prominent in United Nations affairs.

The goals of these new members are egalitarian. The bulk of the wealth, scientific and technological skills, educational talent and productive capacity in the world is concentrated in a relatively few states. As long as this continues, the anti-colonial revolution, in the eyes of the less developed countries, cannot be considered complete.

On their own, most of these countries could do little to make their case persuasively. But in the United Nations, where all states enjoy the same voting rights, the situation is different. By joining forces, the smaller states can, within broad limits, control most of the decisions. To be sure, the word 'decisions' is, in most cases, a misnomer. In the General Assembly there are only recommendations, without binding effect. Even so they are not to be ignored, and over the course of time are bound to influence thought and action.

In order to facilitate the development process, the General Assembly created in 1964 the UN Conference on Trade and Development (UNCTAD). Three years later the UN Assembly established the UN Industrial Development Organization to assist the developing countries. It is now in the process of becoming a fully fledged specialized agency of the UN with its own separately funded budget.

Both the agenda and the membership of the world organization were evolving in a way not foreseen by its founding fathers. It soon became apparent that what the new Third World majority was seeking was nothing less than a revolution in the world economy, to be won less by coercion than by the power of persuasion in the international forum. They demanded fairness and justice: fairness because they did not accept that three-quarters of the world's population living in the under-developed countries should enjoy only one-fifth of its gross income; justice because, in their eyes, the old colonial powers had gained their wealth by exploiting the peoples and resources of their former possessions. To redress the balance they should now agree to a massive transfer of resources to the countries of the south.

There had indeed been examples in post-war history of such acts of enlightened self-interest as the Marshall Plan, the American Alliance for Progress, and European Community arrangements for economic assistance to their former African, Caribbean and Pacific territories under the Lomé Conventions. These programmes had one feature in common: they combined economic aid with the strengthening of alliances, or at least enhanced political affinity.

In contrast, the demands the Third World countries made on the Western industrialized states offered no comparable rewards. Their more radical leaders seldom based their claims in the context of mutual benefits. They spoke of the redressing of wrongs, and economic and social development, not as an aspiration but as a right to which they were entitled. It was an approach which produced confrontation rather than accommodation of views. The Third World could not achieve its purposes without the participation of the industrialized states they were attacking. The result of this policy in the United Nations was chronic acrimony and frustration.

One group, the bloc of Marxist states, stood largely aloof from the whole debate. The Soviet Union and its supporters, and also China, regarded development as a responsibility of the former colonial powers. They supported the argument that it was for the Western countries to compensate the developing nations for the exploitation to which they had been subjected in an earlier era. The Marxist countries hardly participated in the multilateral development activities of the UN. They preferred to pursue their own bilateral aid programmes.

Obviously, the industrialized countries were reluctant to accept blanket liability for the alleged evils of colonialism and imperialism. They were willing to make adjustments in existing institutions and practices to meet the pressing needs of the South, but the improvements they proposed were incremental rather than radical. They insisted that economic development was a complex and lengthy process. They refused to – as they put it – give money and credit, machinery, infrastructure and technical assistance to countries lacking the personnel, organization and experience to absorb them.

It must be said that they did not have to look far to find instances of the failure of ill-considered development projects, or examples of lack of co-ordination among donor agencies and waste and corruption among the recipients. The cost of major aid programmes was high. To grant trade preferences or guarantee higher prices for raw materials, or to extend financial aid on concessional terms, involved a real cost to the industries, consumers and tax-payers of the developed countries. They preferred to rely as far as possible on market forces to increase the productive capacity of the poorer nations.

Both personally and in terms of my constitutional position, I felt considerable sympathy for the basic position of the South. In all good conscience, nations which had subscribed to the UN Charter's pursuit of 'better standards of life in larger freedom' could not stand passively by in the face of massive poverty, hunger, ill-health and illiteracy. The disparity between the two worlds was not diminishing but to a considerable extent increasing. Remedial action was necessary, and in my judgement it could only be carried out on a world scale if the UN organization participated in a major way. The facts were incontrovertible. In the North, one-fourth of the world's population possessed more than nine-tenths of its manufacturing industry and received more than four-fifths of its income. In the South, more than 1.2 billion people lived in countries with a gross national product averaging less than $250 per head per year.

Realistically, however, the process could not be a one-way street. Whatever the help from outside, a critical factor in development would be the self-reliant effort of the countries in the south themselves.

Nothing would be accomplished if the two sides dug in on extreme positions and used the United Nations to launch verbal broadsides at each other. I therefore devoted myself to a search for areas of agreement, the advocacy of moderation and gradualism and the continuation of a dialogue between the parties.

When I assumed office the industrial world was ending a decade of exceptional growth. The UN had established an 'international development strategy' to set economic targets, and while the major industrialized nations had expressed some reservations, they had endorsed the general principle of moving by co-operation towards a more just and rational world economic and social order. The decade of the seventies was one of sharp and painful economic adjustments. The system of fixed exchange rates created by the Bretton Woods Conference in 1944 had collapsed and, in 1973/4, the Organization of Petroleum Exporting Countries ended the era of cheap energy by quadrupling the price of oil. These events shook the world economic system, but their weight fell most heavily on the poorest countries, which lacked the reserves and productive resources to cope. Even the richer nations went into recession, resulting in a combination of inflation and unemployment.

The oil shock galvanized the more outspoken leaders of the Group of 77. They saw that their oil-rich brothers had wrested control of their natural resources from the multinational corporations. They had sharply reversed the adverse terms of trade from which the former colonial territories habitually suffered. The invulnerability of the North had been challenged and the other developing countries, particularly those with other marketable assets, hoped to make comparable gains.

Under the leadership of President Houari Boumédienne of Algeria, at that time the head of the non-aligned group, they called for a special session of the General Assembly in April 1974 'with a view to establishing a new system of relations based on equality and the common interests of all states'. Boumédienne was peremptory, proclaiming the failure of the international development strategy and attributing this to the lack of political will on the part of the developed countries to take the required urgent action, and the inadequacy of the growth targets in relation to the real needs of the South.

He sustained this combative tone in the conversation we had at the outset of this sixth special session in New York. The real issue, he said, was economic domination of the poor by the rich. The Third World now had real bargaining power by virtue of their natural resources. In order to avoid confrontation, both sides should initiate a responsible dialogue. The industrialized nations would have to change their policies and demonstrate a political will to co-operate. What his group hoped for from the Assembly was nothing less than the forging of a new international economic order.

He insisted that the position of the United States would be particularly significant. I told him that I knew from my contacts in Washington that the American administration was taking a passive attitude towards the special session. For my own part I felt that the US must participate actively in the work of the session if it was to have any meaning. It would become highly undesirable for them to be isolated in the Assembly, and I persuaded them to assume a more active role. At the same time I advised Boumédienne to seek a constructive compromise.

The special session in 1974 was not to be guided by counsels of moderation. It adopted a resolution providing for fundamental changes in the entire structure of international economic relations, including provisions on commodities, trade and industrialization, natural resources, food, finance and multinational corporations. The countries of the North were not prepared to respond in depth to these far-reaching proposals. They did not vote against the resulting 'Declaration and Programme of Action on the Establishment of a New Economic Order', but they made it clear through numerous reservations that they would not comply.

At the regular Assembly session the following autumn, the same adversarial spirit prevailed. This time the Group of 77 united behind a proposed 'Charter on the Economic Rights and Duties of States' which had been drafted by President Luis Echeverría of Mexico. This declared that every state had 'the sovereign and inalienable right' to choose its own economic, political, social and cultural systems without any outside interference and should exercise 'full permanent sovereignty' over its wealth, natural resources and economic activities. The developing nations were to have the sole right to decide for themselves the terms for compensating expropriated foreign enterprises.

These demands brought North-South relations in the organization to a new low. Most of the larger industrialized countries resented the verbal attacks and far-reaching demands of the majority. They were unwilling to abandon the existing economic system. If additional aid was to be made available for development, the countries of the North would have to provide most of it. As oil importers they were already making a massive transfer of financial resources to the OPEC countries and they now demanded that these should share in any major programmes to assist those less developed. The session ended in disarray.

The developing countries dismissed the proposal put forward by the West German Chancellor, Helmut Schmidt, that instead of the same old long catalogue of impossible demands they should draw up a list of the things they wanted in some order of priority so that negotiations could start. The representatives of the Third World alone rejected it as patchwork politics where radical action was needed.

Nevertheless, as the months passed, as a result of constant interchanges at the UN passions cooled and more moderate views emerged. A seventh special session of the General Assembly was held in the first half of September 1975. The contrast with its predecessor was remarkable. The developed countries, and particularly the United States, had evidently decided that a purely negative posture would help neither party. In a highlight speech the American Secretary of State, Henry Kissinger, put forward a number of promising proposals in a spirit of reconciliation. Kissinger had begun to recognize the usefulness of the UN for Washington's foreign policies and obviously wanted to make a gesture to reduce Third World scepticism towards the United States.

He outlined a broad range of new international machinery, with offers of additional financial resources in response to the developing countries' needs in the fields of commodities, trade, finance, industrialization and food production. Others adopted a similarly conciliatory tone and an intensive effort began to reach common ground. The special session reached its conclusions by consensus and its work contributed to an improvement of economic relations between North and South.

In all candour I would have to admit that the promise of the seventh special session has not been realized in anything like the form then envisaged.

It was the merit of Henry Kissinger that the relationship between the United Nations and the Nixon administration, which had previously been overshadowed by the controversy over Vietnam, improved progressively, although Nixon himself remained in the background. My relations with the President had been ambivalent. During my first year of office I had put out a public statement concerning the alleged American bombing of the dykes around Hanoi. I appealed on humanitarian grounds to cease operations that led to so much suffering. President Nixon had reacted in sharp tones. The Vietnam War was becoming extremely unpopular and doubtless my intervention was unwelcome, particularly in the period leading up to his second election. Thereafter our contacts remained distinctly cool and distant.

He gave an official luncheon for me at the White House but although we met several times there was never an in-depth exchange of views on world problems. He had little regard for the United Nations. However, I am obliged to say that as to his views and actions in the field of foreign policy one could not but appreciate his knowledge, vision and skill. Of the four presidents with whom I have dealt, he was the best prepared for his diplomatic responsibilities.

I particularly admired the way in which he managed the opening-up of American attitudes towards the People's Republic of China, so ably furthered by Henry Kissinger. I doubt that any American President who did not have strong backing from American conservatives could have run such a high political risk. I also appreciated his management of the *détente* policy towards the Soviet Union. Both these initiatives contributed materially to an improvement in international relations at the time and their effect was quickly and beneficially evident at the United Nations.

I do not know where Nixon's input ended in these and other policies of his administration, and where Henry Kissinger's began. There was no doubt, however, of Kissinger's encompassing influence on American foreign policy during the first half of my tenure at the United Nations.

He also came to office as no friend of the United Nations, indeed as someone highly sceptical of its usefulness. He was certainly no believer in a universal world political order. Yet under the stress of the critical days of the October War of 1973, he began to understand how useful the United Nations could be. He recognized the constructive role the Security Council had played during the crisis and the way it quickly took action to send UN forces as a buffer between the belligerents. As he was fully aware, their prompt dispatch helped to avoid a direct military confrontation between the USA and the Soviet Union.

The reasons for his success and influence are complex. First of all he is a very intelligent man, far above the average, and is aware of his skills. He is a well-trained scholar and historian. Because of his European and Jewish background he has a more specific understanding than many statesmen of world history and the problems of the Middle East.

Even so, in world politics intelligence alone is not the determining factor. What counts is power. It is unrealistic to believe that the era of *Machtpolitik*, the politics of power, is over. The supreme quality of Henry Kissinger was that he had, and knew how to use, power in a productive fashion. In civilized discussion and negotiation he used this power in order to press the parties to accept the proposals he made. Without any bombast or threat, he conveyed to his partners in discussion that he represented the greatest power in the world and that if they did not use the opportunity he was offering, they would get nothing out of the whole exercise. A tough politician, he was able to convince most of his interlocutors that he was sincere and that he genuinely wanted a peaceful settlement; and he never shrank from the heart of the matter. He has an engaging sense of humour, and he never left anyone in any doubt as to where the bottom line in his position lay. His attitude was: 'If you want a solution, I shall go on'; otherwise he made it clear that he would return to Washington. His political power visibly grew with the downfall of Nixon during the Watergate scandal and, of course, afterwards during President Ford's short term in office. The limits which Nixon set on him in the early days of his governmental career became obvious to me in connection with the American bombing of the Vietnamese dykes. When I discussed my public criticism of the US air raids over the phone with Kissinger, he assured me that my statement was well understood and would not have any negative impact on my relations with the President. The next day, however, Nixon convened a special press conference vigorously rejecting my statement and calling me 'naive'.

Kissinger's Egyptian negotiating partner, Foreign Minister Ismail Fahmi, whom I consider one of the best brains in the Arab world, later on blamed him for his 'tendency to manipulate people, his overbearing vanity and his determination to be at centre-stage'. But I personally had no reason to complain about him. Although I was fully aware that he was not in love with the UN, he regularly visited me in my office on the thirty-eighth floor, and made a point of giving joint press briefings after our meetings in front of the famous Chagall window in the UN lobby. Whatever he said on such occasions, I admired his skill in public relations.

Although the seventh special session of the UN Assembly – with Kissinger's thought-provoking speech – in 1975 introduced a greater degree of tolerance and understanding between the developing world and the industrialized nations, this encouraging start did not in itself guarantee a satisfactory outcome. There was still too much suspicion for anything like a complete meeting of minds to occur. I felt very strongly that this favourable beginning must not be frittered away. Worried about the inertia that had characterized these negotiations, in the autumn of 1975 I sent private letters to Kissinger, Foreign Minister Kiichi Miyazawa of Japan, and the Italian Foreign Minister, Mariano Rumor, in his capacity as a president of the European Economic Community, urging them to spare no effort to reach a consensus on the outstanding policy issues. Their replies, although phrased in general terms, were reassuring.

The major resolution that emerged from the seventh special session had been in effect a revision of the Declaration on the establishment of a New International Economic Order of the previous year. Covering most of the same ground, it was couched in a spirit of common effort by the two sides rather than in the peremptory demands of the original declaration and its accompanying programme of action. It stressed the need for greater co-operation between states and proposed 'concerted' action to achieve the goals of the new economic order.

One swallow does not make a summer. The deep-seated difference between North and South was not to be overcome between one month and the next. There was no adequate follow-up. In an attempt to get things moving, the focus of the North-South debate was shifted from the unwieldly General Assembly to a smaller group outside the United Nations – the Conference on International Economic Co-operation, consisting of twenty-seven representatives drawn from both sides, including seven members of OPEC. This body had been organized and convened on the initiative of Giscard d'Estaing and met in Paris. There were high hopes that it might bring about a breakthrough. I attended its initial phase in December 1975, but was soon obliged to come to the conclusion that it was faced with the same problems we had encountered in the United Nations and with the same uncompromising attitudes of the two sides.

The industrialized nations were interested primarily in discussing the energy problem but the developing countries insisted on linking it with general commodity, finance and development issues. The discussions dragged on for eighteen months, with relatively little to show for the effort. The basis was laid for a common fund to assist raw material producers and some money was made available for development programmes. The results were nevertheless meagre.

Ignoring for a moment the strict chronology of this book, I think it would be helpful here to recount later developments in the North-South dialogue. After the disappointing outcome of the Paris talks, the scene of action, if it can be called that, shifted back once more to the United Nations. Over the next few years the developing countries increasingly focused the Assembly's attention on what are called 'global negotiatons' covering the major aspects of economic co-operation and development.

During the last two years of my term of office, I made strenuous efforts to give these negotiations practical form. Working in formal and informal groups, the delegates to the General Assembly tried one expedient after another in search of a formula to enable further progress to be made.

The main thrust of the Third World countries was to attain their ends by seeking radical changes in the United Nations system as at present organized. Currently the levers of financial power lie in the hands of the World Bank, the International Monetary Fund (IMF) and the General Agreement on Tariffs and Trade (GATT), where the voting strength closely reflects economic and financial power. The South would like somehow to shift the venue of decision-making in these matters to the General Assembly, where they have the majority vote. In this they have been unsuccessful, since the specialized agencies concerned were created by separate treaties and are not subordinate to the United Nations. All the exhortations contained in the General Assembly resolutions adopted on these subjects have, by their ineffectiveness, only compounded the frustrations of the developing countries and the irritation of the developed.

I do not mean to imply that all the fault in these attitudes lies on one side. If the developing countries are too rigid in their approach, the industrialized nations have hardly responded with excessive generosity to the proposals of the impoverished South. Their official development aid lags far behind the levels they have themselves accepted as targets. They have been more inclined to stand pat on their negative response to the new international economic order than to make concrete and constructive counter-proposals.

When Rüdiger von Wechmar, Ambassador of the Federal Republic of Germany to the United Nations, became President of the 1980 General Assembly, he made the effort to get a set of global negotiations under way as the central theme of his term of office. There was no one better suited to the task. Wechmar was a disciple of the former German Chancellor Willy Brandt, perhaps the leading Western protagonist of the Third World's development cause. Wechmar represented one of the West's most successful and prosperous countries, enjoying great influence in the counsels of the North.

It was towards the end of the General Assembly in 1980 that some of the leading representatives of the Third World, together with Rüdiger von Wechmar, visited me in my office in an atmosphere of despair, telling me that all their efforts to work out a compromise solution for global negotiations had failed. They referred to my good personal relations with President Jimmy Carter and asked me to intervene with him in order to get America's consent to the latest compromise proposals of the Group of 77. The timing was hardly auspicious. The presidential election was only a few weeks away. Nevertheless I had a long telephone conversation with the President and asked him to take a good look at the proposals, bearing in mind that the developing countries believed that America was the major obstacle in the way of starting negotiations.

This the President said he would do, but he reminded me that it was a difficult period for him. He made three main points. First, he said, the United States could not accept anything that would give the United Nations General Assembly any sort of authority over the IMF, the World Bank or GATT. Second, we should bear in mind that the American Congress took a jaundiced view of the United Nations, so much so that he had serious problems in getting funds appropriated by the Congress for the American contribution. Thirdly, he remarked that because of being in an election campaign he had to be cautious. If we were not careful, our actions could become counter-productive, he warned. It was in the interests of the United Nations not to push him too far.

What alarmed me was that the emotions engendered by the strident demands of the Third World and the recalcitrance, if not indifference, of the West, were destroying the credit of the United Nations and might ultimately even tear it apart. This, I considered, would be a tragedy. Virtually every country in the West agreed in theory that the abyss yawning between the rich and the poor peoples was an evil to be combatted. They agreed also that the process of development would bring benefits to the North as well as to the South. If only both sides were guided by this underlying common interest, I felt that a dialogue could eventually produce at least partial results.

It was Willy Brandt himself who suggested a possible formula. As the head of a distinguished group of former statesmen, including Edward Heath of Great Britain and leading private citizens, he had been instrumental in drawing up an exhaustive, widely publicized report on the need to re-order North-South relations to meet the challenges of the new decade. It envisaged a global agreement resulting from a joint effort of political will and a high degree of trust among the negotiating partners, with a common conviction of mutual interest. An essential step in achieving this objective would be a summit meeting of some twenty world leaders, representative of the major groupings, to produce guide-lines and a new impetus for future negotiations.

The former Chancellor came to see me in New York in February 1980 and handed me a copy of his Commission's report with a request to circulate it to all members. He asked me if I would organize the summit meeting envisaged. I was obliged to tell him that due to the lack of a mandate from any organ of the UN I could not act as the convenor of such a conference. Moreover, it was not for me to select the participants as I knew out of my long experience that this would immediately lead to criticism by those who had not been invited. There would be irresistible pressure to expand the membership so broadly that it would lose focus and effectiveness. We then decided that we would select two co-chairmen for the conference, one from the North and the other from the South. Together they would choose the other participants.

Brandt asked me to proceed along these lines. Our initial choice for the co-chairman from the North was the Austrian Chancellor Bruno Kreisky. As his colleague from the South we decided to approach the President of Mexico, José Lopez Portillo, who had indicated his interest to us. Brandt also asked me to try to persuade the Soviet Union to attend the meeting, but I knew that this would be pointless. The Russians have never considered participating in multilateral economic aid programmes to developing countries. Nevertheless I did take up the matter with Gromyko during my Moscow visit in June 1981. He answered at once that they were not interested and would not attend. I attempted to stress how useful a Soviet contribution to the North-South dialogue would be. Gromyko retorted by insisting that the problems facing the Third World in the economic sphere were the result of colonialism. The Soviet Union had never been a colonial power and had no reason to get involved in the consequences of Western imperialism. 'It is up to them to make up for what they have done to the countries of the Third World,' he said. 'We shall not attend because we do not wish to be placed in the same category as the Western powers.' He did add that the Soviet Union would render economic help to the developing countries. 'We shall of course help them, but we shall do so on a bilateral basis.'

I thought that the easier task would be with my fellow-Austrian Bruno Kreisky, so I approached him first. We had a long talk together in Vienna and he responded positively, but with one reservation: 'I have to be sure that the main industrialized countries support me in this undertaking. I can't do it on my own,' he said. He consulted the Americans, the Germans and the French, and when they responded favourably he went ahead.

Lopez Portillo reacted immediately. As the successor to Luis Echeverría, who had played such a prominent part in the UN special assemblies on this issue, he was predisposed to take an active part, proposed Cancun as the meeting place and joined with Kreisky in issuing the invitations.

Only a few weeks before the conference was due to meet, Bruno Kreisky fell ill. The Austrian government, in consultation with Lopez Portillo and others, invited the Canadian Prime Minister, Pierre Trudeau, to replace him. Fortunately he was able to make himself available and was his usual forceful and effective self. I took part as representative of the United Nations and we foregathered in October 1981.

Instructive for us, and also for him, was the presence of President Reagan. This was his first major exposure to Third World leaders as a group and he told me before we dispersed that he had found it an educational experience. There were twenty-three delegations and the arrangements were both sumptuous and relaxed. The tables in the main conference hall were arranged in a huge circle. Reagan, in a short-sleeved shirt, was inevitably the centre of attention, with all the other participants watching him carefully to see whether he was prepared to yield on any of the points that were so freely made to him. He was exceedingly courteous and genial, but always tough on substance, and yielded very little. The main conference sessions never took on the form of negotiations but there were many bilateral talks in the surrounding offices and at the luncheons, dinners and social occasions, where careful organization ensured that no group was ever the same twice.

I was much impressed by the forcefulness and clarity with which Mrs Gandhi supported the views of her Third World colleagues. She was very outspoken, but always left the way open for some understanding between the main participants. She was a world leader of the highest quality and her recent assassination is a bitter tragedy for all those with the interests of international understanding at heart.

The Chinese delegation was led by their Prime Minister, Zhao Zi Yang. He gave the impression of being a technocrat and administrator rather than the repository of high-level political power. He has a warm and sympathetic personality and gets on well with Europeans. He is also very close to Deng Xiaoping, who comes from the south-western province of Sichuan, of which Zhao was at one time the governor.

During the conference he played a low-key role, listening more than speaking: an attitude which seemed to fit his character and the basic policy of the Peking government. The Chinese still regard themselves as an under-developed country belonging to the Third World, without any ambition to play the role of a major power. They admit publicly that it will take them a long time to catch up with the other main powers. They are far behind in technology and even in technical infrastructure. Their teeming millions are hard-working and one day they will catch up with the Western world and the Soviet Union, but not soon. In my own judgement it will take them several decades; in the meantime they try desperately to acquire know-how from the Western world. Their conflict with the Soviets continues. Whether this will change with the advent of Gorbachev is open to question.

There was a sharp exchange, in the course of the conference, between President Nyerere and Pierre Trudeau. Nyerere, who is never short of words, had launched into a lengthy intervention to establish that although

Tanzania was a socialist country it would welcome private investment. Trudeau was quick to respond. He asked the Tanzanian President whether he really thought that the Western nations would invest more in his country, knowing that sooner or later their investments would be jeopardized by government intervention. Nyerere and his Third World colleagues were momentarily nonplussed by the retort, but suddenly loud laughter broke out, not least from Nyerere himself, and the meeting went on to other matters.

Regrettably the conference did not lead to any major change in the running controversy over the demands of the less developed countries for a new economic order. True to form of summit meetings, Cancun was long on harmonious generalities but short on practical results. Like so many other top-level gatherings, it provided no opportunity for the hard slog of detailed bargaining which must precede any agreement on so complex and controversial a subject. The conference made no provision for following up on its pronouncements or for making a start on global negotiations. With the onset of the recession of the 1980s, the focus shifted to short-term measures needed to save the developing countries from economic collapse. Each side took note of the views of the other and referred the whole matter back to the United Nations, where new efforts of another kind will have to be made if the world is to be relieved of this fundamental and agonizing conflict.

In all the years of my professional life as a diplomat, I learned one basic truth: it is personalities more than anything else which influence the destiny of the world. Out of this conviction, right at the beginning of my term of office as Secretary General I started to visit as many world leaders as possible. These trips to nearly all the capitals of the globe offered me the welcome opportunity not only to meet these personalities, but also to grasp the political environment in which they had to operate. Coming myself from the industrialized North, I made it a particular point to cultivate the leaders of the Third World countries which had swollen the membership of the organization. As they achieved independence, the new political leaders were primarily concerned to establish their control domestically, but most of them quickly realized how valuable the United Nations could be to them. It gave them an international sounding board and a training ground for their officials in modern diplomacy. On their own, their international influence was limited, but united in their regional and non-aligned group they gained importance and sometimes dominated the work of the organization. There was a constant flow of heads of state and other leaders from the Third World countries to the regular annual sessions of the General Assembly. Jointly and individually, they left their mark.

I owe Marshal Tito a posthumous mention for his sturdily independent foreign policy, which established Yugoslavia as a non-aligned country. He always impressed me with his straightforwardness and his strong support for the United Nations. He was frequently critical of it, usually on the grounds that it was too inactive in international affairs and suffered from a lack of clout, but his approach was as constructive as it was frank.

We used to meet in New York and Belgrade and I was a frequent guest of his on the two-island complex of Brioni in the Adriatic off the Yugoslav coast. Under the Austro-Hungarian Empire, the islands had been mosquito-ridden and uninhabited. An Austrian named Kuppelwieser had made them habitable. When Tito came to power, he had constructed handsome hotels and guest houses on the larger island and a residence for himself, surrounded by a beautiful garden, on the smaller. He lived very comfortably there, indulging in his various hobbies, which included a private zoo, where he kept a collection of exotic animals sent to him as gifts by foreign political leaders. His other hobby was to build household furniture in a small workshop set in the midst of vineyards he had himself planted. He was proud of his wines and made a point of serving them with fish caught in the surrounding waters.

Two factors influenced his views on foreign policy. The first was a deep fear of the Russians, particularly after the 1968 'Prague Spring' liberalization movement had been destroyed by Soviet forces. He used to tax us Austrians with what he described as our complacency in the face of the Soviet menace. 'You people are too naive,' he said. 'Don't believe that you are not in danger. I have had my experiences with the Russians. They are capable of doing anything.' He was insistent that we remained on our guard against a Soviet military thrust through Austria and south to the Dalmatian coast.

His second great foreign policy concern was to strengthen the structure of East-West *détente* and the Non-Aligned Movement, thus creating a global equilibrium as a foundation for peace. The last years of his life left him a deeply disappointed man. He witnessed a deterioration in super-power relationships and the erosion of non-alignment as it fell under the increasing influence of the more radical Third World states.

I last saw Tito in a guest house in Havana during the 1979 summit conference of the Non-Aligned Movement. He was obviously physically ill and also deeply depressed. He was particularly concerned over the election of Cuba to chair the meeting, although the host country at these conferences is normally granted that honour. As the more radical leaders established their predominance, Tito's dismay increased. He was deeply exercised as to how the Non-Aligned Movement could maintain its credibility if Cuba, with its close links to the Soviet Union, were its leader.

The Cubans are extremely active in both the United Nations and the Non-Aligned Movement, although I did not meet Fidel Castro personally until I paid an official visit to Havana in January 1979. He is a charismatic figure, with a strong and magnetic personality and quite an attractive spontaneity in his manner. Greeting me at the airport, he asked immediately: 'Do you want the usual diplomatic protocol, complete with receptions and social events, or would you prefer me to take you to some islands where we can have our talks in peace and quiet?'

There was only one answer to such a loaded question and it suited my own preference. We changed our clothes at a nearby guest house and flew by helicopter to the island of La Juventud a few miles to the south. This is where Castro maintains his education and paramilitary centre for young African students, principally from Angola, Mozambique and Namibia. The youngsters were all in uniform and went through their paces with enthusiasm.

Castro had organized a small dinner for my party with only his closest advisers present. After a general discussion on the international situation, he came to what was obviously uppermost in his mind, the state of relations between Cuba and the United States. He launched a bitter attack against the American administration for rejecting all his efforts to establish better contacts. The Americans were not even permitted to export medicines badly needed in Cuba and he had to seek them in Europe and elsewhere. He almost pleaded with me to use all my influence to persuade the American government and people that he really wanted good relations. I assured Castro that I would inform Washington of his views.

The following day we flew to his private island, which he called his 'little Brioni'. It is a lovely spot, although still primitive, and our talks took place on his yacht, which was tied up at a small dock. The business of the day was interrupted by a session of swimming and harpoon fishing, at which our host excelled. We observed that the group of security men who protected him were principally engaged in finding the largest shoals of fish.

As he sat on the edge of the boat, a steward approached with two glasses on a small silver tray, each filled with a dark liquid. Castro first took a sip from one glass, gargled heartily and spat the contents into the sea. Then he took the other glass and swallowed its contents before diving in. I was told later that the first contained Listerine and the other whisky. Apparently this was his manner of fortifying himself against the rigours of skin-diving.

However that may be, he caught several dozen red snappers and lobsters. He personally prepared lunch; it consisted mainly of the raw seafood garnished with lemon juice, which he insisted was the best way to eat it. I have frequently been willing to sacrifice my digestive system in the interest of international understanding, but this went beyond my normal bounds. As I found out later, Fidel Castro's strange way of preparing raw lobster was not so bad after all. Friends of ours did it the same way in Connecticut and loved it.

As on the previous evening, our talks concentrated mainly on Cuban-American relations. If this seemed a case of dialectical overkill, there was doubtless a special reason for it. At Castro's insistence, Bradford Morse, the highly respected administrator of the UN Development Programme, had been invited to all our functions for general discussions and to celebrate the opening of a new sugar mill built with the help of his organization.

Morse was a former American Congressman, well connected in Washington, and Castro doubtless wanted to use him as an additional channel to get his message through to the administration. Morse handled the situation very well.

On our departure Castro noticed my small rented aircraft standing on the airport apron. It was an old and somewhat shabby-looking Falcon, with space for only nine people. Professing astonishment, he asked me with disbelief in his voice: 'Are you going back in that thing? Is it safe enough?' I assured him that it was and that in any event I had no choice. The United Nations does not possess its own aeroplane for the Secretary General or anyone else. It rents and charters the planes it uses. I consoled myself with the thought that, if my dignity had been impaired, I might at least have convinced Castro and his revolutonary comrades of the capitalist frugality of the UN organization.

One figure in the Third World merits special respect: King Hussein of Jordan. I visited him on many occasions and was always impressed by the blend of shrewdness, wisdom and courage which he displayed. Small in stature, precise and careful in speech, he has survived the turmoil besetting his country from outside as well as from its large and unruly Palestinian elements within. He combines courage with cautious diplomacy. A highly intelligent man, he supports a Western style of life while maintaining deep roots in Moslem traditions. Experience has taught him the value of prudence. As a young boy, he saw his father assassinated by Palestinian extremists while standing on the steps of a mosque in Jerusalem. His engagement in the Six-Day War of 1967 cost him Arab Jerusalem and his territory on the West Bank of the Jordan. These were hard lessons indeed.

His reluctance to respond to Western proposals that he should negotiate on behalf of the Palestinians should come as no surprise. He can only do so with the approval of the other Arab states. His *rapprochement* with Arafat and his joint approach to President Mubarek clearly show were his aspirations lie. Mubarek supports Hussein's policies to the best of his abilities, but he too must be wary of provoking his fundamentalists. The joint endeavours to involve Washington actively in the peace process and to negotiate with a joint Jordanian-Palestinian delegation have met with considerable American reserve. For his part, President Reagan is facing a strong Israeli lobby which seeks to thwart all contact with the PLO. It is also no surprise that Muhammad Gaddafi should reject Hussein's proposals.

I received repeated invitations from Colonel Gaddafi to visit him in Libya. It was always one of my problems to visit certain countries at the right time, because such personal encounters are immediately interpreted by the international media as a gesture of support for this or that government. In the case of Gaddafi – whom I met in August 1977 in Tripoli – it was particularly delicate because of his alleged support of terrorist activities. When I brought this up with him, he reacted sharply and indignantly. It was absolutely untrue, he said, that he was supporting international terrorism. All he did and would continue to do was to support liberation movements, which had, he asserted, even under the UN Charter, the right to fight for their independence. That could be done without acts of terrorism. When I left Gaddafi one simple thought again came to my mind: as long as there is no objective distinction between terrorists and freedom fighters, it will always be left to governments and people to make their own subjective assessment. Nevertheless I always find it important to keep contact with all political leaders whatever their ideology and public image may be. It does not help to create a group of political outcasts when one day their co-operation may be needed to solve an international problem.

President Houari Boumédienne of Algeria and I had several encounters over the economic demands of the Third World and the plight of Polisario hostages on his border. He was not an easy man to deal with but I managed to establish good relations with him and he was quite co-operative. He was highly critical of the attitudes of the industrialized nations and known for his tough, rigid approach in the negotiations on the new economic order.

Boumédienne was equally at odds with his neighbour, King Hassan of Morocco, whose army had taken over the former Spanish colony of the Western Sahara. The Algerian President had reacted violently, accusing King Hassan of imperialism. The territory was so sparsely populated that neither the Spanish records, the Algerians, the Moroccans nor the UN were ever able to determine exactly how many people lived there. The best guess was between eighty and one hundred thousand, predominantly nomads, among whom it would have been almost impossible to conduct a referendum to determine their political future.

King Hassan was equally intransigent and almost as difficult to deal with. His firm position that the former Spanish Sahara was an integral part of Morocco – rejecting all claims of the liberation movement Polisario for an independent state – created a deep division within the OAU. When, in 1984, Polisario was admitted under the name 'Arab Democratic Republic of Sahrawi' as a full member to the OAU, Morocco and her friends left the organization, creating a most serious crisis for the OAU. On one visit I had great difficulty in obtaining an appointment with the King. So I indicated to his staff that I wished to present him with the United Nations peace medal, a gold medallion which I made a practice of giving to all the Heads of State I visited during my term of office. The King received me the following morning. He also invited me to join him in the royal train, in which, as it turned out, he was making a tour to mobilize public opinion as part of the 'green march' designed to annex the Spanish Sahara. This placed me in an entirely false position, but fortunately there were no unpleasant repercussions.

The chief victim of this unhappy dispute was the President of Mauritania, Mr Moktar Ould Daddah, who had been persuaded by the Moroccans to occupy the southern part of the territory abandoned by the Spaniards. Daddah was a modest-looking man, educated in France and married to a French lady whose hobby was writing books for children. His official residence had such limited facilities that his reception and dinner for me took place in a tent put up in the garden. We squatted on cushions cross-legged and were served with the traditional racks of lamb, although I managed to avoid eating the eyes when they were served. The Sahara situation was clearly beyond his control and the Polisario liberation units continuously attacked the fragile forces of the Mauritanian army. After a number of palace revolutions Ould Daddah was deposed in a bloodless coup and the Mauritanian government had to surrender its claim to the Western Sahara in 1979.

Much happier were my relationships with two outstanding African leaders, President Léopold Sédar Senghor of Senegal and President Felix Houphouet-Boigny of the Ivory Coast. Both are highly cultivated men, former members of the French National Assembly and experienced statesmen. Their influence in the shaping of African policies towards the former colonial powers was of greatest importance. Senghor is a philosopher and poet of international standing and Houphouët-Boigny one of the wisest men the African continent has produced. Defenders of the free market economy, their countries were among the more prosperous nations in Africa.

Kenneth Kaunda of Zambia is another African leader of great stature. His honesty and personal warmth have created many friends in the United Nations and in the world at large. He is a strong defender of the continent's interests and a determined opponent of South Africa's apartheid policies. He is also a very religious man. At a dinner party during my first official visit, in 1973, he turned to me and asked: 'Are you a Protestant or a Catholic?' I was somewhat surprised by the question and must have shown it, because he went on: 'I have two priests here at the table, one Catholic and one Protestant, to say grace but I have to know on whom I should call.'

Dignity and protocol were not always maintained during these trips. Although it is some time ago now, I cannot forget a visit I paid to Kenya in the summer of 1974 to see President Kenyatta. I was informed that he would receive me in the small village of Nakuru, some way from the capital, where he was opening the agricultural fair. I was flown there in a special aircraft and arrived in the middle of the ceremony. Prizes were being given to the best bulls, and tribal dancers then filled the arena. Suddenly Kenyatta turned to me and asked whether I would like to join him in congratulating them. I saw no harm in this and accompanied him into their midst, where, after a few exchanges, he took me by the hand and suggested we join the dance. This aroused universal enthusiasm and applause but I could not help asking myself whether it had been a worthwhile visit when, instead of having political talks with Kenyatta, I ended up in a cattle show dancing with him.

Perhaps my most embarrassing experience was at Ouagadougou, the capital of Burkina Faso. This was part of a tour of the drought-stricken Sahel region – stretching from Senegal in the west to Ethiopia and Somalia in the east – which I undertook in February 1974. My itinerary included seventeen countries in an attempt to co-ordinate the UN emergency relief operation for tens of thousands who were starving. The co-ordinating committee had been summoned to his modest capital by President Lamizana and it was planned that I should go on to the balcony of his official residence to make an appeal to the international community for further help to these stricken people. Television and radio were in attendance and even before leaving New York I had prepared a dramatic plea to read out to the thousands of people I had been promised would be standing in the square in front of the palace. When we got out on to the balcony there was not a soul to be seen. I turned to the President, asking for an explanation. It soon became clear that the minister in charge of the event had forgotten to make any public announcement of my speech and therefore no one had turned up. In order to salvage something from the occasion I recorded my address for subsequent use.

What would appear to be yet another example of Third World governments in disarray is in fact merely symptomatic of a much more profound
and complicated problem common to all developing countries. It is all too
easy to blame them for their lack of experience and absence of infrastructure, but that only detracts from the root cause of the developing
countries' present plight. The economic, political, social and cultural
problems confronting the developing countries are legion; equally divergent are the means for overcoming hunger, poverty and injustice that are
put forward by the members of the UN in their endeavours to support the
development of the Third World. In the final analysis, all development
models are part and parcel of specific social models. Having seen and
heard a plethora of programmes and concepts during my ten years of
office, I see no merit in adding to the confusion by bringing forward new
proposals. To my mind, and based on my experience, certain basic
principles hold true and must be subscribed to if any long-term
development strategy is to succeed:

Hitherto, development aid, both in its conception and in its
implementation, has adhered to foreign models; such an approach
was doomed, since it made no allowance for those features peculiar to
society in the developing countries. The education system propa-
gated in most developing countries, for example, does not meet real
social needs. Illiteracy rates are still climbing because most developing countries have not been able to introduce primary education on a
general scale. Higher education is often seen as a sign of social
achievement, a kind of status symbol, while technical education and
vocational training are still not considered priorities. A new educational system suited to the specific needs of the individual countries is
a major factor in socio-economic development and should be
recognized as such.
Self-reliance is a deeply rooted tradition in the developing countries;
it offers a firm basis on which sensible aid programmes can be
developed. For example, a plan of action oriented towards the
achievement of self-sufficiency in food should be the guiding
principle for all international efforts to combat famine and starvation, particularly in Africa.
Most developing countries can be seen to be suffering from an
identity crisis which takes on the form of bitter and sometimes violent
attempts to reassert their cultural identity. Unfortunately, this
particular issue is sometimes taken as a pretext for diverting public
attention away from pressing day-to-day problems, and it is
sometimes exploited for purely ideological reasons. In shaping aid

programmes and promoting economic co-operation, the international community should recognize the aspirations of the individual countries and foster their traditional values. Approached from
this angle, a country's assertion of its cultural heritage will proceed
within the right context, rather than be debased to a mere political
slogan.

The gap between rural and urban areas is forever widening:
development, services and infrastructure are wanting in rural areas,
with the result that the unending waves of urban immigration give
rise to awesome conurbations and new social problems. Rural
development should thus take on priority in any development plan.
The absence of planned infrastructure incurs a wastage of valuable
resources and under-utilization of machinery and equipment. Steps
should thus be taken on an international scale to assist the
developing countries in building up the infrastructure needed to
absorb new technologies and subsequently to adapt them to
prevailing conditions.

National security is a major concern in the developing countries,
whose independence is for the most part still young. Unfortunately,
in their search for external and internal security the majority of them
fall within the super-powers' sphere of influence. Given this situation, an atmosphere of relative peace and security conducive to
development is one of the most important preconditions for improving the living standards of the poor nations.

As I write, the North-South issue is as far from resolution as ever. The
recovery of the industrialized states from the most recent recession has
been uneven and precarious. Most of the poorest developing countries,
and even many of those more prosperous, are in dire straits, while a
number of them are weighed down by onerous debt burdens and high
interest rates. The quest for a new international economic order has
perforce given way to more immediate, practical concerns. Developed and
developing countries alike are striving to prevent massive defaults on
international loans, and an increasing mood of protectionism is jeopardizing international markets.

In a crisis situation emergency measures are required. But deep-seated
maladjustments and persistent world economic difficulties call for longer-
term solutions. If world prosperity is to be restored on a sustainable basis,
all concerned must take responsible and concerted action: North and
South, market and centrally-planned economies, oil-exporting and oil-
importing countries, governments, international organizations and the
private sector, including the banks. Only through the co-ordinated efforts

of all these institutions shall we be able to shake off our present difficulties and advance anew.

However necessary and however beneficial the spontaneous raising of funds throughout the world may be in terms of saving the lives of hundreds of thousands in Africa and Asia, it has nothing to do with the kind of development policy under discussion here. Long-term development aid should in no way be considered a form of charity to any country. It should be based on enlightened self-interest in the industrialized countries. The recognition of global economic interdependence, which has emerged particularly in the past decade, has established a direct and strong link between the developed and the developing world.

Whereas the South needs help to help itself if it is to overcome hunger and misery, the North needs the markets and purchasing power of the South. The prosperity of the Third World is, therefore, ineluctably linked to global trade. If trade expands, the world economy expands. Moreover, I cannot foresee international security being firmly established for generations to come as long as islands of wealth persist in a sea of world poverty. The basic truth remains – neither side can prosper without the other.

9

Human Rights and Wrongs

One of the most regrettable consequences of the schism between the developing countries and those of the industrialized Western democracies was the deep divide that opened up in the interpretation of what constituted human rights. This is particularly to be lamented because the United Nations will go down in history as the first international organization to concern itself in a sustained and serious way with the rights of all human beings.

In its preamble the UN Charter reaffirmed 'faith in fundamental human rights, in the dignity and worth of the human person, in the equal rights of men and women and of nations large and small'. That principle was codified in the Universal Declaration of Human Rights of 1948. This was no more than the first step in a lengthy journey. The UN can accept a reasonable share of the credit for imprinting this concept of human rights on the consciousness of mankind. It is the principal agency for focusing world attention on the gravest violations of such rights, but even now it has only just begun to grapple with the problem of applying its proclaimed standards when they are most flagrantly disregarded.

It would be unreasonable to expect more in a world still dominated by sovereign nation states. The ambivalence in the Charter established forty years ago persists to the present day. On the one hand members pledge themselves 'to take joint and separate action in co-operation with the Organization to promote universal respect for and observance of human rights and fundamental freedoms for all without distinction as to race, sex, language or religion'. On the other, the organization is not authorized 'to intervene in matters which are essentially within the domestic jurisdiction of any state . . .' This provision is too often used to override any specific human rights obligation a state may have accepted. When the organization seeks to induce members to observe universal standards, it moves into a delicate and often inflammatory area of activity.

Implementation, inevitably, will continue to lag far behind good intentions. Since the United Nations is not a world government, it could hardly be otherwise. The organization has nevertheless succeeded in encouraging member states to accept voluntarily binding legal obligations to apply accepted standards of human rights within their territories. The general provisions of the Universal Declaration were elaborated in 1966 in legally binding 'covenants', one on civil and political rights and a second on economic, social and cultural rights. It had taken eighteen years to reach even this stage. The covenants were to come into effect when ratified by thirty-five states and it took another ten years before, with my encouragement, the necessary number of ratifications was secured in 1976. The number has continued to grow but as I write I have to note to my great regret that less than half the total membership has adhered to the covenants. There have been some curious anomalies. The Soviet bloc states have found it possible to ratify, but the United States, normally in the forefront where human rights are concerned, has not so far adopted either of them.

The covenants were carefully drafted to allow considerable flexibility in their application and reflected the situation at the time they were drawn up in the sixties, at the climax of the de-colonization process and the creation of so many new independent states. The first article of each covenant proclaimed, in identical terms, the rights of all *peoples* to self-determination and the free disposal of their natural wealth and resources. The language was significant and lies at the root of the present differences of interpretation. It reflected the desire of the emerging states to emphasize their sovereignty and challenged the Western democratic view that a sound human rights structure must of necessity be based on the inherent civil and political rights of the individual. The Third World countries assert that such rights, preserved in isolation, merely sanction and perpetuate privilege and exploitation. Of what use is the right to vote, they ask, if a person is starving, or the right to free expression if he is illiterate? Millions of people in Africa and Asia die of hunger and starvation and are deprived of education and economic progress. Their problem is survival, and they are less exercised by violations of individual human rights whether it be in totalitarian or authoritarian regimes. It is this appearance of double standards that exasperates and alienates the West.

The inter-relationship between economic and social rights on the one hand and civil and political rights on the other finds continuing expression in every UN declaration and resolution over the years. The Third World majority has consistently emphasized the former at the expense of the latter. Their priority has been the promotion of collective rights: opposition to racial discrimination, anti-colonialism, full sovereignty over national wealth and resources, economic development and other real or assumed requirements for the progress of the nations of the developing world. The defence of individual liberties has been pushed into the background. The imperatives of self-determination were even held to justify the denial of individual rights and freedoms to enable these new countries to move more quickly towards their desired goals. They defined their major needs and objectives as entitlements rather than as aspirations, coupled with the demand that the countries of the North should redress the situation by the transfer of resources to the South, a claim that more conservative Western states would not accept.

I found this a distressing controversy. Each side had a valid point, but each was looking at only half the picture. In fact, no amount of peace and 'development' can compensate for the loss of individual liberty, just as the absence of 'development' is itself a violation of human rights. I made it my concern to devote equal and urgent attention to all aspects of human rights, taking into account the absolute necessity to promote development and peace. The international community must speak out against torture, the 'disappearance' of political opponents, arbitrary arrest and detention, slavery and similar abuses in the contemporary political scene. At the same time it must concern itself with such social objectives as adequate care for children, the aged and the disabled, with minorities and migrant workers and with the rights of women. In all these fields, the United Nations has begun to establish guidelines and promote their observance.

Whenever human rights questions were discussed in the United Nations, the Western governments accused the world organization of double standards, dealing more or less exclusively with violations in the Western hemisphere and ignoring the human rights problems in the Communist countries. However, there has been some shift in emphasis recently and the accusations in this regard have less justification. When Soviet forces moved into Afghanistan and the Vietnamese invaded Kampuchea, their governments were severely criticized both by the West and by the countries of the Third World in unison. The treatment of Soviet dissidents and trade union rights in Poland have occupied the attention of the UN human rights agencies. The organization cannot compel member states to take, or to refrain from taking, action dealing with the human rights of their populations. Declaratory resolutions are seldom immediately effective, but, as the strong reaction of governments subjected to criticism shows, they do have an impact.

Under the human rights covenants, member states are required to report to the appropriate United Nations agencies through the Secretary General on the measures they take. A few have agreed that the Human Rights Committee may consider communications from their nationals claiming to be the victims of violations. The despatch of special rapporteurs or represenatives and expert working parties to countries under scrutiny has proved an effective means of marshalling factual information. Confidential reviews of complaints or petitions from individual citizens against their own governments, although often fruitless, have frequently led to confidential intercession, which has proved helpful. Quiet diplomacy is often the indicated method for handling human rights problems in order to avoid inflammatory public discussion, which could be counter-productive. It is easy to lose patience with these necessarily tangential methods of operation. Much effort is still required to utilize them more effectively, but as the procedures become more firmly established I have no doubt that their effect will increase.

I was able to intervene personally on a number of occasions to obtain the release of political prisoners or alleviate the conditions in which they were held. I was approached frequently in New York or in their national capitals by governments requesting me to take an initiative in particular cases. Some of my appeals were public, many more had to be carried out in private; I exercised my good offices on a humanitarian basis whenever I felt I could be of assistance to individual victims of abuse.

I made countless official visits to member countries and, as part of the general discussion of substantive problems with the head of government and top officials, it was not difficult, even in the most unlikely places, to raise privately specific individual cases that had been brought to my attention. Whenever appropriate I would present to my hosts a list of the names of people who had been unlawfully imprisoned or prevented from emigrating to join their families abroad. In a surprising number of cases this quiet diplomacy was successful. There was always the danger that my appeals would complicate the negotiations on substantive matters, but I felt that was a risk well worth taking. Requests which had been brushed aside when made by subordinate officials would receive a hearing when presented by the Secretary General of the United Nations. If the government in question refused to take action on these private representations, I could always 'go public' as a further means of influence.

Before my first visit to Guinea in March 1974, the West German government had asked me to intercede on behalf of three of their nationals who had been imprisoned for alleged participation in an anti-government plot. The President was Sekou Touré, a Marxist hard-liner considered to be most difficult to deal with. He came personally to the airport to meet me, a tall, good-looking, rather impressive figure. (It should be said that he later became somewhat more moderate in his attitudes and the skilful chairman of several of the mediating committees of the Organization of African Unity.) On this occasion circumstances became distinctly bizarre.

He conducted me to his own car and I automatically made for one of the back seats, expecting that he would sit next to me. 'No, no, Mr Secretary General,' he said, 'I am going to drive. Please come and join me in front.' It was a huge open American car, which he drove with one hand while waving a white handkerchief with the other at the many thousands of people who had doubtless been instructed to line the streets.

Our first destination was a huge stadium, holding tens of thousands of people, and my party was conducted up to the presidential box. This formed no part of the previously arranged official programme, but I watched the displays and processions patiently. The women were all wearing long white robes, dancing up to below the box to show their reverence to the great leader of their country, when suddenly he turned to me and said: 'You see that lady there? She is dancing to show her gratitude because I had her husband executed – a traitor who was denounced by his own family. People understand that I did the right thing, because he was a traitor, and they know and feel that the interests of the country have priority over family links. I think this is one of our greatest achievements.' I was absolutely appalled by this statement, which made me realize the pressure under which these people had to live.

Then, to my dismay, he stood up and made a very long speech, criticizing colonialists and imperialists in the accustomed fashion. I was obviously going to be called upon to reply, so the only thing I could do was to get one of my aides to find the text of the speech that I had prepared for the official dinner the following day, hurriedly adapt it and express general anodyne sentiments.

Our conversations did not go at all well. He insisted that the German prisoners, who had worked as development experts, were guilty; he was not at first disposed to let them go. Eventually he agreed to do so, on condition that the German government sent him a communication accepting responsibility for the abortive coup and apologizing for the behaviour of the nationals. There was obviously no possibility of obtaining such a message. However, it seemed to me that in order to get its citizens released the German government might be willing to approve a letter containing some more ambiguous formulation. This would require delicate negotiations not to be concluded during my three-day visit.

I therefore left behind my press spokesman, André Lewin, a very competent French career diplomat seconded to the UN Secretariat. It took him a few weeks, but he eventually obtained a formula acceptable to both parties. The prisoners were released and flown back to Germany just in time, as they were in very bad physical shape. Lewin also undertook a similar exercise on behalf of eighteen French nationals held in Guinea under the same charges. Again he was successful and the prisoners – some of them in deplorable condition – were released.

There were diplomatic overtones in all this. Sekou Touré had obviously made up his mind that he needed to mend his political fences with the French and this was his way of breaking the ice. There was an interesting sequel. André Lewin was later named by the French government as Ambassador to Guinea when diplomatic relationships were resumed. Since the embassy residence had been destroyed, he had the unique diplomatic experience of setting up his first household in a tent.

I was only partially successful when I interceded personally after the 1974 revolution in Ethiopia. There was still a large United Nations regional headquarters in Addis Ababa and they were able to keep me fully informed about the persecution and imprisonment of thousands of political opponents and the harsh treatment of the aged ex-Emperor Haile Selassie and the former Prime Minister Makonnen, whom I had known during his time as Ambassador to the UN.

I was able to visit the Ethiopian capital and talk to Mengistu Haile Mariam, the leader of the Marxist revolution. He was courteous, but intractable and difficult. Makonnen was executed and although I like to think there was some amelioration in the conditions of the Imperial family, the Emperor died shortly after as the result of an operation. Under pressure from the United Nations and the intervention of governments and regional organizations, the regime did later moderate its attitude towards its political opponents and the mass killings without trial were to a large extent halted.

During my term of office human rights aspects were also discussed in 1975 at one of the most important conferences, the Helsinki Conference on Security and Co-operation in Europe. Finland, the host country, invited me to attend as representative of the United Nations. It was mainly a European conference, East and West, with the participation of the two super-powers and Canada.

Although I was invited to make an opening speech at the conference, it was indicated to me, even before my departure from New York, that I would not have the status of a participant. After having made my speech, I intended to stay a day or two longer in order to listen to some of the more important speeches, such as Gromyko's and Kissinger's. When I enquired where I could sit in order to do that, I was informed that there was no seat reserved for me in the conference hall because – although I was invited as an honoured guest – it was not intended to have me, as an exponent of the United Nations, participating in the conference. It became clear to me that my role had been envisaged more as a ceremonial one than anything else. This was reflected in the fact that in the opening ceremony I was seated in a separate box at the theatre where the conference took place, next to

President Kekkonen and other non-participating dignitaries.

Nevertheless, I was apparently able to solve some of their protocol problems. On the evening of the opening day a big State dinner was given by Kekkonen for the conference participants. Despite my somewhat nebulous status, I was informed by the Finnish Chief of Protocol, shortly before the dinner, that I would be seated in the ranking position to the right of the host and that the Finnish President would be grateful if I could answer his toast on behalf of the conference delegations. This is another example of the ambiguous status a Secretary General of the United Nations has to accept. Under the United Nations protocol, he has the rank of Prime Minister and is very often given, especially in Third World countries, the treatment of a head of state. Not so in the Western world, where the maximum protocol he receives is one of head of government. However, in the capitals of the super-powers he is treated merely as a Foreign Minister. The only exception occurred on the occasion of my first official visit to President Carter early in 1977 – he visibly wanted to upgrade the role of the United Nations and its Secretary General. Needless to say, I was always glad to attend international meetings, whatever the status accorded me, as long as I felt that my role could be useful.

The Helsinki Conference gave me the opportunity for a brief exchange of views with the American President, Gerald Ford. During this encounter I came to the conclusion that he was occupied almost exclusively with binding up the domestic wounds of the Watergate affair after the resignation of President Nixon, and that he had no substantial foreign policy initiatives in mind. During his short term of office, his relations with the United Nations were relatively routine. He showed very little interest in our activities and although he was not negative or hostile, he was certainly not a strong supporter of the world organization.

The conference itself was a major landmark in the history of post-war Europe. Its lengthy proceedings and interminable follow-up sessions in other cities would have been daunting to all but the most patient diplomats, but it has served the interests of both Eastern and Western Europe reasonably well. The countries of the Soviet bloc, particularly East Germany, gained a degree of legitimacy for their boundaries and regimes, while the West was able to use the conference for persistent attacks on the human rights record of the eastern European states and the Soviet Union itself.

Despite my rather ceremonial role in Helsinki, I went on working quietly for human rights, making representations where I could, and had more success than might be supposed with the Soviets. In September 1977, during a visit to Moscow, I presented to Foreign Minister Gromyko a list of ten requests drawn up by Jewish community leaders in New York for fellow religionaries to be allowed to emigrate from the USSR in order to be re-united with their families. While I did not receive an immediate response, we discovered in due course that positive action had been taken in a number of the cases.

I repeated this initiative on several occasions, usually with the assistance of a Soviet member of the Secretariat named Viktor Lesiovsky, whom I had inherited from my predecessor U Thant as a personal assistant. His appointment derived from the pressure that Moscow exerted from time to time to be properly represented in senior appointments within the organization. He was the only Russian with an office on the thirty-eighth floor of the UN building, which was where my senior colleagues worked. Lesiovsky had no very clearly defined function, and it was said that he belonged to the KGB. This was not a source of worry as he was not involved in the immediate day-to-day work of the Secretary General.

He had become something of a fixture and spent his time building up a whole range of surprising contacts. He was not only a useful channel to the countries of the eastern bloc and other Marxist governments, but being a very easy-going, cultivated man he had a remarkable range of acquaintances in American business and society. One day he even invited Mrs Kennedy, the widow of the President, to have lunch with him in the delegates' dining-room on the occasion of the opening of the General Assembly.

Whenever I had assembled a list of would-be Jewish emigrants from the Soviet Union I called in Lesiovsky and told him to send it off to his government with my request to release them. In a great many cases positive results were achieved. In the end the number of people involved amounted to several hundred, but Lesiovsky was always at pains to say to me: 'Please, no publicity, otherwise that is the end of it.'

During my last visit to Moscow in 1981 I privately raised with Gromyko the problem of two or three dissidents, including that of Andrei Sakharov. Gromyko stiffened visibly, but he was courteous and said it would be better if I were to put this down on paper for his persoal assistant, Vladimir Fedorovich Petrovsky, head of the Department for International Organizations in the Soviet Foreign Ministry. Clearly I was no more successful than others have been. The Soviets are impervious to arguments about their dissidents. Their attitude is that as long as they obey the laws of the state and do not establish contacts with the outside world, no action is taken against them. If the dissidents engage in what the Soviets consider subversive activities involving the interests of state security, then action is taken against them. In such cases the authorities are almost impossible to move.

One of the most difficult and yet rewarding initiatives I was able to take concerned eight French hostages who had been working in Mauritania when they were seized by elements of the Polisario liberation movement during the fighting in the western Sahara. The French government was deeply worried about their fate and asked me to see if I could bring influence to bear.

It was an extremely delicate situation because the Moroccan government regarded Polisario as a terrorist organization and opposed any attempt by third parties to establish direct contacts with them. The Algerians supported the movement, but since both countries were represented in the United Nations I had to tread warily. I claimed authority as Secretary General to act for the best on humanitarian grounds and found myself receiving a Polisario delegation in New York headed by their foreign spokesman, Ibrahim Hakim, as they called him, a tall, good-looking, quite young man with a halo of white hair. After many months of difficult negotiations, agreement was reached that the hostages would be released personally to me. They doubtless calculated that this would contribute to their *de facto* recognition as a national liberation movement; it placed me at the centre of an acute political controversy. I decided to go ahead, always insisting that my motives were purely humanitarian.

The Algerians had by now decided that there was no further advantage to them in prolonging a situation which was attracting wide publicity, and began to co-operate. I flew into Algiers in December 1977 and was received by President Boumédienne, who had seemingly conceived a good opinion of my impartiality in the long years during which the Third World had been asserting its new-found majority. He had by now taken to affecting a large black toga, which he wore over his European suit, and, with this garment billowing round him, he invited me to an open-air grilled luncheon in his palace and then drove me to the office of the United Nations representative in the capital. There the Polisario delegation was waiting with the hostages. The leader made a long, controversial, highly political statement, to which I was compelled to listen. I made a brief response expressing my satisfaction at the release of the hostages, and we drove straight to the airport.

The French government had provided an aircraft to fly us to Orly, where we were greeted by my old United Nations colleague, now the French Foreign Minister, Louis de Guiringaud. All the relatives of the hostages were there. It was Christmas Eve. The atmosphere was electric with emotion and it was one of the most heart-warming occasions I have ever experienced.

I would not wish this account to become too much of a catalogue, but I achieved several unexpected results. I was able to obtain the release from imprisonment of José Esteban Gonzalez, who had been co-ordinator of the Commission of Human Rights in Nicaragua. The President of the Republic of Korea, Chun Doo-Hwan, commuted the death sentence on opposition leader Kim Dae Jung to life imprisonment at my request and in response to the appeals from many other leaders. I even persuaded Fidel Castro, with whom I worked up quite a personal relationship over the years, to release a number of individuals from custody for re-unification with their families in the United States.

After Pinochet came to power in Chile, we did what we could under very difficult circumstances. Hundreds of political refugees found asylum at the headquarters of the UN Economic Commission for Latin America (ECLA) in Santiago de Chile. Its brave Executive Director, Enrique Iglesias, did not hesitate – despite heavy pressure from the military junta – to extend help and humanitarian assistance to many Chileans fearing for their lives. He and his staff worked day and night to alleviate the human suffering of countless people and visited political detainees in the country's prisons.

One of the most tragic aspects of the Chilean situation was the unknown fate of thousands of people who had disappeared after the violent death of Salvador Allende. Numerous UN missions tried to throw light on that tragedy. The answer, after years of intensive efforts, was usually to register their death or their disappearance without any further knowledge of their whereabouts.

Allende's widow came to visit me several times in New York, praising the efforts of the United Nations and thanking me for my personal humanitarian commitment.

My most distressing – and most abortive – attempt at intervention concerned the Italian Prime Minister Aldo Moro when he was kidnapped by the Red Brigades in March 1978 and held hostage. He and I had worked together in 1969 when I was the Austrian Foreign Minister to conclude the agreement that attempted to settle the problem of the South Tyrol and I had the highest regard for him.

I desperately tried to help him through a series of contacts with the Italian government and through private channels. It very soon became clear that the government in Rome was adamantly opposed to any contact with the Red Brigades, being anxious about possible domestic complications if accused of giving status to this terrorist movement. In view of the deteriorating situation and repeated pleas by the Moro family, I finally decided to make a dramatic personal appeal to the Red Brigades. It was my colleague, Bill Buffum, the American Under Secretary for General Assembly Affairs, who suggested a possible method of approach. He knew I spoke a little Italian and proposed that I should record an appeal for Aldo Moro's release to be broadcast over Italian radio and television.

After carefully weighing human considerations and possible political implications, I decided to go ahead with the appeal. The Italian government was not too pleased with my appearing to give status to the terrorists in this fashion and criticized me publicly, despite my clear statement that my intervention was made on purely humanitarian grounds.

Shortly after this intervention, to my surprise I received a personal letter from Aldo Moro written in captivity on simple lined paper like the exercise books used in school. It was sent to me by his son. Moro asked me for my personal intervention to save his life. Referring in his letter to the rigid attitude of the Italian government, he asked me to use my influence with it to accommodate the terrorists. He stressed that time was running out but he still hoped for a possible solution not only for his own sake but also in the interest of his family. Reading the letter several times it became clear to me that it had probably been screened by his captors. At any rate, I was deeply moved by the human tragedy enacted in such a dramatic way through this letter. I immediately informed the government in Rome of its contents, despite the critical reactions I had received concerning my earlier initiatives. Unfortunately, all my efforts did not save the life of Aldo Moro, whose body was later found in the boot of a parked car.

His widow had been deeply shocked and disappointed by what she regarded as the failure of the Italian government and her husband's own Christian Democrat party to negotiate with the terrorists in order to obtain his release. When I visited Rome a year later she asked if she could call on me at the neutral territory of the Austrian embassy to the Holy See. She wished to keep our meeting completely private and did not want to go through either Italian government or United Nations channels. It was a most moving encounter. With tears in her eyes, she thanked me for all my efforts to save her husband's life.

The election of President Carter in 1977 brought a welcome thaw in the relationship between the United Nations and the American administration. From the first Jimmy Carter was a strong supporter of the United Nations. Shortly after his election, he expressed a wish to address the General Assembly. This was unusual, since it was not in session at the time. We were, however, eager to comply with this request and in March I arranged a special meeting of all the permanent representatives and members of the Secretariat staff in order to provide him with the best possible platform. His visit to New York was a most impressive event. Not a seat was vacant in the large General Assembly Hall and the corridors were packed with people who had come to hear his address. He went out of his way to support the role of the United Nations and its staff in New York and this produced an immediate and much-needed lift in Secretariat morale.

The new President was quick to reciprocate my gesture by convening a special meeting and taking me into his confidence on a wide range of foreign policy problems. My wife and I were invited to pay an official visit to the White House. Symbolism is important on these occasions, and we were gratified by the obvious intention of President and Mrs Carter to demonstrate their regard for the organization and for us personally by according us the treatment normally reserved for a head of state. As our limousine swept up the semi-circular drive, an honour guard was in place to welcome us and we were received by the Carters at the main entrance. Ushered into the spacious reception rooms, the President and I then retired to his Oval Office for extensive talks.

I could not but be impressed by the keen interest he took in literally everything I could tell him about the problems of the United Nations. An excellent listener and a sharp questioner, he obviously digested and retained complex matters of detail with great ease and speed. Even more satisfactory, it became manifest to me that his private words were matched by his public utterances in support of international co-operation in general and the work of the United Nations in particular.

Carter made the issue of human rights one of the most prominent themes in his policy and there is no doubt that this brought considerable pressure to bear on Moscow and on dictatorships in Latin America. It is said of him that this was an enthusiasm that waned. In my experience, this was not so. What he did find was that public condemnation and resounding official statements did not really achieve anything. He changed his tactics, but not his policy. He remained a strong supporter of human rights but preferred to use diplomatic channels to discuss these problems with the governments directly concerned. I furthered his approaches whenever he called for my collaboration and we remained in close communication during his whole period in office.

Our efforts in the United Nations to help individuals on a humanitarian basis touched on only a small portion of the mass of injustice we see in the world around us. It was a source of great satisfaction to me to be able to seize moments of opportunity when they arose and to register some gains, however minor, in the quest for a more free and equitable society.

In their different ways, a number of religious leaders as well as non-governmental organizations are similarly active in the human rights field – first and foremost is the Pope. In my repeated contacts with John Paul II in Rome and during his memorable visit to the United Nations in October 1979, I was deeply impressed by his profound dedication to the protection of human rights, his enormous interest in the problems of the Third World and in the existing conflicts in the world, especially in the Middle East. He was eager to hear my insights and my experience in these fields. Of course I did not hide some of the frustrations of my work, at which point he always tried to encourage me, comparing his experiences with my own. I was taken by his personality – a very warm-hearted, open-minded and humorous man who radiated confidence and optimism. During our meetings he made a point of talking German, which he speaks fluently. Whenever he received me at the Vatican, he insisted on seeing my family after our talks, which usually lasted much longer than scheduled. On his visit to the United Nations the Pope made a moving speech in the packed General Assembly Hall and showed his personal interest in the well-being of the UN staff: when he heard of a secretary who was fatally ill, he immediately asked to see her and gave her his special blessing. John Paul never left any doubt that he was a strong believer in the United Nations, which he considered to be an excellent forum for conveying his message to the world community.

We owe a debt to Amnesty International, the International Organization of Jurists and other similar groups, for their success in turning the spotlight of public opinion on individual and collective abuses. This is a field in which one often risks being overcome by the enormity of man's inhumanity to man. Limited as it is by the constraints of national sovereignty, the United Nations has taken only the first few faltering steps towards fulfilling the goal of advancing fundamental human rights enshrined in the Charter. It has, however, won the support of a significant group of people. Human rights committees, manned mostly by young people, have mushroomed throughout the world over the past ten years – not only in the protected areas of democracy, but also on the hard, barren ground of dictatorship.

In retrospect, the feeling of repeated disappointment in human rights matters tends to obscure the moments of success. As much as I cherish the letters of appreciation from people we helped or whose suffering we alleviated, I am very aware – much to my regret – that our endeavours merely scratched the surface, while the rule of injustice and terror still holds sway.

10

Stranded Millions

Nothing else in my ten years with the United Nations is so deeply branded on my memory as the countless visits to refugee camps all over the world. I cannot tell how many despairing people I met. Memory has transformed them into an endless procession of misery. I can still see the children with their swollen bellies, outstretched hands and pleading eyes. I can see the mass graves, the swarms of flies. Refugees are the flotsam of all the wars, crises and conflicts of the Third World. Nothing was worse than the certainty of knowing how little we could do to help – despite Herculean efforts by the United Nations and countless private organizations. Nothing was more oppressive than to realize what hopes these people had set in the United Nations. And nothing was more satisfying than the feeling of having at least helped to alleviate the lot of millions of desperate people. For, with all the weaknesses and faults of the world organization, there can scarcely be any doubt of this one truth: the flow of millions of refugees could never have been alleviated without the massive and timely intervention of the United Nations and its agencies. In spite of all the material advances of society and government in this modern age, many communities have not yet reached a stage in which all their inhabitants can live together in peace and harmony. One of the agonies of our human condition has been the uprooting of whole populations from their homes to flee to other countries in the face of unknown dangers, want and despair. The conscience of mankind is appalled by the magnitude of their suffering. This is no temporary phenomenon. Experience has demonstrated that we must be prepared to deal with these tides of humanity as they continue to flow across national borders for the foreseeable future.

The United Nations took an early lead in coping with these emergencies, and since 1950 the office of the United Nations High Commissioner for Refugees has been the principal agency for protecting their legal rights and maintaining them while their return to their old homes or re-settlement in new ones was being arranged. Originally, the High Commissioner's work was centred in Europe, to complete the return or re-settlement of Second World War refugees and assist the people fleeing from the countries of eastern Europe. Most of them found asylum in the western European countries, the United States, the old British Common-wealth and Israel. Even these movements have since been dwarfed by the human tides fleeing from the tribal conflicts attendant on de-colonization and the wars in the Horn of Africa, the Indian sub-continent and South-East Asia. During my term of office, successive crises in Asia and Africa continually taxed our resources, our ability to mobilize material assistance and our administrative capacities.

The first of these crises grew out of the civil war in East Pakistan, later Bangladesh, in 1971 and the Indo-Pakistan war which broke out at the end of that year. As a result of the hostilities, some eight million refugees fled into India, where they had to be maintained temporarily in camps. Simultaneously, the densely populated area of East Pakistan was threat-ened with a devastating famine.

The first UN measures had been initiated by my predecessor U Thant. Our urgent need was for funds. I made an appeal to all member states and within a year we had received pledges amounting to $1,275,000,000. The High Commissioner for Refugees, Prince Sadruddin Aga Khan, was entrusted with the co-ordination of the Indian operation, which involved most of the UN and private agencies capable of furnishing food and relief supplies.

In what had now become Bangladesh itself, we established special relief operations to obtain stocks of food and the means of transporting and distributing them. It was Victor Umbricht, a former executive of a Swiss chemical concern, who was in charge of our relief operation in Dacca. He did an outstanding job despite the tremendous difficulties he faced. His managerial skill and his great dedication made a decisive contribution to the positive outcome of this challenging venture. As the scope of the operation went far beyond Bangladesh, I appointed Sir Robert Jackson of Australia as my special co-ordinator. His qualifications in this field had long been recognized as outstanding. During the Second World War he had been responsible for the important and difficult support operation to maintain the island of Malta when it was isolated by the German and Italian presence on the nearby Italian peninsula and in North Africa. Sir Robert did a remarkable job and I was to call on him in similar circumstances over the years.

An almost Herculean task confronted the UN in Bangladesh. It was literally a question of saving 75 million Bengalis from starvation – hard on the heels of a terrible war had come the catastrophic harvest of 1972. On top of all that, arrangements had to be made for more than 90,000 Pakistani soldiers who had been detained in prisoner-of-war camps by the victorious Indian army. Finally, provision had to be made to assist in re-integrating all those who had been separated from their communities during the hostilities. Many Bengalis stranded in West Pakistan wished to return to Bangladesh. Non-Bengalis caught there, such as the Biharis, wished to cross India into Pakistan.

In February 1973, at the height of the dramatic events on the Indian subcontinent, I decided to visit the countries that had been affected by the vicissitudes of war. It was a journey that offers some insight into the difficulties and strange circumstances that confronted the UN and myself alike on so many humanitarian missions.

I first flew to New Delhi in a small chartered aircraft because I was convinced that the key to a solution lay there. The Indian army's victory had placed Indira Gandhi and her government in a decisive position. She listened to me with the composure of a sovereign victor, secure in the knowledge that she could set the terms. However, I received certain assurances that India would co-operate with our relief operations, insofar as they bore no undesirable political implications which might upset the new military reality.

The real trouble started in Pakistan. Our flight had been cleared to fly direct from New Delhi to Islamabad, thus avoiding a circuitous route via Karachi. In mid-flight the pilot, who was just getting over a kidney attack, was instructed by the Pakistani air traffic controller to return to the normal air corridor since our special clearance had been withdrawn. After checking the gauges, the pilot realized that he did not have the fuel for the re-routing and asked me in desperation what he should do. I told him to inform the tower in Islamabad that I would return to New Delhi immediately should our original flight plan not be re-confirmed. After a few tense minutes on board, our clearance finally came through.

Ali Bhutto, President of Pakistan, awaited us in a hangar, where he had taken shelter from the pouring rain. As we drove to the Presidential Palace he began to lament about the Indians, who, he claimed, were starving his captive soldiers and had even shot many of them as they tried to escape. Huge crowds lined the road, trying desperately to get close to me and display their grief: wives and mothers pleaded with me to obtain the release of their husbands or sons from Indian captivity. After dinner, Bhutto invited us to watch some films – clearly, we thought, an attempt to substantiate his claims about the tragic outcome of the war with documentary evidence. However, we were mistaken – we were treated to a long series of newsreel shots taken of his last election campaign, showing him in his shirt sleeves addressing enormous crowds in different parts of the country. The defeated leader obviously wanted to convince me and my companions of the extent of his popularity and charisma, with the result that valuable time was lost that could have been spent discussing urgent problems. It was this self-assured arrogance and showmanship that contributed finally to his downfall.

Immediately after my visit to Islamabad, I flew on to Bangladesh, hoping to find in my talks with Prime Minister Mudjibur Rahman some practical solutions to the horrendous political and economic problems facing his country. The very survival of his newly-born nation was at stake. But even there I found it almost impossible to negotiate because of the somewhat bizarre atmosphere in his provisional headquarters. Just as we had started our talks, a stream of private citizens poured into his office, presenting him with all kinds of problems and asking for his help. My visit turned out to be a sort of open-house reception interrupted constantly by outsiders who had nothing whatsoever to do with my talks. I finally left the meeting after more than two hours with the sad feeling that the country lacked an effective administrative structure and that Mudjibur Rahman, albeit an excellent politician, failed to grasp the need to organize himself and the problems of his country in a practical way. Disappointed at the outcome of the talks, I returned to New York. The UN relief operation, however, was a resounding success. We had organized a massive repatriation exercise. More than 200,000 people had been moved back and forth, almost entirely by air.

The full extent of the successful UN relief operation in Bangladesh is not generally known. It was one of the rare occasions where the organization was able to draw upon the joint services of the Americans and the Soviets. For instance, Soviet teams cleared the port of Chittagong, the largest harbour in Bangladesh, while American teams set about reconstruction work in Dacca and other parts of the country. They were assisted in this venture by several European countries and international relief agencies. Under the overall guidance of UN experts, the work was completed within a relatively short period of time. Ships were able to use the harbours again and offload the supplies so desperately needed in the country – success was thus assured.

Another major area of concern was South-East Asia. Years of war and political upheaval in the Indo-China peninsula had created an outflow of refugees that outstripped the capacity of the neighbouring countries to absorb them. The climax was reached in 1979 when the world was horrified by the sufferings of the so-called 'boat people', predominantly ethnic Chinese fleeing from Vietnam, only to be shipwrecked or inter-cepted by pirates, robbed and killed. Even more distressing was the refusal of many passing vessels to rescue these unfortunates, since the countries where the ships were registered would not accept them. Other refugees, fleeing the new regimes in Indo-China by land, were harshly treated in makeshift camps in Thailand and other countries of first asylum.

Shortly after she was elected to office, the British Prime Minister, Margaret Thatcher, sent me a personal message through her admirable new Ambassador in New York, Sir Anthony Parsons, urging me to take action to alleviate the sufferings of these people. I was obliged to explain in my first response that since the UN Economic and Social Council was not in session I was not authorized under the Charter and the rules of procedure to take an initiative. Encouraged by Mrs Thatcher, and after consultation with other governments, including those of the Eastern bloc, who raised no difficulties, I decided to cut through the red tape and to summon, on my own initiative and authority, a special conference to consider effective remedies.

In consultation with the High Commissioner for Refugees, I convened a high-level meeting in Geneva with representatives of those countries willing to take part. My position was delicate. I had no mandate from the General Assembly and if I had permitted the discussions to spill over from humanitarian considerations to the political issues involved, our task would have been made impossible. Some countries in the Association of South-East Asian Nations wished to take this step and I had to discourage them. I told them that if they wished to raise political matters, they would have to go direct to the Security Council. Fortunately, the great majority of the participants respected my appeal and the conference was a success.

Over the course of two days, offers of re-settlement doubled from 125,000 to 260,000. Substantial new pledges of assistance in cash and kind were made, totalling more than $160 million, a sum later increased. Thailand, Malaysia and Indonesia agreed to stop expelling refugees. Japan increased its financial support. The United States doubled its monthly quota for receiving refugees from Indo-China and sent rescue ships to the South China Sea. I was able to work out a plan with the Vietnamese authorities to reduce the exodus of some 70,000 persons a month to about 10,000, thus permitting their orderly departure in a humane fashion and their swift transportation to countries of final settlement.

I was subjected to some criticism for making these arrangements. Was it proper, I was asked, to conclude an agreement that appeared to condone Vietnam's refusal to comply with standard United Nations principles on human rights? Were we interfering with the right of individuals to free choice over whether to emigrate or not? Would those released under the orderly departure procedures qualify for assistance as refugees, that is to say people who had fled because of fear of persecution? Serious issues of law and ethical judgement were indeed involved, but it seemed to me better to have arrived at a workable solution than at none at all.

Later in 1979 we were confronted by yet another refugee problem of major proportions in South-East Asia. As a result of war and famine in Kampuchea, the former Cambodia, some 400,000 people had crossed the border into Thailand and found refuge in entirely inadequate facilities. The Thai authorities were making every effort to cope, but they were overwhelmed. The situation was complicated by the fact that we could not deal directly with the Kampuchean authorities under Heng Samrin as the UN General Assembly did not recognize his regime as the legitimate government of the country, insisting that it had been imposed by the Vietnamese army, with which we could not co-operate either.

To emphasize the purely humanitarian character of our assistance, I placed the children's fund, UNICEF, in charge of the relief operations. With the help of other UN agencies, particularly the Food and Agriculture Organization, and a number of non-governmental relief bodies, we began to co-ordinate the flow of aid. In the midst of this I received a telephone call one morning from Mrs Rosalynn Carter. I was well aware of her interest in humanitarian activities and also of her substantial rôle in providing advice and support to the President, which went far beyond the normal image of a First Lady.

She had just returned from a refugee camp set up in Thailand and told me that she had found the international relief operation in confusion. There was no co-ordination of the large number of international organizations, both public and non-governmental, working in the field and as a result resources were being squandered and those most in need of help were not getting the assistance they required. She suggested a meeting to see if there was not some manner in which I could intervene. At her request she came to my official residence in New York and we sat down over a Viennese coffee.

I was aware that there had been a lack of co-ordination between the UN agencies and a number of private relief organizations operating in the area. Therefore I was not surprised that Mrs Carter had reached the same conclusion. My problem was that not only did I have no authority over the non-governmental agencies such as OXFAM and the various religious relief services participating in the operation, but, under the United Nations system of independent specialized agencies, I had no legal authority to direct the activities of bodies like the Food and Agriculture Organization which were working in the camps. One solution had worked in the past, and this I had already made up my mind to adopt – to appoint a high-level personality who, through his personal stature, could co-ordinate a more efficient operation. Putting the right man on the spot would serve as a catalyst for more effective performance.

I therefore turned again to Sir Robert Jackson, who, together with Victor Umbricht, had made an outstanding success of the Bangladesh operation. He quickly set up headquarters in Bangkok and got to work. Thanks to his firmness and courtesy, a dramatic improvement in the situation occurred in very short order. Unfortunately, as I write, there has been no political settlement in Kampuchea. It has therefore remained impossible to dispose of the refugee problem by repatriating them or re-settling them permanently elsewhere. The camps are still in existence but they are being run much more efficiently than had initially seemed possible.

I embarked on an extensive tour of these Asian trouble spots at the end of 1979 to satisfy myself that our own operations were proceeding as smoothly as possible. I also took the occasion to visit both North and South Korea to see if there was any way of furthering negotiations between the two hostile halves of the country. It was too much to expect that I would succeed where so many others had failed. My next port of call was Singapore and its Prime Minister Lee Kuan Yew. He is nothing if not outspoken. I gave him an account of my discussions and impressions and when I had finished, instead of asking questions in order to clarify some aspect of my extensive report, he said: 'Well, if I understand correctly nothing came out of your visit' – a statement which took me by surprise. Frankly, I did not share his views. Obviously nobody expected me to change the political and strategical map of East Asia in a few days, but, as it turned out later, there was indeed a beginning of a dialogue between North and South Korea in the making. It was Deng Xiaoping who in his conversation with me had, for the first time, suggested that Kim Il Sung, the leader of North Korea, should resume the talks with South Korea. A series of follow-up meetings took place in New York which later on led to a cautious dialogue between the two countries.

During the whole of this period, the refugee problem was assuming increasing prominence in a third area – Africa. A number of the newly independent nations there had become mired in serious political disturb-ances which caused massive movements of population across their frontiers. Conflicts in the Horn of Africa, involving Ethiopia, Somalia, Djibouti and the Sudan, were causing chaos. Violence in Chad and Uganda was causing more people to flee. Tribal warfare in Burundi, drought and famine in western Africa were both causing large-scale migration and serious problems.

Impressed by the success of our efforts in South-East Asia, the African representatives urged me to organize similar channels of assistance for their own compatriots. The situation had become the most serious with which we were confronted. When I assumed office in 1972, the number of African refugees was estimated at approximately three-quarters of a million. By 1981, we were attempting to assist no fewer than five million African displaced persons in eighteen different countries. This represented about half the world total of such unfortunates. They had crossed frontiers but they did not leave the African continent. The neighbours where they had found some refuge had behaved very well within their own very limited resources. They were being fed and accommodated, and not rejected as had happened in Asia. Nevertheless, their plight was and continues to be pitiful.

I alerted all the independent United Nations agencies to co-ordinate information and, on my recommendation to the General Assembly, was authorized to organize yet another conference in Geneva in April 1981 to consider the problem, attended by the representatives of ninety-nine governments. The results were heartening. More than $550 million in aid was pledged and we were able greatly to expand our relief operations. Africa has now emerged as the worst problem of all and resources continue to lag far behind needs.

This account cannot become a mere catalogue. Suffice it to say that when I left office at the beginning of 1982, there were probably more refugees and displaced persons in the world than at any time since the end of World War II. The High Commissioner's programme for Afghan refugees in Pakistan and Iran is designed to assist more than two million people. The number of Palistinian refugees has increased as a result of the turmoil in the Lebanon. Conditions in Central and South America are adding their quota to the number of refugees and the problems increase rather than diminish.

Although the United Nations has worked wonders, every one of its refugee operations has been complicated by political, economic and legal factors connected with the underlying causes. To thrust aside political considerations and be guided only by the humanitarian factors has been to walk a tightrope. Yet it has been absolutely necessary to do so. The only possible course of action was to damp down the divisiveness of political conflict, appeal to the better instincts of member governments and their populations and gain at least the tolerance of the parties concerned. This did not mean that the organization would ignore the political implications but rather that it would handle them in entirely separate channels. When wearing our refugee hats, we had to avoid discussing the causes of the great human tragedies with which we were trying to cope.

We were also faced by the dilemma of the extent to which we should allow our refugee operations to go beyond the provision of subsistence, re-settlement or repatriation to include development programmes contribut-ing to the self-sufficiency of the refugees and the economic growth of their host country. In general terms, and I think wisely, the High Commissioner for Refugees, now Mr Poul Hartling, has resisted such proposals. Their acceptance would increase the budget of refugee operations and their complexity beyond any funds available to the organization. In theory, this, as I have already indicated, is how plans for the future should be worked out, but they will need to be funded and executed as entirely separate projects.

There is even a legal problem. The original United Nations convention concerning the status of refugees defined the word quite narrowly, so as to exclude those who wish to migrate for economic or other reasons considered less compelling. Refugees are defined as people outside the country of their nationality, driven away by well-founded fear of persecution for racial, religious, political or social reasons. This does not even cover victims of natural disaster in or outside their own countries or those fleeing from major public disorder. We were always at pains to avoid the pitfalls caused by this narrow definition by choosing the appropriate agency to carry out the necessary operation without allowing legal considerations to override the elementary humanitarian objectives that motivated us.

The problem of co-ordinating relief and re-settlement efforts remains unresolved. Each operation presents its own particular problems. The establishment of smooth co-operation between the specialized agencies and voluntary organizations concerned with the feeding, health, trans-portation, education and other needs of displaced persons presented us with a constant challenge. There have been accusations that food and other relief material have ended up in the hands of the very authorities and their soldiers involved in the persecution. Where nations and communities are disordered, no outside agency has control of the country. Even the indigenous authorities are beset. The relief workers risk and sometimes lose their lives amidst the chaos surrounding them and they respond tardily and unwillingly to any suggestion that they should be subjected to overall authority, which in any case the United Nations has no franchise to exert. On the whole, and given the circumstances, the practical arrange-ments we were able to make on the ground have always functioned with reasonable efficiency. We learned from experience and, what is most important, we saved lives. I dare to assert that if there is a continuous success story of the United Nations, which unfortunately is widely underrated, it is this vital support for the stranded millions.

11

Carter and the Hostages

My most intensive period of common endeavour with President Carter was during the Iranian hostage crisis. After my alarming and seemingly abortive experiences in Teheran, which had taken up the first three days of the new year of 1980, I arrived back in New York on 4 January. I felt as if I had been away for weeks and certainly had no inkling that the crisis was to last another thirteen months.

In the sanity of the familiar surroundings of the UN headquarters, I took stock of the ordeal I had undergone. I had not obtained the release of the hostages, and that was indeed discouraging. Every effort by the secular leaders, Bani-Sadr and Ghotbzadeh, to negotiate seriously had been undermined. The revolutionary fanaticism of the street crowds and the students, the bitter rivalries within the fragmented leadership, and the deep-seated hatred for the United States as an implacable enemy were obstacles that could not be quickly overcome. Iran was simply not ready to take any action on the issue and certainly was in no mood to compromise.

There was some criticism of my mission. I had achieved nothing, the hostages remained incarcerated, why had I gone? That seemed to me unreasonable. I was perfectly aware before I went that there was no possibility of my returning with a plane full of hostages. The alternatives – and the risks – were quite clear-cut. I could either have remained in New York and relied on diplomatic gestures or I could put my person and position in jeopardy and attempt to discover on the ground whether there was a loophole that might provide a solution. The initiative had been entrusted to me; I chose the latter course because I considered it the responsibility of the Secretary General to use every avenue which might lead to a solution of the crisis.

My visit had provided much enlightenment. It had given me an acute sense of the national psychology of revolutionary Iran and particularly of its leadership; of the turmoil and confusion in all quarters, of the precarious position of the civilian authorities, of the endless jockeying for power. I had not come back empty-handed, because the painful and laborious process that was to follow was based on the results of my visit. If the Iranians were to be brought to move at all, the arrival of the UN commission of enquiry to hear their grievances would have to precede the release of the hostages, or at least to coincide with it, and I had to persuade the American administration that this was the only way to avoid complete deadlock. The odds against it were great but with perseverance it still seemed possible to reach a settlement. The establishment of the commission would have to be the first step. Accordingly, I reported to the Security Council on 7 January that my trip had been useful.

Two days later I flew to Washington for a two-hour meeting with President Carter in the Oval Office. He had come back early from Camp David, bringing with him his Secretary of Sate, Cyrus Vance, his National Security Adviser, Zbigniew Brzezinski, and his Press Secretary, Jody Powell. Donald McHenry, the American Ambassador to the UN, was also present. Don, as we called him, was a skilled diplomat with great human warmth, on whose good judgement and co-operation I relied heavily during that difficult period. I was warmly received and the President expressed great appreciation of my efforts and of the risks I had run. I gave him a comprehensive account of the chaos and turmoil I had encountered. He said later in his memoirs that at one point I had tears in my eyes. That is poetic licence. It is not easy for me to cry, although I doubtless became emotional. In spite of the detailed briefing I was able to give, the President and his entourage continued to underestimate the appalling mess in Teheran. 'You see, Mr President,' I said, 'there is no clear line of authority. Neither Bani-Sadr nor Ghotbzadeh have any control over the militant students in the embassy compound. Only Khomeini can bring influence to bear and he is holding back because he does not wish to antagonize them. Until we can establish contact with the Ayatollah, there is no way to solve this problem.'

Vance was his usual steady, enquiring self. Brzezinski played very little part in the discussion at all. He just sat listening. For his part the President said that the extradition of the Shah, who was by now very ill, was completely out of the question. He was by then in Panama but, if that country were to consider his extradition, Carter would invite him to return to the United States. The President said he was determined to press for sanctions against Iran at the Security Council as this was the only way of maintaining the prestige of the United States as well as that of the United Nations and the World Court. 'We cannot sit idly by for weeks,' he warned.

He then intimated that his administration had evolved a new set of proposals 'through other intermediaries'. Who they were he did not at that time disclose. It was to become only too clear within a few days. Cyrus Vance outlined what the proposals were before I left and, although they preserved the basic elements of the points I had taken to Iran, there was a significant shift of emphasis. The Americans were prepared to co-operate in seeking through the auspices of the United Nations to establish 'a forum or commission to hear Iran's grievances and to produce a report on them'. This was a more precise proposal for airing Iran's case than had previously been put forward. The Americans were also prepared to consider with the Iranians what could be done to strengthen their security in the light of the Soviet intervention in Afghanistan, which was a new and disturbing element in the situation.

What now follows is a sequence of events of almost Byzantine complexity, but if the course of this crisis is to be understood and its lessons learnt for the future, the chronology needs to be established.

The Security Council was due to meet on 11 January to consider the imposition of sanctions on the Iranian regime. That very morning, Mansur Farhang, the Iranian Ambassador to the UN, brought in a message from Ghotbzadeh that appeared to signify a major change in the Iranian attitude. Its purport was that the hostages could be released before the return of the Shah and his assets, providing that the enquiry commission could be sent to Teheran as soon as possible. Ghotbzadeh asserted that Ayatollah Khomeini had agreed with this approach.

Farhang had been something of a problem before my visit to Teheran. The most recent of a series of temporary appointments as Iran's delegate to the United Nations, he had been plucked out of a professorship in sociology at the University of California. He was an émigré who had long been opposed to the Shah's regime and, although he had a good understanding of the American mentality, he had been out of contact with his own authorities. He was a tall, good-looking, rather impressive personality, very quiet and courteous in his manner, but given to well-meaning initiatives which were not backed by his government. One such initiative had misled me before my mission and we had something of a brush as a result. I was therefore wary of his communications.

I wondered what lay behind the urgency of this sudden appeal for action. Could it be a first reaction to the new American effort through 'intermediaries' to which President Carter had referred? I recalled his jocular parting words to me: 'Perhaps you should go to Teheran every two weeks and eventually there would be a solution.' Presumably someone was carrying on where I had left off.

I had disclosed the new Iranian 'clarifications' in my private consultations with the members of the Security Council, including Ambassador

McHenry of the US, and sent a letter to Ghotbzadeh on 11 January reflecting their attitudes. I asked whether Iran would release the hostages if a Council resolution recognized their right to seek a return of the Shah and his assets or alternatively whether they would permit the hostages to leave upon the establishment of an international commission of enquiry. Ghotbzadeh responded the following day, insisting that Iran wanted the Security Council to recognize its right not merely to seek but to obtain the return of the former monarch and his funds. This communication made no mention of the fate of the hostages.

Farhang admitted that his government's attitude was ambiguous and pleaded with me to understand the atmosphere in Teheran, of which I was only too well aware. Revealingly, he said that if Ghotbzadeh even mentioned the release of the hostages in any specific time frame 'he would not remain Foreign Minister for two hours'. Nevertheless Farhang insisted that the significance of the interchange was that Iran had accepted the United Nations as mediator in its dispute with the United States.

The Security Council, which had twice postponed its session to await the outcome of this new exchange of messages, did not wish to delay any longer. It met to consider the imposition of sanctions on 13 January. Despite majority support the Soviet veto prevented its passage.

Curiously, the failure of the American campaign to impose sanctions did not increase Iranian intransigence. The reason for this became a little clearer on 29 January when Secretary of State Vance again visited me at my residence in New York. He was confident that a 'scenario' worked out for transmission through the 'intermediaries' President Carter had mentioned to me – 'some Frenchmen who had been close to Khomeini and his followers in Paris' – would result in the release of the hostages.

In one respect, this scenario marked an important change in the American position. The US no longer insisted that the hostages be released before a commission of enquiry was created or simultaneously with its creation. The commission would be a fact-finding body to hear Iran's grievances and not a judicial tribunal, would have private discussions with the Iranian authorities and visit each of the hostages. It would not return to New York to report to me until it had informed the Revolutionary Council that it considered the hostages were being held under inhumane conditions and that, under Khomeini's orders, they should be removed from the control of the militants and transferred to a hospital under the joint control of the Iranian government and the commission. Khomeini would then 'pardon' and expel the hostages on some festive occasion such as the mid-February anniversary of the Iranian revolution.

This all seemed to me to have a distinct Alice in Wonderland quality. I was sceptical about it from the first. Under existing conditions in Iran, it was highly unlikely that the authorities would carry it through. In particular, it seemed to me doubtful that Khomeini's support would be forthcoming. Nevertheless I was willing to play my part in putting the scheme into operation. I called in Ambassador Farhang on 31 January and outlined the plan to him, stressing that the United States had made a major concession in giving up its insistence on prior release of the hostages. He was clearly not well informed about these new developments and, instead of reacting with a sense of urgency, suggested that I should go slowly. His main and pointless contribution was to point out that Bani-Sadr was about to be elected as Iranian President and that this would open up a period of transition.

This was no help. Bani-Sadr and Ghotbzadeh were already beginning to back-pedal. In public pronouncements in Teheran, Bani-Sadr was denying any knowledge of the proposal for an enquiry commission, even though he had been present at my meeting with the Revolutionary Council when I raised the subject. I enquired direct of Ghotbzadeh whether it was indeed correct that agreement had been reached for the commission to meet the hostages and he replied that this was 'a possibility'. It was a typical Iranian performance.

Cyrus Vance gave me the 'final version' of the scenario worked out with the 'French intermediaries' at another meeting on 11 February in New York. Hamilton Jordan, Chief of Staff at the White House, was with him. He had just returned from talks with these intermediaries in Berne and this was the first occasion that I even learned their names – Christian Bourguet, a French lawyer, and his associate Hector Villalon, an Argentine businessman living in Paris. They had been associates and intimates of Ayatollah Khomeini and Bani-Sadr during their period of exile in France. Both the 'lawyers', as we began to call them at the UN, were of left-wing persuasion. They had clearly kept up their contacts, although we never did discover who was paying for their travel and subsistence or what their basic motivations were.

I was by no means pleased to discover how much had been going on behind the scenes and resented being faced suddenly by this *fait accompli*. The American administration should have kept me confidentially informed in more detail so that I was not working in the dark.

What we subsequently found out was that the initial contact had occurred as far back as 25 December, when two 'lawyers' had flown to Panama in an abortive attempt to serve extradition papers for the return of the Shah. Hamilton Jordan had intercepted them there and begun to work out the main lines of the 'scenario' with which we were now confronted. My part was limited to the establishment and work of the UN commission. I was asked to send a message to Ghotbzadeh that very day, 11 February, stating that I was ready to send the commission within a week. The following day Ghotbzadeh would reply affirmatively, stating that Iran desired to have its members speak to the hostages. I would then send a follow-up message, confirming that the comission would be a fact-finding body. Then on 15 Februrary, Bani-Sadr would report by telephone that the Ayatollah had instructed the Revolutionary Council to take the necessary action or would himself issue a statement to that effect. I would then be free to announce the establishment of the commission on 15 Februrary at 4 pm New York time. This would enable Bani-Sadr to describe the result as a victory for Iranian diplomacy and the United States to emphasize that the commission was going on a fact-finding mission to hear both sides and meet the hostages and then report back to me.

I listened with increasing doubt to this elaborate theatrical script. Hamilton Jordan appeared quite confident of success and of the co-operation of both the civilian and the religious authorities in Teheran. I remained unconvinced. My experience of the Iranians was that promises were not kept. It was an extremely complicated scenario, full of traps and ambiguity, and I could not see it working. I asked Cyrus Vance bluntly if Khomeini had given his consent to the operation. The Secretary of State indirectly confirmed my hesitation. 'All we know is,' he said, 'the Ayatollah has been informed. That is all I can tell you.'

I felt that this was not really good enough, but I agreed to play my part, hoping that my scepticism would prove to be mistaken. I sent my first agreed message to Ghotbzadeh. His response the next day did not follow the script. It did not include any reference to the release of the hostages. Instead it stressed once again the 'crimes of the deposed Shah and the funds stolen by him and his family'. The following day, 13 Februrary, we received a second message, this time the correct one. It came, of all places, from Athens, Ghotbzadeh's first stop on a brief European trip. It seemed odd that he should choose this very moment for what was described as a routine tour of European capitals. Unknown to me, its true purpose was for him to meet secretly with Hamilton Jordan in Paris on 17 Februrary, where, as has subsequently been revealed, his main suggestion was that the United States should resolve the whole problem by arranging for the Shah's assassination.

In retrospect I have to assume that the Americans were acting in good faith and were pursuing every possible channel to resolve the agonizing dilemma in which they found themselves. Keeping in mind the generous remarks of Cyrus Vance, who later publicly stated: 'We are eternally grateful to Waldheim for his support!', I harbour some resentment at the lack of information about these shadowy negotiations. Full and frank disclosure would have made my task much easier.

Amidst this thickening confusion, I still felt obliged to go ahead with the limited role which had been allotted to the United Nations. As soon as the correct response arrived from the Iranian side, I sent a draft of my planned public announcement on the establishment of the commission to Bani-Sadr. He sent back his approval with only one change, and on 20 Feburary, two days later, I issued the statement as planned. The commission was 'to undertake a fact-finding mission to Iran to hear Iran's grievances and to allow for an early solution of the crisis between Iran and the United States'. I then added: 'Iran desires to have the commission speak to each of the hostages.' I listed the commission members: Andres Aguilar of Venezuela and Mohammed Bedjaoui of Algeria, the two co-chairmen, Adib Daoudy of Syria, H. W. Jayawardene, the distinguished jurist and brother of the President of Sri Lanka, and Louis-Edmond Pettiti of France.

I explained to them that they were to visit the hostages, but not to interrogate them. Their objective was to complete their entire task in a week. They were then to inform the Revolutionary Council that they were ready to return to New York to submit their findings, including the evidence and documents supplied by the Iranians. Their report would not be published until the hostages had been released or at least taken out of the hands of the militants and placed under the protection of the government. At the request of the United States, which was apprehensive about leaks, I did not reveal to the commission the further elements of the larger 'package plan' which had been worked out through Bourguet and Villalon.

I appointed the very able young Assistant Secretary General, Diego Cordovez of Ecuador, to accompany them and co-ordinate their mission. He was responsible at the UN for liaison with the independent agencies such as UNESCO, FAO, the World Health Organization and the other specialized agencies. I had formed a high opinion of his competence and hoped that he would be able to guide them through the jungle that awaited them.

The party left New York for Geneva that very day. After minor delays imposed by the Iranians they left for Teheran three days later. It was while they were in the air that we received the stunning news that Ayatollah Khomeini had announced that the fate of the hostages would be decided by the Majlis, the Iranian parliament, which had not yet even been constituted. This was a major setback, but very much in keeping with the well-established pattern of Iranian diversionary tactics.

At their first meeting with Bani-Sadr and Ghotbzadeh, the commission was joined by Bourguet and Villalon, intent on playing their part as intermediaries. Putting the best face on the Imam's announcement, Bani-Sadr tried to reassure the members of the commission that they should view it as a positive step because there was no longer any connection in Khomeini's mind between the release of the hostages and the extradition of the Shah. When Aguilar interjected that the introduction of the Majlis into the process would delay the release until April or even longer, Bani-Sadr referred to the 'secret plan which has been agreed upon and which Iran intends to carry out'. That let the cat out of the bag. The members of the commission suddenly realized that they were going through pre-planned paces, and wondered whether they were not participating in an artificial scenario rather than carrying out a meaningful assignment. The complicated scenario, as I feared, was starting to fall apart. There was dissension within the commission. Cordovez reported to me that the two co-chairmen were not seeing eye to eye, with Bedjaoui apparently willing to go altogether too far in meeting the Iranians' demands.

Everything now depended on the ability of Bani-Sadr and Ghotbzadeh to arrange a meeting with the hostages. It was set for 27 February, but two days earlier Ghotbzadeh informed the commission that he had run into problems. The students had reverted to the demand that the commission should interrogate the hostages. Since this had met with fundamental American opposition, the commission refused to agree. True to form, Ghotbzadeh suggested that they should accept the condition in order to gain access to the embassy but do as they wished once they got inside.

Wisely, the commission rejected this piece of duplicity. They began to realize that they would not gain access and that Ghotbzadeh once again was in no position to deliver on the Iranian pledges. He even hinted to them that, by being designated to make the necessary arrangements, the rival factions were setting him up as a convenient scapegoat.

The commission turned its attention to taking testimony from alleged SAVAK victims and the collection of information about Iranian grievances and alleged American misdeeds. They saw bank officials and the Iranian Attorney General, but obtained little documentary evidence of any value. Sensing that their house of cards was starting to collapse, Bourguet and Villalon began to look for excuses. They chose to accuse me of having departed from the scenario in my opening announcement, an accusation which was completely unfounded, as I had followed down to the last comma exactly what Bani-Sadr and the United States had wanted me to say. They also rounded on Ghotbzadeh and Bani-Sadr for always promising but never fulfilling their promises. Their own credit with Hamilton Jordan was at stake. They simply could not deliver, as I had expected from the start.

It seemed pointless for the commission to remain. On 4 March, more in hope than expectation, I suggested that they should stay a few more days. I felt that their presence gave us the only leverage we had with the authorities. Once they had gone, the pressure would be off. A couple of days later we thought that our patience might be rewarded. The militant students suddenly announced that the hostages would be turned over to the government. We drew up plans for their transfer and sent a physician to Teheran. Our optimism was short-lived.

On 10 March a broadcast in Khomeini's name demanded that the commission issue a statement on the crimes of the Shah and the history of United States intervention in Iran. Only after the Iranian people had by some means approved this statement would the commission be allowed to visit the hostages. Thus bolstered, the militants controlling the embassy disavowed their earlier agreement. Ghotbzadeh came on the telephone and implored me to persuade the commission to accept Khomeini's terms; he appeared much offended when I told him that this was out of the question. It was the end of the affair. The commission decided that it could do no more, although Bedjaoui objected, talking vaguely of some compromise formula. He was overruled by the other members and the commission left for New York on 12 March.

We held a post-mortem with Secretary Vance, discussing the obscure motivations of the principal participants and speculating fruitlessly on further action. The commission had been thwarted. Ghotbzadeh and Bani-Sadr had made commitments which they could not fulfil. And, as it turned out, Bourget and Villalon had no influence on the real power centre – Teheran. The Revolutionary Council had remained recalcitrant and Khomeini, always the powerful figure in the background, had played a cat-and-mouse game with everyone.

I instructed the commission not even to prepare a report. The enormous expenditure of effort, the complex arrangements, the Byzantine man-oeuvres had all come to nothing. The American government resorted to unilateral action. It broke off diplomatic relations with Iran, invalidated visas for its nationals and applied its own economic constraints.

I made one final attempt to revive contact. I met Ghotbzadeh in Belgrade on 8 May at the funeral of Marshal Tito. We agreed that one member of the commission might go back to Teheran to resume contact. His nomination was Adib Daoudy of Syria, whom they trusted and who was indeed an uncommonly level-headed man. He spent three weeks in Iran later in the month, but it was the same useless exercise, mired once again in a morass of confusion, intrigue and double-dealing. As far as action by the United Nations was concerned, we had reached the end of the line.

I had also provided a rod for my own back. Mohammed Bedjaoui was incensed at not being chosen for this one-man mission. The plain fact was that the Americans would not hear of it. Bedjaoui took it as a personal affront and I had no way of explaining the true reason to him. He reacted very bitterly and, when the question of my re-election as Secretary General for a third term arose, he went out of his way to mobilize as many representatives of the Third World against me as he could.

I have hardly any comment to make about the attempted American rescue by helicopter. Since it was organized in total secrecy, I obviously had no prior knowledge of it. That was probably just as well, as I would have opposed the whole operation. I had been in Teheran and knew the topography: to my mind there was no conceivable military plan which would have succeeded in extracting the hostages from their compound surrounded by their captors. The casualties would have been appalling.

The Shah died on 27 July 1980. In late September the Iraqis attacked Iran, initiating the long tragedy – the Gulf War. In the ensuing turmoil, the mullahs established even more firmly their dominance over the civilian officials. When the Security Council met to consider the outbreak of hostilities, the new Iranian Prime Minister, Mohammed Ali Rajai, came to New York to present his country's case. A faithful adherent of the religious leadership, a former teacher, he had never before set foot outside Iran.

He could not understand why the Iranians, so evidently the victims of aggression, did not get a more sympathetic reception. He complained of the injustice of the United Nations, but in two days of long talks with him I made it clear that as long as Iran continued to hold the hostages in the face of universal condemnation, he could expect little support for his griev-ances. Most of the representatives of the non-aligned countries made the same point. Rajai remained in New York only two days. He then returned home with the message that unless the hostages were released, Iran could expect scant support at the United Nations in its resistance to the Iraqi invasion.

In my opinion this was the turning point in the Iranian hostage crisis. Rajai was visibly shocked by the luke-warm reception he received in New York, not only by the Western representatives but also by his friends from the Third World. Everybody told him that he had to solve the hostage crisis in order to be accepted again by the international community. He was apparently able to convince Khomeini and the mullahs that the problem had to be solved without any further delay. The Iranians therefore decided to negotiate in earnest with the United States, and chose the Algerians as their intermediaries. The requirements for the satisfaction of Iranian grievances and admission of guilt by the United States went by the board. The negotiations were bilateral and the United Nations was not called upon to intervene.

Elaborate arrangements were made for settlement of the financial claims of each party against the other. A special international tribunal was set up under the auspices of the International Court of Justice to handle them. The hostages were finally freed on 20 January 1981, an operation timed to make sure that they did not arrive home until just after the inauguration of the new American President. It was a final act of vengeance against Jimmy Carter, whose political fortunes had come to be so closely linked with the fate of the captive Americans.

After the hostages had been released, Pierre Salinger of the American Broadcasting Company sharply criticized me and my actions in a television broadcast widely seen in the United States. Referring to a taped version of my meeting with the Revolutionary Council, he charged that I had not discussed the American proposals and had consequently misled them. It is literally true that I did not enumerate the proposals to the Council. This was because I had already presented them in full to Foreign Minister Ghotbzadeh in my two extensive meetings with him.

After explaining to me that he had fully informed and consulted with the Council, Ghotbzadeh had twice rejected the American proposals. There was no point, therefore, in my repeating them. The most useful thing I could do, it seemed to me, was to obtain the clearest possible exposition of the Council's views, for communication to the United States government. I knew that Ghotbzadeh had suggested to the Council that it should present the Iranian proposals to me.

I went over this ground with Pierre Salinger and showed him the record of my meetings with Ghotbzadeh. As a result of this discussion he did not repeat these accusations in his book, which was published a few months later. Soon afterward, I was told that it was Bourguet and Villalon who had sent the tapes of my meeting with the Revolutionary Council to President Carter in order to demonstrate how close their relations were with the Iranian rulers, rather than to discredit my mission.

The accusation of having panicked under the threat against my life lost all its credibility when President Carter himself and Secretary of State Cyrus Vance strongly condemned this allegation. They praised my courage and skilful behaviour during my stay in Teheran. I shall always be grateful to these two distinguished leaders for having spoken out so forcefully and without hesitation, thus putting the record straight.

What lessons can be drawn from the hostage crisis as far as the United Nations is concerned? In the early phases of the dispute, it had performed well. Through the Security Council and the International Court of Justice it had established the legal and political unacceptability of the forcible detention of diplomatic personnel and of the violation of diplomatic premises with the connivance of the host government. It had focused world-wide opprobrium on Iran. The Soviet veto had frustrated the imposition of economic sanctions and neither inside nor outside the United Nations had it been possible to organize collective economic measures against the Iranians.

The Americans took advantage of the United Nations machinery to seek a settlement of the problem by peaceful means. I did everything I could with my trip to Teheran, my many discussions with Iranian leaders and my sponsorship of the international commission of enquiry to keep the process alive. I do not see how we could have done more. No other channel of communication was any more successful in effecting the release of the hostages until the Iranians, on their own, decided the time had come to do so. The United Nations played no direct part in the *dénouement*.

We are left, to our dismay, with the upsurge of religious fundamentalism as an element in world politics. It carries a threat to the international community because of the acts of violence and terrorism it engenders. It is not only the Western world that feels endangered. Many moderate Arab governments are deeply worried by this development, particularly those round the Gulf like Saudi Arabia, Kuwait, Qatar and the United Arab Emirates. The invasion of the holy mosque at Mecca required a very serious effort on the part of the government of Saudi Arabia to defeat the terrorists.

We should not suppose that what is happening in the Moslem world is a new phenomenon. During the Crusades and the era of the Thirty Years' War, violence was endemic, totally at variance with the Christian doctrine of tolerance, understanding and love for one another. Its resurgence is a threat to world tranquillity.

In many Moslem countries, and not only Iran, the resurgence of fundamentalist thinking has political overtones. There is resistance to the Western way of life, which they fear can demoralize their inherited traditions and threaten their social fabric. Even those countries which have not succumbed to purely religious leadership tend to adopt a strict Moslem approach in order to stabilize their internal political situation. This fundamentalist movement has become a factor in international affairs which even the super-powers and their allies can ignore only at their peril.

Despite some reservations concerning certain procedures followed by American diplomacy to bring the hostages back, I enjoyed a closer and more intimate relationship with President Carter and the members of his administration than with his predecessors or successor. This was largely due to the more constructive view that he took of the part the United

Nations could play in international affairs and the absence of any reservations on his part concerning the posture the UN Organization had to adopt from time to time in view of its substantial majority of Third World and non-aligned nations.

He was particularly well served by his Secretary of State, Cyrus Vance. He and I had been sincere friends before the Iranian crisis and during its long course our rapport became even closer. He was possessed of high intelligence and a clear legal mind, a modest and unassuming manner and a refreshing willingness to cut through protocol to accomplish an objective. We were in frequent communication on the telephone. If I was not available he was happy to relay his messages through one of my subordinates in the interest of making rapid progress. He spoke and acted with dignity and restraint. He did not stand on ceremony, but was quietly tenacious in pursuing his ends, always assured and relaxed whenever we met. He had a strongly developed sense of the long-range importance of the United Nations if it was used in the right way. His approach to the matters that came before us was never carping and always constructive.

He was a strong influence at the beginning of the Carter administration and enjoyed the full confidence of the President. The Iranian hostage crisis brought a gradual erosion of that position. The commando operation in Iran was the watershed. He was on vacation when it was launched and he shared my doubts about its wisdom. As much as I liked Edmund Muskie as an experienced and honest parliamentarian, I was stunned by the courageous decision of Cyrus Vance to quit. In the final months of the presidency, it was the national security adviser, Zbigniew Brzezinski, who superseded him in the President's counsels.

The complex machinations in which President Carter became involved in an attempt to resolve the Iranian hostage crisis, of which I considered myself to some extent to be the victim, must not be allowed to detract from the broader feelings of warmth I had for his personality. His humanitarian concern for the fate of his countrymen held hostage in Iran was extraordinary. The American ethos lays great stress on the welfare of the individual. The rage and frustration felt by the American public at the powerlessness of its government to redress the insult to its national dignity had to be the primary concern of any President in office.

Jimmy Carter's reactions went far beyond considerations of political expediency. There was no mistaking his spiritual agony during the long-drawn-out process of obtaining the hostages' release. It is an irony of history that the supreme efforts made by his administration to resolve this problem were perhaps the major factor in bringing it to defeat in the election of 1980.

Like other mortal men, Jimmy Carter had his flaws. Mastery of detail was one of his strongest assets, sometimes, it seemed, to the point that he could not see the wood for the trees. Perhaps because of his honesty and a deep sense of justice he was given to indecisiveness, or at least a tendency to change course at a time or in ways harmful to his stature.

At the personal level, Carter seemed to lack the ability to perceive himself and his office as others did. His habit of jogging in public, especially in foreign capitals, did little to enhance his prestige. In the solitude of Camp David it was unobjectionable, but the public display of the Head of State of the most powerful country in the world running about the streets in a sweat shirt, shorts and headband was counter-productive.

Much stands to his credit and will in due course find recognition. The Panama Canal treaty removed an irritant in the United States' relationship with Latin America, and the Camp David agreement with President Sadat and Prime Minister Begin provided an impressive demonstration of negotiating skill under the most difficult circumstances. The SALT II treaty, although unfortuantely never ratified, represented a rare breakthrough in the field of arms control. Carter was a kind-hearted, well-meaning man with an abhorrence of violence, whose obsession with negotiation and communication was not understood by the American people. As a born-again Christian with a belief in the perfectibility of man, his views on international problems were shaped by an underlying idealism which contrasted sharply with the orientation of American policy towards the United Nations in the immediately preceding years. This idealism was tempered, not unnaturally, by the subsequent buffeting of hard realities. My own feeling is that history will be much kinder to Jimmy Carter than his contemporaries have been as a result of his far-sighted policy initiatives.

12

Anarchy in the Gulf

The outbreak of war between Iraq and Iran in September 1980 may have been the catalyst that helped to solve the American hostage crisis in Teheran. However, it has developed into a major conflict, seriously undermining the tranquillity of the riparian states of the Persian Gulf in particular and the Middle East in general, and adversely affecting the interests of all oil-importing nations.

As with most regional conflicts, the seeds of war were sown long ago. Iraq and Iran have long disputed the location of the common border which runs along the confluence of the Tigris and Euphrates rivers – the Shatt-el-Arab. Starting as a confrontation between the Ottoman rulers (in Iraq) and the Persian Empire, the continuing issue was whether the frontier followed the river's median line or the low-water mark on the Iranian shore. It was in 1969 that Iran denounced the last of a series of boundary treaties, dating from 1939, which once more failed to demarcate clearly the border between the two countries. Nearly five years later, in February 1974, Iraq complained to the Security Council of acts of military aggression by Iran against its territory. In response, Iran claimed that Iraq had violated its frontiers and was engaged in terrorism, sabotage, the expulsion of Iranian nationals and the encouragemnet of movements opposed to the regime of the Shah. The United Nations was able to intervene in this earlier conflict with signal success. The Security Council instructed me to appoint a special representative to investigate the situation and I chose Ambassador Luis Weckmann-Muñoz, whom I had known as the Mexican envoy to Austria when I was Foreign Minister in 1968. He paid several visits to Baghdad and Teheran, made field trips to the frontier areas where the skirmishes had taken place and persuaded the two governments to reach an agreement.

Each undertook to observe a cease-fire, withdraw their armed forces from the border areas, refrain from hostile actions and resume negotiations for a comprehensive settlement of all bilateral issues. This was ostensibly formalized in 1975, when agreement was reached between President Saddam Hussein of Iraq and the late Shah Mohamed Reza Pahlavi of Iran: the border would conform to the median line. Other elements of the accord, however, led to the tragic conflict which later generated strategic waves far from the shores of the Gulf. The provision that Iran would cease aiding the Kurdish rebels in Iraq led by Mullah Mustafa al-Barzani posed no significant difficulty. But, for its part, Baghdad promised to expel the exiled Iranian cleric Ayatollah Ruhollah Khomeini. The fundamentalist religious leader of Iran's Shi'ite Moslem majority, long an avowed opponent of the Shah as well as of any secular regime in the Persian state, had been living in southern Iraq, from where he continued his messianic campaign. After having been banished by Hussein, the Ayatollah moved to Paris, where he began to fashion the revolution which ultimately drove the Shah from the Peacock Throne. The successful Khomeini, however, also brought with him to Teheran an abiding hatred for Saddam Hussein and a determination to see his government brought down and replaced by a fundamentalist Islamic regime similar to the one Khomeini was busily imposing on Iran.

Indeed, relations between the two neighbouring countries deteriorated when Khomeini's Islamic exhortations inevitably aroused favourable sentiments among the Shi'ites in southern Iraq. The mullahs' revolution in Teheran threatened the secular, Sunni-dominated Iraqi government with a sectarian upheaval. It jeopardized Saddam Hussein's aspirations to build a strong, unified country and it threatened Iraq's bid to dominate the Gulf region and lead the Arab world. President Hussein and his advisers no doubt thought a quick victory was possible when Iran, after the Shah's collapse, appeared to dissolve in turmoil and disorganization, being internationally isolated and with a demoralized army.

Long before the Iraqi President miscalculated so badly, I had met him in Baghdad. He was a somewhat impressive personality. He was tall and looked like a heavyweight boxer. He had a disconcerting habit. We were all sitting round a huge conference table in his office when he suddenly jumped up in the middle of our conversation and started to run round the table. I must have looked surprised, but he smiled and said, 'I am sorry, but I have a problem with a slipped disc. If I sit for more than an hour, I have to get up to stretch my legs and do some exercises to loosen my back' – which is exactly what he did, walking and trotting round the table several times, whirling his arms, before he sat down again and continued the conversation.

He did not hide his dissatisfaction with the 1975 agreement which, signed as he said under duress, restricted the Iraqis to the western bank of the disputed waterway, with the Iranians on the eastern bank and the national border running down the middle of the river.

After weeks of sporadic clashes and bitter rhetoric in the media, in which Iran invoked religious slogans against the 'atheistic' rulers of Iraq and Baghdad countered with nationalistic slogans against 'the Persian racists' harbouring 'a buried resentment for the Arabs', Iraqi forces struck across the border on 22 September 1980 in a massive invasion of Iranian territory.

Iraq managed to occupy some territory on the eastern bank of the Shatt-al-Arab, but it failed to capture the strategic city of Abadan. And as long as the Iranians held it, the waterway could be blockaded and Iraq's major objective would remain unfulfilled. So, after some initial gains, stalemate ensued. Urged on by the mullahs, the Iranians summoned up a wave of military fervour and the Iraqi President found that he had a major war on his hands.

The Security Council passed resolutions and issued appeals, the Organization of the Islamic Conference and the Non-Aligned Movement attempted to intervene but, as in all these cases when the instigating party has not reached its goals and the defender has not been able to recoup its losses, neither side is likely to listen to pleas for peace. I was in direct contact with both parties. Iraq at this phase still enjoyed the military advantage and Hussein informed me on 29 September 1980 that he was ready to halt hostilities immediately if Iran did the same. The Iranian reply from my old sparring partner, President Bani-Sadr, was much less accommodating. As long as Iraqi aggression continued, the proposals of the Security Council could not be considered.

The Iranians were deeply aggrieved because the Security Council resolution had not demanded the withdrawal of Iraqi forces to the positions they had occupied before the start of hostilities. This underlined the difficulties confronting a would-be peace-maker. Neither the Council nor I wished to take up a position on the substance of the dispute at this early stage. To have done so would have prejudiced the possibility of mediation. We intended our silence to reflect a neutral position. It was regarded as hostile by the Iranians. It was a dilemma from which there was no escape.

The problem took on international dimensions. As a result of the fighting, eighty-six ships flying twenty-two different flags had been immobilized in the Shatt-al-Arab with bombs and shells falling all round them. I appealed to both governments to respect the security of peaceful shipping and agree to a local cease-fire until the vessels could leave. Bani-Sadr indicated that Iran would not hinder safe passage under the United Nations flag. Hussein would not agree. The ships must fly the Iraqi flag as long as they were in the waterway, since it was an Iraqi river. The flag question alone became one of the most complex issues with which we had to deal.

We were thus faced with complete deadlock. In my judgement the best chance to break it lay not with the cumbersome and largely public proceedings of the Security Council but in a patient mediation effort conducted by a disinterested, high-level political figure. We went through lists of names, and one day, as I was chatting informally with the deputy US representative in New York, Ambassador William Van den Heuvel, he suggested the name of Olof Palme of Sweden. It was in many ways a generous and unexpected proposal. Palme had been the Socialist Prime Minister of his country, well known for his very outspoken foreign policy, a great defender of the Arab cause in the Middle East, a supporter of the Palestine Liberation Organization, an opponent of the American intervention in Vietnam, and something of a thorn in the side of successive American administrations.

If the Americans would tolerate him, I saw a loophole. I proceeded with infinite caution, first contacting Palme through the Swedish Ambassador in New York. He responded positively. Palme was at that time the leader of the opposition, and I was not certain that the successor government, headed by Prime Minister Thorbjörn Fälldin, would welcome the appointment of their principal political opponent as a mediator. No problem arose, and the Conservative government in Sweden was most co-operative.

Palme accepted the mission, to which I also assigned Diego Cordovez, who had represented the Secretariat with such merit and skill as the co-ordinator of the UN mission on the hostage crisis. The prospect was daunting. Palme came to New York and we worked out a detailed plan of action for halting the hostilities and setting up negotiations to arrive at a general settlement. The contestants accepted his appointment and Palme left for the scene of conflict.

Olof Palme was assiduous and dedicated. He conducted no less than five separate rounds of negotiations in the two capitals during my remaining term of office and even after. The first phase was complicated by the parallel efforts of the Cuban Foreign Minister, whose country was in the chair of the Non-Aligned Movement, and Yasser Arafat, head of the Palestine Liberation Organization, with their rival schemes. Palme contented himself with listening rather than making detailed proposals.

When he reported back, we felt we might be able to isolate the problem of the blockaded merchant ships. The UN offered to provide observers to monitor a cease-fire over the Shatt-al-Arab waterway. This proved unacceptable. Then they attempted to organize a sailing schedule which would ensure their safe passage. The expense involved would have been high and this gave rise to an extraordinary set of competing mathematical calculations. Normally, in such instances, the parties concerned seek to hold their financial commitments to a minimum. In this instance the reverse was true. Iraq, claiming sovereignty over the Shatt-al-Arab, insisted that it must meet the entire cost of the operation. Iran, asserting its sovereignty, was just as adamant in insisting that the cost must be shared equally. Palme was indefatigable. He suggested a joint fund, or alternatively contributions from other UN members. Lloyd's of London were brought in to organize funding from the maritime insurance companies. Neither country would accept any of these proposals.

Iraq rejected the use of the United Nations flag on the ground that it would internationalize what should be a domestic matter. When we floated the idea of flying the Red Cross, the International Committee objected that its use had to be restricted to purely humanitarian purposes. In the end even they agreed, but the plan foundered on the original question of cost-sharing.

The diplomatic and military negotiations were even more tortuous. We tried to get agreement on broad generalities and the establishment of buffer zones. That collapsed in disagreement on where the actual boundary lines lay. Neither side was disposed to make compromises for the sake of a settlement. The Iraqis acted as if they were negotiating from strength. They expected the Iranians to show flexibility. The Revolutionary Government in Teheran approached the conflict from an absolutist outlook. For them it was straightforward – good against evil – hardly compatible with a mediator's search for balance and mutual accommodation. The situation was then confounded by internal dissension in Teheran, with the dismissal of President Bani-Sadr by the parliament and the assassination of senior clerical leaders.

When administrative order had been restored and the Iranians had succeeded in recouping some of their original military losses, Palme paid another visit to the area in February 1982 to present a further refinement of his proposals. Again this effort failed and faced by the impasse, Olof Palme told both governments that he saw no purpose in returning to their capitals unless they could give him clear signs of a political will to reach a negotiated settlement.

The Gulf War has taught politicians, diplomats and generals all over the world a whole series of lessons. Presumably the most important of these is that, despite the daily growth in the armaments of the two super-powers, they are themselves unable or unwilling to prevent the occurrence of a shooting war or of stopping one that has broken out. This contradicts the earlier view – widely held – of the effectiveness of the 'peace through fear' guaranteed by the balance of atomic deterrence of the super-powers in areas where their fundamental interests are at stake.

Many explanations have been offered of their failure to mediate. The attention of both super-powers was distracted by other events in the first phase of the Gulf War – the USSR was preoccupied with developments in Afghanistan and Poland, and the USA with the hostage affair and the changing of the guard at the White House. Also, the growing frostiness of East-West relations seemed to make both super-powers reluctant to enter into a dialogue about joint crisis-management in the Gulf. Both found it better, in view of the high risk of more active intervention in the Gulf drama, to observe the Irani-Iraqi war from a safe distance – and to keep a watchful eye on the reactions of the other – but not to intervene in favour of either party. Both speak of their 'strict neutrality'. True, the USA tends rather to support Iraq, in order to lay a pro-American *cordon sanitaire* of Arab countries along the Gulf some day and thus also to consolidate the independence of the small Gulf States. But at the same time, Washington does not wish to take any action against Khomeini's revolutionary regime in Iran, so as not to provoke a *rapprochement* between Teheran and Moscow. Equally, while the Soviet Union is disinclined to drop Iraq, which has been its ally so far, in view of the political unpredictability of Iran it demurs at giving up its option in Iran completely, especially with an eye to the time after Khomeini.

Failure to bring about a diplomatic solution to the Gulf War does not lie exclusively with the intransigence of the belligerents and the super-powers' inability to agree to some form of crisis management. The longer the fighting continues, the more convinced some observers have become that certain international parties find it most opportune and will continue to do so as long as the battle remains geographically limited and without any clear issue.

Some fifty states have shown themselves willing to supply arms on a large or small scale and thus fan the flames of conflict in the Gulf. Countless governments and sections of the economy publicly welcome the weakening of the Organization of Oil Exporting Countries as a result of the war. Furthermore, the oil-rich states' revenue, which upset the major financial markets in the 1970s, is now being invested in the purchase of arms.

The conflict between Iraq and Iran has led to festerings elsewhere, not only in the Lebanon. The friction between the Iranian revolution and the Iraqi pan-Arabism has led to a new rift in the Arab world and a new imponderable in the Israeli-Palestinian drama.

Many governments in East and West had hoped that the marathon war in the Gulf would check, if not sink, the advance of the anti-Western and anti-Communist Islamic revolution. This was a significant error: each day's fighting brought with it anew the global threat of religious fanaticism that had long been thought dead. If the conflict cannot be solved through negotiations, the whole world could one day find itself held hostage to an awesome Holy War.

13

Afghanistan: Reagan v. Brezhnev

It was my first meeting with Ronald Reagan at the White House – for the fourth time during my term of office a new President in the Oval Office; for the fourth time the sounding-out process, testing each other's reactions. The fire crackled softly in the hearth. It was in the last days of April 1981. I was fully aware that Reagan was no great admirer of the United Nations. Although his attitude was friendly, even cordial, he immediately started to criticize the world organization. 'It is heavily biased in favour of the Third World,' he said, 'and lacks the moral authority which the world expects from it.' Alexander Haig, the Secretary of State, and Jeane Kirkpatrick, the US Ambassador to the United Nations, nodded approvingly. Reagan was not against resuming the dialogue with Moscow but, as he quickly added, 'certainly not under the present circumstances. The Soviets have gravely violated international law,' he said, 'invading Afghanistan, supporting the Vietnamese invasion in Kampuchea and engaging in subversive activities in Central America. Clearly this is something the United States cannot tolerate.' After I had seemingly unsuccessfully tried to convince the President of the merits of the world organization, I asked him whether there was any kind of message he wanted me to convey to General Secretary Leonid Brezhnev, whom I would be seeing a few days later. 'Tell him,' he said, in a rather relaxed mood, leaning comfortably back in his chair, 'that I am not against the dialogue with Moscow. However, this can only be done if the Russians make some positive gestures towards us. The field of gestures is wide open from Afghanistan to Kampuchea or Central America.'

Six days later, on 5 May 1981, I was seated in Leonid Brezhnev's office in the Kremlin. The whole atmosphere was more formal, but the attitude towards the United Nations less critical than in Washington. When I conveyed Reagan's message, Brezhnev blushed and jumped up from his seat, walking round the conference table in a highly emotional way. He rejected Reagan's demand for some gesture in advance of new negotiations. Gromyko and Brezhnev's *chef de cabinet*, Aleksandrov, reacted to this angry response with stony faces.

The problem of Afghanistan heavily overshadowed the last two years of my Secretary Generalship. While the United Nations in its long history was repeatedly able to play a helpful role in regional disputes, it lacked any real influence in regard to the Afghanistan question – despite all the strenuous efforts by such excellent UN diplomats as Pérez de Cuellar and, after him, Diego Cordovez.

The Soviet Union had been attempting to stabilize the Marxist rule in Afghanistan ever since it was established in 1978, but struggles for power among the local factions and resistance from fundamentalist Moslem tribesmen had hampered the attainment of this objective. In the last week of December 1979, when the internal power struggle reached its peak, Soviet troops entered the country. An Afghan Communist leader, Babrak Karmal, was brought back from Czechoslovakia and installed as Prime Minister.

This was the first Soviet military invasion outside the post-World-War-II boundaries of the Communist bloc. It provoked a sharp reaction in the international community and broke the tacit alliance of the Marxist countries with the Third World majority in the United Nations, ranged against the industrialized West. Now it was the Soviets who became the object of the United Nations disapproval. Spearheaded by the Moslem members supporting their Afghan co-religionaries, the non-aligned nations brought the invasion before the Security Council, requiring that foreign forces should immediately be withdrawn from Afghanistan. They rejected the Soviet contention that their troops had entered the country at the request of the newly constituted Afghan government to protect it from intervention in the country's internal affairs by the United States, China and others.

The smaller members of the United Nations were gripped by a sense of fear. Who knew which of them might some day suffer occupation by the forces of a major power? They felt a need to respond vigorously; the United Nations was the most effective instrument at their disposal. On 7 January 1980, a Security Council resolution calling for the withdrawal of all foreign troops to enable the people of Afghanistan to establish their own form of government was vetoed by the Soviet Union. The majority on the Council therefore decided, by a procedural resolution not subject to the veto, to summon a special session of the General Assembly.

Within a week the Assembly had passed a similar resolution by a vote of 104 to 18, with eighteen abstentions. It also appealed to all countries to respect the non-aligned character of Afghanistan and to refrain from interference in its internal affairs, and it urged all parties to bring about conditions permitting the speedy return of refugees and the organization of humanitarian aid.

At the beginning of February I received a letter from President Karmal containing the standard statement of his position:

> The Minister of Foreign Affairs of the Democratic Republic of Afghanistan during his recent visit to New York and meeting Your Excellency had occasion to explain facts concerning recent developments in Afghanistan and flagrant interventions by imperialism headed by US imperialism, international reaction and reaction in regions and circles related to it in Afghanistan's internal affairs, creating dangers on Afghanistan's frontier and compelling the Democratic Republic of Afghanistan to request, in conformity with provisions of the Treaty of Friendship, Good Neighbourliness and Co-operation between the Democratic Republic of Afghanistan and the Soviet Union, and provisions under Article 51 of the UN Charter, limited contingents of Soviet Union armed forces for repelling threats to the independence, national sovereignty and territorial integrity of Afghanistan.
>
> I should like to bring to Your Excellency's attention some of the new measures taken by the Democratic Republic of Afghanistan following the release of more than 15,000 political prisoners. Realizing that a number of Afghans, due to oppression and brutality by Amin's band, were compelled to leave their beloved country Afghanistan and take refuge abroad, the Democratic Republic of Afghanistan, in an official statement, sincerely and categorically declares that all clergy, mullahs, scholars, tribes' elders and all nationals of the country will be accorded full respect when they return. Their freedom and full security is guaranteed and their rank, position and property will be restored . . .

The General Assembly resolution had requested me to keep its members informed of progress in its implementation but had given no guidance as to how its provisions might be carried out. Although it did not specifically mention the USSR, there was no mistaking where the Assembly's sympathies lay. It would clearly be resented by Moscow and the Karmal regime and it would not be easy to gain their co-operation in useful action.

The American government was pressing me to devise some form of approach and within the Secretariat we explored a number of avenues that might be useful. The difficulty was how to initiate a dialogue between the parties involved when we clearly could not link our initiative in any explicit way with a General Assembly resolution which had been adopted over the objections of one side. We considered sending a mission to Kabul, either on its own or in conjunction with the International Committee of the Red Cross. This, however, offered no immediate hope of progress.

The Non-Aligned Movement, under Cuban leadership that year, was still too divided for concerted action. The Islamic Conference of Foreign Ministers, meeting in Islamabad, suspended Afghanistan's membership and invited its members to withhold recognition of Karmal's regime as well as denying it economic aid. The Foreign Ministers of the European Community endorsed the General Assembly resolution and urged the Soviet Union to comply. In April 1980 President Castro of Cuba informed me he was seeking to exercise his good offices on the basis that the problem was one between Afghanistan and Pakistan, an interpretation that ran counter to the opinion of the international community and especially of the Islamic Conference. None of these initiatives made any headway.

The Soviet Union and the Afghan authorities insisted that the root problem was one of outside interference from Pakistani territory, for which the United States and China were blamed. They did announce a plan for a political settlement in May 1980 involving trilateral talks between Afghanistan, Iran and Pakistan, the return of Afghan refugees under an amnesty, an end to outside interference, and political guarantees from other states, including the United States and the Soviet Union. This would lead to the withdrawal of Soviet troops, but only once a political settlement had been reached. The United Nations majority insisted on the reverse order: for them the main emphasis was laid on Soviet withdrawal.

Close to three million refugees, approximately one fifth of the entire population of the country, had meanwhile fled from Afghanistan, predominantly to Pakistan and to a lesser extent to Iran. In Pakistan the cost of feeding them approached a million dollars a day. With the help of the office of the High Commissioner for Refugees and the World Food Programme, together with other international agencies, about half that sum has been raised by the world community. The other half remains a burden on the country of asylum. The task of Poul Hartling, the dedicated High Commissioner for Refugees, was not made easier by Soviet and Afghan accusations that the refugees were receiving military training and arms and returning to take part in the resistance movement. I have no doubt that this is an element in the conflict but no one connected with the United Nations has had any part in it.

I had numerous conversations with the Soviet Ambassador in New York, Oleg Troyanovskiy, and succeeded to some extent in bringing home to him the serious effect on Soviet standing at the UN if Moscow continued to adopt a negative attitude to the expressed feelings of the non-aligned majority. I have to say that Troyanovsky, a quiet, shrewd, highly intelligent man, handled his difficult brief well. He never acknowledged that the USSR had done anything wrong, but claimed that they and their friends in Afghanistan were the victims of imperialist threats from outside. However, I did get him to indicate that Moscow might be willing to accept some kind of United Nations mission providing it was not directly connected with the General Assembly resolution and that it dealt with the alleged threat to Afghanistan's frontiers as one of its concerns. I found myself subjected to mounting Western criticism for the lack of any concrete action, but I held to my view that the clash of opposing views was still too acute for any peace-making initiative to get very far. My position was much reinforced on 20 November 1980 when the General Assembly adopted a supplementary resolution specifically authorizing me to appoint a special representative to promote a political solution.

We were still not out of the wood. The Soviet delegation made it absolutely clear that it rejected the text of the resolution and particularly the appointment of a special representative. The Afghan authorities indicated that the only way to start negotiations would be for me to visit the area personally in order to reconcile the provisions of their own proposals in May and those of the General Assembly. This was not a procedure that commended itself to the Western countries, who felt that any visit of mine would further legitimize the Karmal regime. (I had in mind the discouraging precedent of the failure, after the national uprising in Hungary in 1956, to persuade the authorities there to accept a UN special representative. The unfortunate Sir Leslie Munroe of New Zealand had been nominated prematurely and never even got to the country.)

I obtained a hint of the intransigent Russian attitude from Mr Gromyko and his aides when they came to New York in the autumn of 1980 to attend the General Assembly. This was mainly done at private meetings or social events and I was able to impress on them the damage that was being done to the Soviet reputation at the United Nations. I have always had a very good working relationship with Gromyko. From my talks with him I got the impression that although Moscow would not agree formally to the appointment of a special representative, in certain circumstances they might not object to it.

In the new year of 1981, the pieces began to fall into place. The Pakistani President, Zia Ul Haq, made his own representations to the Russians and the Afghans and moved them in the direction of a dialogue under the aegis of the United Nations, on the understanding that the Kabul representatives would act in their capacity as party leaders in order to ease the problem of their international status.

In February 1981 I met them all in New Delhi, where I had arrived to deliver an address at the meeting commemorating the twentieth anniversary of the Non-Aligned Movement. The principal antagonists were still poles apart on matters of substance but they were willing to talk about the possibilities of a settlement. The problem remained of appointing a representative when one side would have nothing to do with it.

In diplomacy, finding the right phraseology often permits a compromise. It occurred to me that by describing my envoy as a 'personal representative' rather than the 'special representative' called for in the UN resolution we could have it both ways. This deliberate ambiguity would allow one side to assume that I was proceeding as directed by the Assembly while the other side could assume that I was not. This indeed solved the problem. All sides, including the Soviets, indicated their agreement. My choice was Javier Pérez de Cuellar, who had acquitted himself so well in Cyprus and Zimbabwe. He found his title ingenious. 'You should announce it at once,' he said, 'before there is any time for the parties to split hairs about its significance.'

We tried first to involve the Iranians, but the Revolutionary Government resisted strongly any attempt to bring them in. They had religious ties with the Afghans and had become a country of first asylum for hundreds of thousands of refugees. They regarded the Karmal regime as mere puppets of the Soviet Union and saw no reason to participate in any negotiations. They did come in later, but not with any commitment.

Pérez de Cuellar visited Kabul and Islamabad in April 1981 to get the talks started on the basis of the General Assembly resolution. The Afghans stated that they were prepared to accept the good offices of the Secretary General, and there was general agreement that for the time being at least Afghan resistance representatives would not participate in the talks. In May 1981 I went to Moscow accompanied by Pérez de Cuellar. This was a welcome opportunity to discuss the delicate situation with the Kremlin leaders. In my talks with Andrey Gromyko I obtained Soviet acquiescence to negotiations between Afghanistan and Pakistan, 'with the partici-pation' of the Secretary General's personal representative.

In a follow-up mission made by Perez de Cuellar in August 1981, it turned out that the parties, except for some procedural concessions, were unwilling to change their basic attitude. Since then the Mujahaddin and the Soviet forces have dominated the scene.

My visit to Moscow brought my last encounter with Leonid Brezhnev before I left office at the end of that year. On my various visits to the Soviet Union, Brezhnev impressed me as one of the most careful and conservative of men. His advent in the seventies had produced a pronounced change in the Soviet style of leadership. There was, contrary to Khrushchev's approach, no likelihood of his antagonizing the Soviet power structure and he would not move until he was sure of support from his own ranks.

The meetings at the Kremlin were very formal, across a long table, with Brezhnev leading at the top of the line, Gromyko to his left and his *chef de cabinet*, Aleksandrov, next to him. I sat opposite Brezhnev, with Pérez de Cuellar to my right, followed by Ustinov, my Soviet Under Secretary General.

Brezhnev always followed his brief closely, speaking from a prepared text very slowly, and sometimes stopping, because he already had problems with his breathing. I would respond and whenever I made a point he did not like he would discard his script and comment spontaneously, as he did when I conveyed Reagan's message to him. Brezhnev's emotional reaction, already mentioned earlier in this chapter, illustrated the experience of most Westerners called upon to deal with the Kremlin. Whatever the reason, the Soviets are highly sensitive to questions of status and prestige where the two super-powers are concerned. Anything implying less than full equality or reciprocity of treatment is unacceptable to them. How could Reagan ask for some gesture in Afghanistan, Kampuchea or Central America? The USSR was a sovereign power and could not accept conditions put forward by another. That was really the end of this particular initiative, and although I had long talks subsequently with Gromyko in his office, on Afghanistan he was immovable.

Apart from rare outbursts of this nature, Brezhnev was normally restrained and soft-spoken, though direct in his personal conversations. The leaders of most major nations behave with a personal modesty and simplicity that belies their heavy responsibilities. My last view of Brezhnev was typical. Soon after our formal meeting, Gromyko invited me to freshen up in a private room not far from Brezhnev's office, since my party was due to go on to a performance of Tolstoi's *War and Peace* by the Bolshoi Theatre in the main Kremlin hall. Emerging with my colleagues a few minutes later, I noticed Brezhnev walking alone in the corridor ahead of me, quietly and slowly and apparently with some difficulty. He was heading towards the elevator, which had been held at that level for me so that I could leave the building.

As I passed him, I turned round to bid him farewell for the second time. He clearly thought I had already left and looked surprised. Since I do not speak Russian and the interpreters had gone, I could do little but say '*dos vidanya*'. He responded with a few words in Russian, smiled and shuffled to the elevator. The attendant apologized. They thought I had departed earlier and the lift was required for President Brezhnev. I understood perfectly. Walking downstairs was no problem, but my final sight of Brezhnev was that of a sick man, walking alone towards his destiny.

Brezhnev's physical condition was deteriorating visibly, although I have to say that on this occasion he appeared to me to be in somewhat better shape than during my previous visit. In a democratic society a man with his infirmities would long since have left office. He presumably stayed on because of the traumatic problem of succession in the USSR. Once the Chairman controls the levers of power, it is very difficult to ease him out. The same appears to be true of the majority of the top leadership. Most of the senior Soviet officials are old men and their conservatism is not surprising.

If there was one deep impression which I took away from Moscow after this visit of 1981, it was that of the enormous continuity which was so visible not only through the presence of the Soviet old guard, but also through the approach to all the basic political problems of the world. In fact, this was no surprise to me. What I saw and heard was reconfirmation of my previous experience. Whenever age, illness or death requires a change of leadership, there may be a change of style but surely not of substance.

It was only a few months before my visit to Moscow that, with the inauguration of President Reagan in January 1981, the political pendulum of the other super-power took one of those sharp swings which sometimes bewilder foreigners. The new administration was at best wary and distrustful of the United Nations and at worst downright hostile and contemptuous. The new President's term of office coincided with the remainder of mine for only a year, but it became abundantly clear that a complete reorientation of policy was under way. There was a much greater emphasis on a bilateral approach in foreign affairs.

Although I met President Reagan on a number of occasions, my contacts with him were limited. Having met him at the Oval Office and, in a much more relaxed manner, at Cancun, my general assessment of him is mixed. He has an admirable, easy personal presence and an unsurpassed ability to use and enjoy humour as an element in political discourse, but his lack of prior diplomatic experience and his conservative approach to political affairs initially shaped his thinking in a very basic way. I believe he has little appreciation for multilateral diplomacy and its role in the solution of global problems. His mind appears to run to traditional diplomacy, supplemented in some cases by regional action. Ideology bulks large in his decisions. For him the Afghan crisis was, I believe, a showcase of Moscow's disregard for the principles of international behaviour. To counter his fear that on most issues the UN membership appeared hostile to the US because of the organization's 'automatic majority' of unfriendly Third World countries, I pointed out to him that the great majority of them had voted with the United States and the West, condemned the presence of foreign forces in Afghanistan and Kampuchea and called for their withdrawal.

The President remained sceptical. His mind was obviously made up and he was not much moved by my arguments. However, I could not but be impressed by his friendly tone throughout our conversation and the understanding he expressed for my personal efforts to find solutions to these problems.

As one of his first official acts, the President had appointed Professor Jeane Kirkpatrick of Georgetown University as the US Ambassador to the United Nations. We viewed her nomination with a degree of unease and suspicion, for she was known as the exponent of a hard-line conservative approach to foreign policy. Indeed, she quickly established herself as a most outspoken and highly undiplomatic representative. She had neither UN nor bi-lateral diplomatic experience, and the same was true of many of her new staff. She was distinctly reserved and somewhat condescending in some of her personal contacts, a considerable handicap at the UN, where the representatives mingle and talk freely, even when their governments are on bad terms. She was continually shuttling between New York and Washington to fulfil her duties as a member of the cabinet and the National Security Council. This cut down on the time she had available for meeting other UN Ambassadors, and this was resented. As in other realms of officialdom, there is no substitute for contacts at the top.

She discussed this with me, complaining of what she termed her 'no-win situation'. She was constantly being forced to choose between losing her access to and influence with the administration in Washington and restricting contacts with colleagues in the United Nations. She regarded the latter as a lesser evil – an understandable choice, but it did not improve her relationships in New York.

She was a powerful, often brilliant spokesperson for the policies of the Reagan administration. A strong supporter of Israel, she resisted the attacks on South Africa and on right-wing dictatorships in Central and South America, nor did she shy away from criticism of the Third World. She particularly resented the actions of those delegates who, yielding to group pressures in New York, violently castigated the United States and voted against it in the Security Council or the General Assembly at the same time as their Heads of State or Foreign Ministers were assuring the American Ambassadors in their own capitals of firm support. She insisted at considerable length that if these countries wanted co-operation and assistance from the United States they should match it by acting in a more friendly spirit at the United Nations. It was not an argument calculated to evoke warm enthusiasm among her colleagues.

I have to say in her defence that she was a quick learner. She did not change her basic attitudes but became much more accommodating in manner. Long before she left the UN she recognized the importance of establishing friendly personal co-operation and, without abandoning her tough substantive position, her methods became noticeably more flexible with the passage of time.

If I have dwelt at some length on the peace-making process in the Gulf and Afghanistan, and on the attitude of some of the key players in

Washington and Moscow, it has been to illustrate how laborious and often unrewarding such activities of the United Nations can be. It is only too easy to brush aside as meaningless the seemingly interminable, sometimes ritualistic steps the world organization has to take in these situations. That is a misreading of our work. In every international dispute, a window of opportunity eventually opens and the moment occurs when accommodation is possible. If, through quiet, intensive diplomacy, the issues have been clarified, the potential points of compromise explored, the underlying objectives and priorities of the contending parties investigated, the possibility of agreement is enhanced. We can seldom foresee with clarity when such opportunities will present themselves, but it is the duty of the United Nations to be prepared to make the most of them when they do.

The Soviet intervention in Afghanistan was a turning point in the political mechanics of the United Nations. The alliance between the non-aligned Third World countries and the Soviet bloc has been weakened by the crisis in Afghanistan and the invasion of Kampuchea. One of the tragic ironies of this problem is the fact that the United Nations, purely for legalistic reasons, still recognizes the deposed regime of Pol Pot as the legitimate government of Kampuchea, despite the hideous massacre of half the population by those leaders.

Obviously there are changes in the political climate of the world organization. The United Nations human rights agencies, which once carefully avoided any mention of Marxist practices, have begun to discuss them openly. It can no longer be said that the United Nations condemns authoritarian practices in right-wing dictatorships only, while turning a blind eye towards the authoritarianism of the left.

14

The Lebanon Tragedy

For many reasons, the Lebanon crisis was one of the greatest and most unusual challenges I had to face. The status of the PLO, one of the main belligerents, was in dispute. Lebanon, the scene of the war, was in complete disarray. The UN peace-keeping force, sent by me on the instructions of the Security Council, was in permanent danger and suffered more casualties than at any time since the Congo operation. Moreover, the events of the war seriously strained relations between Israel and the United Nations – and me personally.

The world organization has been troubled during its entire existence by the volatile and explosive situation in the Middle East, long before, during and now after my term as Secretary General. My first five years in office found us embroiled in the October War of 1973 and its aftermath and my second five years were occupied by the acutely deteriorating situation in the Lebanon. This was particularly distressing and dangerous, as for over twenty years after the 1949 armistice agreements the frontier between Israel and Lebanon had been relatively quiet. With a political structure carefully balanced between Christian and Moslem sects, the Lebanese government was a centre of moderation among the Arab states.

With the onset of the seventies, the balance between the communities began to break down. The delicately adjusted distribution of power between the numerous religious groups no longer reflected the numerical strength of the different minorities. Factional rivalries increased and the tensions were compounded by the militancy of the Palestine liberation forces which had settled there. Civil war broke out and was quelled in 1976 only with the aid of an Arab League deterrent force, composed predominantly of Syrian troops. Israeli influence was paramount in southern Lebanon, particularly among the Christian elements resident there. There were frequent skirmishes with the Palestinians and other Moslem groups and the situation became increasingly unstable.

After a particularly destructive Palestinian commando raid at the beginning of March 1978, which killed thirty-eight Israeli civilians on the highway between Tel Aviv and Haifa, the Israelis struck back with a full-scale invasion and occupied some 500 square miles of Lebanese territory as far north as the Litani river. The Lebanese government protested strongly to the Security Council, claiming not to be responsible for the actions of the Palestinians or for their bases in the south. The Security Council reacted swiftly. Andrew Young, at that time the American Ambassador, suggested the formation of a United Nations peace-keeping force, and this was supported by other Western powers and Arab states, particularly Lebanon itself.

On 19 March the Security Council adopted Resolution 425, calling on Israel to withdraw its forces from the Lebanon and establishing a United Nations interim force, henceforth known as UNIFIL (United Nations Interim Force in Lebanon) to restore tranquillity to the area. I was under no illusion about the difficulties such a force would encounter. This was not a conflict between two states, as in the Sinai, but between Israel and the guerrilla forces of the PLO, whom the Israelis regarded as terrorists. A peace-keeping force would have to cope not only with them but with the feuding Christian and Moslem communities and their armed militias.

I did not fail to explain my concern to the members of the Security Council – however, they decided to go ahead. Of course I told the Council that we in the Secretariat were ready to take all necessary steps in order to set up such a force as quickly as possible. The overall directive required the force to 'confirm' the withdrawal of Israeli forces, assist the government of Lebanon in restoring its authority and exert its best efforts to prevent the recurrence of fighting. As in the case of UNEF (Sinai) and UNDOF (Golan), UNIFIL was to use force only in self-defence, which was defined to include resistance to attempts by forceful means to prevent it from discharging its duties. UNIFIL was not to assume governmental functions; these remained the responsibility of the Lebanese authorities.

Once again we proved how fast we could move given the necessary backing and authority. Our initial projection was for a force of about 4,000 men, made up of five contingents of battalion strength and the necessary logistic units. It was important that they be put in place as quickly as possible. The Israelis were manning the line of the Litani river and PLO units had re-grouped, with much of their heavy equipment, in the coastal strip known as the Tyre pocket and north of the river in the strongholds of Nabatiya and the old crusaders' Château de Beaufort. Active skirmishing was still in progress.

Speed was of the essence. The nearest available troops were the Austrian and Iranian contingents serving in UNDOF, the disengagement force on the Golan Heights. They could be transported overland by truck convoy and reach their new deployment area within a few hours. However, I could not transfer them without the consent of their governments.

I first contacted the Austrian government, which let me know that they rather preferred to have their troops stay where they were. So I turned to the Iranians. The Shah was still in power and had been most helpful in previous peace-keeping activities. I reached him easily on the telephone, he gave his assent, and within twenty-four hours the Iranian contingent was on its way. We withdrew the Swedes from UNEF and soon reached the approved strength of 4,000 men. General Erskine of Ghana was in command and strongly recommended an increase to 6,000. It was a prudent request. The force was operating in two largely separate and extensive areas, in rugged terrain and often in situations of great danger. Over the months, the Security Council agreed to a further reinforcement of up to 7,000 men.

The individual battalions were subject to rotation. Sometimes they were replaced by units from the same country, sometimes by personnel from new contributor nations. We could not always plan these transfers on a routine basis. For some time after the revolution in Iran, its contingent remained in place, probably because the Khomeini regime had overlooked its existence while it grappled with more urgent matters. But of course there came the day when he had to airlift them back home. We had a different problem with the Nepalese battalion, whose return was requested because they were needed to participate in the coronation ceremonies of the new king. After an interval they came back. The Nepalese were a fine body of men, and Brian Urquhart used to remind me with pardonable pride that they were 'British trained'. So were the Fijians, a first-class unit, particularly popular with the local population, establishing a special bond with Arab children through their fatherly and helpful bearing. The Fijians were prone to resist interference with their mission, and suffered substantial casualties as a result.

Political considerations compelled me to make other changes. The Netherlands government, traditionally friendly to the Israelis, provided a contingent, yet, when they began to take casualties in skirmishes with Major Haddad's Christian militia and the PLO, the Dutch began to criticize the Israelis for failing to control their satellite. The Netherlands government found it necessary to pacify growing domestic opposition over the casualties and over embroilment with the Israelis. Their contingent was finally withdrawn.

The French played an important part in UNIFIL from the first. They furnished more men for the force than any other single nation. An elite group of French paratroopers arrived among the very first contingents under the command of Colonel Salvan, a wounded veteran of the climactic Vietnam battle at Dien Bien Phu. He was appointed chief of staff to General Erskine, but a few months later his car was ambushed and he was seriously injured.

The personal relations I had always been at such pains to build up with heads of state and government stood me in good stead. With English- and French-speaking contingents in UNIFIL we needed a bilingual logistics unit. The obvious country to approach was Canada. At first they declined our request, so I immediately put through a personal call to Prime Minister Trudeau, with whom I had established a close relationship over the years, and explained our problem to him. Within minutes Trudeau agreed to send the required unit to Lebanon, and the Canadians were flown to the area without further delay.

The Israelis had suspended major military operations, but they complained that the Palestinian forces were continuing to launch rockets against Israeli settlements at the rate of approximately a hundred a day. The Israeli commander, Lieutenant General Gur, insisted that unless this was stopped Israel would have no option but to resume full-scale hostilities. Interestingly enough, it was Gur himself who urged UNIFIL to use its channels of communication to obtain PLO compliance with the cease-fire. This request presented us with a problem of some delicacy. As a matter of policy, Israel had always criticized contacts between the United Nations and the PLO, even though several General Assembly resolutions had authorized me to maintain them. In his turn Yasser Arafat, the PLO leader, had taken offence at the failure of the Security Council to mention his organization as a party to the conflict. At times, he asserted, the PLO had been the only force resisting the Israelis. Therefore he did not feel bound by a resolution which ignored his organization.

We had to move fast. I issued an appeal for a general cease-fire and instructed General Erskine to meet Arafat in Beirut, together with my personal representative, James Jonah. At first Arafat was obdurate, but in the end he authorized General Erskine to inform me that the PLO would accede to my appeal. He coupled this with an expression of appreciation for my efforts to restore peace in the Middle East. Of course Arafat only exercised uncertain control over the more extreme factions of the PLO and the armed Moslem groups, but this was the first time the PLO had agreed to a cease-fire in its attacks against Israel. Rocket firing from Lebanon into northern Israel diminished appreciably, and UNIFIL was thus able to begin the task of stabilizing the cease-fire. General Gur recognized the value of this achievement, transitory though it was. At that time my loyal and dedicated press spokesman for many years, Rudi Stajduhar, drew my attention to Gur's statement in the *Jerusalem Post* of 30 March that one of the results of Israel's incursion into Southern Lebanon had been to make the PLO a *de facto* party to any agreement in that area.

Interestingly enough, seven years later, as I write these lines, Ezer Weizman, who was then Minister of Defence, has admitted publicly that Israel negotiated indirectly with the PLO in 1978 in order to stop Palestinian hostilities across the northern Israeli border. Because of this, he stated, no enemy shells hit the north of Israel. At the time, nevertheless, the Israelis were reluctant to withdraw their troops in spite of the fact that the Security Council resolution called on them to do so 'forthwith'. They planned a phased pull-back, a procedure not envisaged in the cease-fire arrangements, insisting that – as they told us – they could not leave Lebanon because UNIFIL was not yet able to protect them against terrorist attacks from across their northern border. We did everything we could to control the Palestinians. The area involved was so large and the terrain so difficult that it was never possible to be certain that infiltration could be completely halted. We could not give the Israelis an air-tight guarantee, and they would not be satisfied with anything less. We were accused of showing partiality to the Palestinians, a charge we resented, as we were trying faithfully to carry out our mission.

The entire experience was a frustrating ordeal for me and my aides in the UN Secretariat. For weeks, day and night, we were buffeted by the complaints of Israelis, Palestinians, Christians and Moslems as we tried to damp down the pervading violence. However hard we worked, we could only claim limited success. We seemed to be made the culprit for every mishap and the target for a host of extreme and irreconcilable claims. In April 1978, just four weeks after our peace-keeping forces had arrived in south Lebanon, I came to the conclusion that a personal visit to the area might be helpful to discuss the complicated situation with the political and military leaders in the region and to establish personal contacts with our force. My first stop was in Beirut, where I had meetings with President Sarkis, who was in a very gloomy mood and did not hide his scepticism about the future of his country. One of the subjects of our discussion was the question of a more active role for the Lebanese army, which would have been necessary to re-establish – at least symbolically – the authority of the government in the south. Sarkis expressed doubts about the practical possibilities of setting up even one battalion and sending it down to the south, taking into account the fact that the road from Beirut to the Israeli frontier was firmly blocked by numerous rival factions.

Leaving the Presidential Palace in the hills outside Beirut, I drove to the UN office in the Lebanese capital, where I was to meet with PLO leader Yasser Arafat. On arrival I was surprised by a phone call from Arafat's headquarters, informing me that because of security reasons he could not show up. He asked whether it would be possible for me to see him in his premises somewhere in the city. Sidestepping questions of protocol and political implication I decided to go – because I considered it imperative to talk to the man who played such an important role in the Lebanese quagmire, and also in the interests of the success of UNIFIL. The ride in a UN car to Arafat's headquarters was, to say the least, an exciting experience. Our guards *en route* changed from UN observers to Lebanese government units and finally, as we approached our destination, to Arafat's people. Our arrival there was greeted with tremendous shooting and rifle fire – fortunately in the air – doubtless a ceremonial welcome for my visit.

Our talks took place in an austere room, decorated only with a few pictures of PLO fighters killed in action. The substance of our discussion turned on the infiltration of PLO forces into and through UNIFIL's zone of control. I put it to Arafat as strongly as I could that incidents of this type undermined UNIFIL's credibility and provoked Israeli reactions which could not benefit the PLO in the long run.

Arafat maintained that the PLO launched no attacks from Lebanese territory, but that occasional and casual infiltrations were difficult to control. Whenever he was informed of violations of agreements reached with the UN, he said, he would not hesitate to take the necessary measures. Without actually saying so, Arafat conveyed the impression that he had difficulties within his own ranks and simply could not control extremist elements who ignored his instructions.

Arafat was no stranger to me. Over the years I met him frequently and found him one of the most unusual figures with whom I dealt as Secretary General. He fitted into none of the ordinary categories of UN personalities. He represented no existing government or state and held legitimized control over no territory. The movement he led, the Palestine Liberation Organization, was a conglomeration of loosely linked politico-military groups with a wide range of doctrinal and tactical differences. They were united only in their espousal of a Palestinian state for the Palestinian Arabs.

To the Israelis Arafat was no more than the terrorist leader of an illegal terrorist organization with which it was in a perpetual state of conflict. But other UN members accorded him quite different treatment. Arab states, and some others, gave him financial, logistical and diplomatic support. In many countries his representatives had quasi-diplomatic status. In the UN he was widely regarded as the leader of a national liberation movement entitled to such assistance as the organization could give him by way of refugee relief, the moral support of resolutions adopted by overwhelming majorities, and the ceaseless activity of various promotional agencies set up by the General Assembly.

The ambiguous status of Arafat and the Palestine Liberation Organization frequently caused us difficulties. Normally we could handle them with a little ingenuity and some fast-footwork diplomacy. But when Arafat's partisans tried to give him the treatment reserved for heads of state or government, touchy problems could arise.

The most notable instance of this kind occurred when the General Assembly invited Arafat to address it in 1974. As the host government, the United States was obliged to permit Arafat to come to New York and to protect him there. But the prospect of doing so in such a hostile environment obviously caused the United States some concern. At about 2 am on the morning of his arrival, the American Ambassador telephoned me enquiring whether it would be possible to put Arafat up somewhere in the UN buildings, since it would be risky to transport him through New York's traffic-choked streets back and forth between the Waldorf (the midtown hotel used by the United States government) and the General Assembly building.

I approved the idea but recalled that UN headquarters had no sleeping accommodation. The only beds we had were those in the UN clinic. These, we agreed, would have to serve; and so Arafat was whisked by helicopter to the garden at headquarters and from there to the clinic for a few hours of rest before he was to address the Assembly. When I went to greet him at the opening of business, I jokingly asked him how he liked hospital beds. Rising to the spirit of the occasion, he assured me that the bed was the best he had slept in for a long time.

But our biggest problem was still ahead. While I was sitting in my office on the thirty-eighth floor of the Secretariat building, I received a hurried telephone call from Bradford Morse, who was at that time the UN Under-Secretary responsible for General Assembly affairs. The President of the General Assembly, Morse informed me, had instructed the Secretariat to put in its special place on the podium of the General Assembly hall the chair used exclusively for visiting heads of state, from which they rise to address the Assembly and to which they return on concluding their remarks.

The General Assembly President in 1974 was Abdul Aziz Bouteflika, the Foreign Minister of Algeria. Without any consultation, Bouteflika had decided to grant Arafat the protocol courtesies accorded to a head of state. Such procedural steps can have serious political consequences.

I hurried down to the second floor, where I had a small office directly behind the podium, and met with Bouteflika in his office next to mine. He insisted on leaving the chair where it was. In any event, it was connected to various communications cables so the occupant could make use of the simultaneous translation system. Thus to remove it in front of an already crowded hall would have been a complicated operation likely to give rise to questions and objections.

As the delegates were in their seats waiting for Arafat to speak, I proposed a compromise: Arafat was to remain standing while the President greeted him and also while the President made his concluding remarks after Arafat's statement. Told of this, Arafat joked that he was not so weary as to need a chair and complied with the agreement, except that after his speech he leaned on the back of the chair.

The Assembly gave Arafat an enthusiastic welcome, and he raised his arm in acknowledgement. There, before the television cameras, a holster flashed into sight – triggering a further clamour in the press about whether Arafat had carried a firearm into the Assembly Hall. This, of course, is prohibited under the security rules of the United Nations. Fortunately, UN photographs later proved that the holster was empty. But, as is so often the case, the evidence never really caught up with the charge.

I found Arafat to be quite an intriguing character. One had to admire his skill in juggling the many factional and governmental forces impinging on the PLO in the rapidly changing and tumultuous conditions of the Middle East situation. His distinctive garb and his unshaven presence concealed an educated, intelligent individual of exceptional political ability. From my meetings with him I have the impression that with time and experience he adopted increasingly moderate views. But he has had to shape his conduct so as to maintain control over some very unruly associates. In seeking a solution for the Palestine problem, I believe he would consider a political victory more important, or at least more attainable, than a military one. I think, too, that he would prefer to have the PLO seek its goals by negotiation rather than to rely on terrorism as its primary weapon.

I first met Arafat in Damascus in 1972, during an official visit to President Hafiz al-Assad. He came to see me at night, with a group of political advisers and security guards. We started off with a formal and stiff exchange of views, during which Arafat explained at length the PLO's basic position. I pressed him as to why he could not accept the existence of the state of Israel. If he could not recognize it, I asked, why could he not make at least a preliminary gesture in that direction. If he did so, the PLO would improve its standing in many quarters and would have a much better chance of attaining its objectives. In particular the PLO should do something to clarify what I understood to be the provision in its charter concerning its intent to destroy Israel.

This provoked an emotional response from Arafat. He denied that the PLO charter contained such a statement. And he asserted that recognition of Israel was the only card he had in his hands. 'Why should I play that card now,' he inquired, 'without getting in return any recognition of our legitimate right of self-determination?'

In all our subsequent meetings we never closed this gap in our perceptions. But I did establish a kind of rapport with Arafat which facilitated our dealings in connection with the October 1973 war and the subsequent UN peace-keeping operations.

Somewhat encouraged by my talks with Arafat concerning the infiltration of PLO forces through UNIFIL lines in southern Lebanon, I left Beirut on 17 April 1978 and flew in a special aircraft to Tel Aviv, where a United Nations convoy was waiting to take me north across the Lebanese border to General Erskine's headquarters in Naqoura. After an extensive briefing, we drove on towards Tyre. The first part of the ride was more or less uneventful. There were three checkpoints on the road, the first Israeli, the second UNIFIL, manned by the French, and then the PLO barrier. They attached a liaison officer to us.

As we went on, the number of people on the roadside steadily increased, as well as the level of armaments, especially weapons carried by children. The road passed Rachidiye refugee camp, known to contain a large and militant PLO element and the target of repeated Israeli air and naval bombardment attacks, including cluster bombs, a potent anti-personnel weapon.

Then the road became completely blocked by a large demonstration of people waving placards and banners, including a number of heavily armed paramilitary militia. Prominently displayed were large olive-drab pieces of metal casing which my military companions recognized as the containers of cluster bombs. Children were running up and down, waving at the windows of our cars what appeared to be bunches of green golf balls. One of my Austrian colleagues, Albert Rohan, riding in another car of the convoy, told me later that one of the boys thrust his hand through the window. The Irish major at the wheel of the car remarked drily, 'Cluster bombs, sir.'

Our convoy was completely immobilized for some minutes, since the French UNIFIL armoured cars accompanying us did not dare to move for fear of running over the demonstrators. The crowd jumped on to my car, pounded on the roof, screamed and yelled for immediate Israeli with-drawal and against the use of the cluster bombs. Small-arms shooting began, happily into the air. Even Colonel Salvan became exercised. He was worried that one of the demonstrators might drop a cluster bomblet. He and General Erskine assured me that they had not expected this kind of incident. They had traversed the same road many times without any difficulty. I could not resist pointing out that the UN Secretary General probably provided a more rewarding target.

After expostulating with the demonstrators, and with the help of the armoured cars, we managed to get through the crowd and reach the gates of the UNIFIL barracks on the outskirts of Tyre, where there was another large demonstration with more small arms being fired into the air. The French paratroopers opened the gates to let my car through and then immediately shut them again, excluding the rest of the party.

The French had originally arranged for me to visit the city itself but it was now clear that this was impossible. They had arranged for the large Norwegian helicopters attached to the force to take me on an inspection tour of UNIFIL outposts. They had landed near the bridge over the Litani river, but there was no way of getting there. While I inspected the barracks, my staff arranged to have one of the helicopters fly right into the compound to pick me up. The crowd outside reacted with considerable anger and made threatening gestures towards the remaining helicopter and the others in my party, who had to fight their way through the demonstrators to get to it. After we had taken off we noticed guerrillas firing at us from the ground. Fortunately there were no hits.

Yasser Arafat later told a UN official that he had been appalled at the decision to take me to Tyre. He said that there was a conspiracy to kill me as a protest against the continued Israeli presence, and claimed that he had sent his own special guard down to arrest the ringleaders. Only the helicopters had saved our lives.

After my return to New York, I sent Under Secretary Roberto Guyer, the experienced Argentine diplomat, to negotiate with the parties concerned. He had an extremely difficult task, but in the end, on 13 June 1978, the Israelis left Lebanese territory. In doing so they paradoxically created a new problem. In the earlier stages of the withdrawal they had handed over their positions to UNIFIL. In the final phase they relinquished their posts to Major Haddad's Christian militia, justifying this action on the highly debatable grounds that he was a legitimate representative of the Lebanese government, although he had always ignored their instructions to co-operate with us.

The Israeli Foreign Minister, Moshe Dayan, informed me on 13 June 1978 that his government considered that by its withdrawal it had done its part in carrying out the Security Council's resolution. I was compelled to reply that the failure to turn over control of the evacuated area to UNIFIL certainly did not facilitate its future tasks. It was a prophetic and perhaps too diplomatic comment. When, in April 1979, the Lebanese government sent a small force into the area to reassert its sovereignty, the Christian militia shelled and rocketed UNIFIL headquarters near Naqoura and declared the 'independence' of the border strip they occupied.

This was an outrageous and purposeless act. Naqoura was hardly a worthwhile target. When I saw it in 1978 it was a hamlet of a few half-destroyed small houses, not one of them habitable. The UNIFIL forces were lodged in tents and General Erskine's headquarters consisted of a mobile home towed north from Israel. Our troops were not equipped as a fighting force, and were incapable of meeting an organized attack. Fortunately the shelling had caused only a few casualties. The Israelis had to be held accountable for Haddad's actions, and unless they kept him under control it was difficult to see how we could carry out our mandate. I called in Ambassador Yehuda Blum, Israel's permanent representative to the UN, and told him in the strongest terms that I was tired of the harassment of the United Nations forces by Haddad and his Israeli-supplied tanks and rockets. Blum replied that Haddad was an independent authority, a palpable falsehood. I am not prone to a show of emotion when I engage in diplomatic negotiations, but on this occasion I felt that my patience had been impossibly tried. I told Ambassador Blum in vigorous language that we knew Israel was supporting Haddad and that it was putting us in an impossible position. I told him that this sort of activity simply had to stop.

I was on good personal terms with Blum, who was born in Bratislava, right on the Austrian border, and who spoke fluent German. He took exception to my attitude and tried to bluster his way out of our altercation by engaging in the usual catalogue of complaints about the activities of the PLO.

These differences of opinion marked something of a turning point in my relations with the Israelis. Previously, the Israeli government had drawn a sharp distinction between the anti-Israeli posture of the voting majorities in the various United Nations organizations on the one hand and the impartial attitude of the Secretariat and myself on the other. The Israelis now began to include us in their condemnation; our contacts became distinctly cool.

Ambassador Blum and I were on family visiting terms and when his Prime Minister, Menachem Begin, came to New York, I decided to try to mend some fences. At a private dinner at Blum's residence, Begin and I had a long talk. I had met him on various previous occasions and he was well aware that I considered that the right-wing policies of his Likud Party were going to make any Middle East settlement even more difficult. In his deeply obsessed way he was an honest man, not devious at all. He had the intensity of a religious fanatic and was immovable on such issues as the settlement of the West Bank, which he insisted on calling Judaea and Samaria. When Begin later called on me in my office, he insisted that if the Israelis did not co-operate with Haddad's forces the Christian population in south Lebanon would be wiped out by the PLO. He even had a map of the area with him, marking all the Christian villages, to show how essential it was to protect them. He was deeply concerned at the volume of criticism which his government's actions were attracting and was using every possible argument to justify his position. There was another interesting aspect to this conversation. When we touched upon the Israeli-occupied West Bank of the Jordan river, the question of autonomy for the Palestinians came up. I told Begin about my personal experiences with autonomy problems – referring to the negotiations I had conducted between Austria and Italy concerning South Tyrol. I suggested that this – while not constituting a precedent – might be of some interest to him. He immediately asked me to explain the whole process in detail and wanted to have a copy of the agreement between Italy and Austria. I told him that I could send him one the next day out of our library, which I did. Later I was told that he studied it very carefully but had come to the conclusion that the two situations were different. I was not surprised.

However great the differences between the United Nations and Israeli government policy, my talks with Begin were always calm and correct. In appearance he was not a striking figure, though extremely well groomed. He gave an impression of being weary and depressed – at least at our last meeting in New York. What impressed me about Begin was the strength of his self-control in emotional situations, when only his eyes betrayed his feelings. In our conversations I never heard him utter an unconsidered word or one charged with personal emotion. Although there was no doubt of the extent to which his political philosophy was marked by his people's faith and tragic history, he nevertheless tried to put forward his policy clearly and with the greatest possible deference to legalistic principles. Unlike my contacts with Golda Meir, who had once served me Viennese-style coffee and cakes in the garden of her house in Jerusalem, my relationship with Begin was formal and cool. He did not rail against the United Nations – he simply considered it to be flawed in its structure, dominated by Arab interests, and largely unfit for mediation. But even Begin knew when and where the United Nations was a partner for whom there was no substitute.

In southern Lebanon, Begin and his Christian ally, Major Haddad, were not our only problem. Relations with the PLO and the Lebanese Moslem groups in the area were hardly better. Yasser Arafat had repeatedly promised that the PLO would co-operate with UNIFIL and not initiate hostile acts against Israel from southern Lebanon, although it would continue to do so from the sea and across Israel's other frontiers. He still refused to withdraw some limited PLO forces from the UNIFIL zone, where they were situated in small enclaves surrounded by UNIFIL-controlled territory. When they were detected they were disarmed, but since they would not leave the area voluntarily, UNIFIL had to furnish them with water, food and non-military supplies.

For the next couple of years guerrilla attacks and counter-raids continued. UNIFIL's capacity for total surveillance was less than complete and hardly provided a textbook case of United Nations peace-keeping activity. If anything, it highlighted the limitations of such operations rather than their potential. My repeated admonitions to the contending parties and my threats to withdraw the UN force had only a marginal effect. There was an increasing feeling in the Secretariat that we should have dubbed UNIFIL 'Mission Impossible'.

Its efforts were thwarted repeatedly and I often wondered whether it would not have been better at an early stage to have made a clear-cut request to the Security Council to terminate UNIFIL's mandate. There was every justification for doing so. It was an exercise in frustration and the drumfire of criticism was galling to those of us who were devoted heart and soul to making it effective. UNIFIL suffered more casualties than any UN operation since the Congo.

Even so it would have been irresponsible to have yielded to this temptation. The Lebanese government desperately wanted us to maintain the UN force as the only stabilizing influence in the country. UNIFIL cannot be judged against a standard of flawless performance but against the situation that would have existed if it had never been created. It prevented literally hundreds of attempted infiltrations across the Israeli border and for a considerable period discouraged the outbreak of more general hostilities.

In my last year of office, I was able to render one further service. In April 1981, a new cycle of violence broke out in Lebanon. In answer to the Syrian military intervention in the Lebanese civil war the Israel air force had attacked Syrian ground-to-air missile sites as well as Palestinian targets in south Lebanon. Ambassador Philip Habib, President Reagan's special emissary to the region, attempted to mediate in both conflicts. However, he could not deal with the PLO, with which neither the United States nor Israel would have anything to do. Consequently, Secretary of State Alexander Haig telephoned me to request that the United Nations approach the PLO and obtain its agreement to a cease-fire. The United States, he told me, was dealing with the Israelis.

We tackled the problem on two fronts. In New York we worked with the PLO observer, Zehdi Terzi, while on my instructions the UNIFIL commander, General Callaghan, took the matter up with Arafat. As a result, the latter informed us of his acceptance of the cease-fire two days before the

Israelis agreed. This was an important contribution, and when I told Secretary Haig of it he expressed his appreciation for what we had done. Haig asked me, however, not to make public the part the United Nations had played in obtaining PLO compliance. This might, he said, create problems with the Israelis. We never did make an announcement in New York of our *démarches*. We were seeking results, not publicity.

For us it was a bitter-sweet outcome. As was often the case, when we helped to achieve something good we could not take our share of the credit for it. But when we could not carry out our missions, however unreasonable they might be, we were sharply criticized in the press and media.

The lull was only temporary. In June 1982, Israel embarked on a major invasion of Lebanon, passing through the UNIFIL zone. This action precipitated a chain of events, still vivid in all our minds, that had as one consequence the creation of a new multinational force around Beirut, composed of units from the United States and three other Western powers. These military measures were entirely separate from the United Nations effort. Perhaps their devastating experiences will provide the international community with a better perspective from which to assess the value of using the UN for peace-keeping purposes.

My own reaction was that such a force in Lebanon could not by itself do much to help the parties to achieve a political solution. A multinational force organized outside the United Nations can function successfully when, as in the Sinai, the governments agree to its deployment and control their own armed forces accordingly. Under such conditions a United Nations force can do just as well. In a country where there is a complete lack of co-operation by warring communal elements and where the authority of the legitimate government is confined to a very small area, the outlook is entirely different. In such a case, the psychological influence of the peace-keeping force's presence is virtually reduced to nil.

The problem is compounded when the force represents major powers. Its every action is suspect. It will be accused of defending national interests and not the cause of peace-keeping. Its very presence on foreign soil becomes part of the problem, however praiseworthy the intentions of the participants. If, as in Lebanon, the forces of the Western powers are in close proximity to Syrian forces backed by the Soviet Union, the search for a political solution is complicated by the overtones of super-power rivalry.

I do not contend that if the countries concerned had made a different decision and chosen to use UNIFIL in the Beirut area the situation would have been materially different. UNIFIL could not have been expected to stop determined antagonists engaged in bitter inter-communal warfare. But a UN force would not have been a major factor in the conflict. No one would have found it worth-while to plan an appalling terrorist attack on, let us say, forces from Fiji or Senegal, as was done against the United States marines and the French contingent.

The solution in Lebanon must be a political solution. It cannot be negotiated in isolation from the other problems of the Middle East. Whatever the fate of the PLO and Yasser Arafat, the Palestine issue will inevitably have to figure prominently in any settlement in the area. In the end, peace in the Middle East requires a comprehensive agreement on a whole complex of inter-related problems. The step-by-step approach can help bring that eventuality closer, but it can never by itself be a substitute for a general agreement.

Syria's role in the Middle East conflict has grown in importance. President Assad and his government feel left out of the negotiating process. It is naive to think that Syria will agree to withdraw its troops from Lebanon before the Israelis retire to within their own borders in the south. Moreover, Assad will engage in no negotiations which do not include a settlement of the Israeli occupation of the Golan Heights.

Assad is a proud man who attaches great importance to prestige and honour. He wants to be treated as an equal. He felt deeply hurt when, after Lebanon and Israel had signed a withdrawal agreement, the American Secretary of State Schultz did not come to see him in Damascus personally but left it to the Lebanese President Gemayel to inform Assad of the outcome of the negotiations. Psychological considerations play an important part in Arab countries. To ignore them is the surest recipe for failure.

We are still, as I write, in the presence of a tragedy in the history of nations. The state of Israel was brought to birth by the decision of the United Nations. By its very existence it has polarized the course of events in the Middle East since its foundation. No other subject has engaged so fully the energies of the world organization or presented it with more intractable problems. Despite the most exhaustive efforts, there is no good reason to believe that a settlement of the basic Arab-Israeli conflict is in sight.

The failure of Israel and its Arab neighbours to reach a general settlement is a calamity of epic proportions. Both sides have suffered enormous losses in five fully-fledged wars and countless episodes of violence over a period of nearly forty years. This is only part of the story. Only when we consider what might have happened in conditions of peace can we appreciate fully the opportunities that have been lost and the damage that has been done.

In a world of rational men, it should have been possible to accommodate the justified aspirations of the two sides. Israel's quest for recognition, territory and security could have been realized without undue damage to any existing Arab state. With the assistance of the international community, Arab concern for the displaced Palestinians could have been met without unacceptable losses to Israel. Political and economic collaboration between Israel and the Arab states could have led to a stronger and better balanced development of natural resources and human capabilities in this quarter of the globe. Men of vision might reasonably have hoped for co-operation between the two Semitic peoples to make the desert bloom.

The harsh reality is different. Israel survives in a state of perpetual siege, sustained by the military and economic support of the United States. The Arab countries are diverted from more constructive activities by the permanent campaign against Israel. While it is a rallying point that unites them, its fruits are all too often sterile.

What is even worse, the conflict has served to blight the nobler characteristics of both antagonists. From its creation, Israel has been a humanistic and democratic Socialist state; however, with its existence under constant threat and driven by the need to win, the seeds of expansionism and narrow chauvinism were sown. By relentlessly establishing new settlements in the West Bank, Israel is obstructing progress towards peace. In the Arab countries, the burdens of war and the frustrations of defeat have fostered authoritarianism and militarism. The prospects for serious peace-making are still bleak.

The rise of the Palestinian Liberation Organization was furthered by an Arab League summit decision in 1974 confirming its status as the sole legitimate representative of the Palestinian people. Critics have insisted that the PLO is a loose collection of political and military sub-organizations of widely differing character and beliefs. The open rebellion against Yasser Arafat, during its period of adversity in Lebanon in and after 1982 has highlighted the fragility of its composition.

Even if its structure is unstable, the PLO has been for years the only Palestinian Arab voice that has spoken with authenticity. Efforts to create an alternative Palestinian leadership in the Israeli-occupied West Bank have not been successful. This may have been partly due to pressure from the more radical paramilitary elements of the PLO, but, for whatever reasons, the PLO has come to be widely regarded as the only established spokesman. The Arab states have been united in its support. Over the course of time virtually all other members of the United Nations have accepted it as a quasi-governmental organization, notwithstanding its lack of territorial base and its failure to establish itself as a government in exile.

My own position in this matter has long been clear. Israel's existence and independence must be maintained. But the rights to self-determination of the Palestinian Arabs living in the territories occupied by Israel in the 1967 war and of Arabs displaced from their homes in Israel must also be recognized. I would have hoped that Israel, which has so recently achieved nationhood, would be more receptive to Arab demands for similar self-determination and political entity for the Palestinians. I do not condone terrorism or resort to war as a means of altering the status quo. But neither can I condone creeping Israeli expansionism through the implantation of Israeli settlements in the Arab-inhabited West Bank and the annexation of east Jerusalem.

Irrespective of the merits of the case, the form in which the subject has been considered in the United Nations must be regarded as unfortunate and not helpful in working out a peaceful settlement. The Arab members of the organization have worked closely with other delegations and indeed the entire non-aligned majority to form a solid anti-Israeli bloc. Eastern bloc countries have supported them strongly and at times some or all of the Western states have joined them. A frequent voting pattern ranges almost the entire membership against Israel, with the exception of the United States and one or two others, and sometimes not even that.

This situation has led to a bitter, highly emotional confrontation within the organization and damaged its chances to play a helpful role in this dispute. On repeated occasions various countries and regional groups have endeavoured to exclude Israel from the meetings of the UN organs. Wherever possible, I have spoken out against such an approach. Not only do such manoeuvres skirt the bounds of legality, but they also put at risk the very existence of the world organization, since they bear the seeds of rift and dissent. It would only destroy or gravely undermine the sole global organization to which the weaker states can turn for support against injustice.

We are left with a continuing threat to peace and stability. I would not exclude any promising approach in attempts to overcome it. If and when bi-lateral diplomacy can pursue a step-by-step process towards an eventual settlement, that will be highly important. I am convinced that, in the end, each step must lead towards a general, comprehensive settlement and that the United Nations must play its part in reaching and confirming such an agreement on the basis of the principles of its Charter. It is the responsibility of all member states to bring this about, and particularly the permanent members of the Security Council.

The argument is put forward that the United Nations is disqualified from taking effective action in the Middle East because its voting majorities fall so preponderantly on one side in the conflict. In the Security Council, the organ principally responsible for the maintenance of international peace and security, the power of veto precludes anything that could be regarded as a tyranny of the majority. This veto power obliges the great powers, when action is needed, to reach agreement by mutual accommodation. In this dangerous world, a settlement obtained in this way offers the best hope for a lasting solution.

15

Managing the Unmanageable

It was Thomas Jefferson, I believe, who after eight years in office described the American Presidency as a 'splendid misery'. After ten years as UN Secretary General, I was tempted to share his lamentation. This is not because the two positions have much in common: they do not. But in one respect they are alike: the occupants of both are chief executive officers operating under legal and political constraints that guarantee high levels of frustration. There the resemblance, by and large, ends. The administrative head of an international organization does not enjoy the power and perquisites of the chief executive officer of even a moderate-sized state.

Nations guard few things more jealously than their sovereignty. In a world scarred by violence, they have agreed, in accepting UN membership, on the general need for some form of collective action in order to avoid being overwhelmed by anarchy and chaos. In specific cases, however, they are often most reluctant to surrender their freedom of action or to endow international agencies with powers of compulsion.

The United Nations is founded on the practice of negotiation, recommendation and consent. For the most part, national states handle their various interest groups in the same way; but they hold in reserve the power to enforce compliance by the dissenter or the outlaw if they must. Lacking this capability, the United Nations falters because its members so often refuse to take the steps needed to make the general interest prevail.

This reluctance is reflected in the circumscribed authority the Charter grants the Secretary General. He is 'the Chief Administrative Officer of the Organization'. He is to act in that capacity and 'perform such other functions' as the organs of the United Nations entrust to him. He appoints the staff of the Secretariat under increasingly detailed regulations laid down by the General Assembly. He and his subordinates are to act as international officials responsible only to the United Nations.

The Charter gives the Secretary General two additional prerogatives, which have provided the foundation for a tenuous but nevertheless appreciable increase in his authority since 1945. He is authorized under Article 99 of the Charter to bring to the attention of the Security Council any matter which may threaten the maintenance of international peace and security. And he is directed to make an annual report to the General Assembly.

In themselves these provisions are relatively modest. Yet they underlie the evolution of his office to a point well beyond mere nuts-and-bolts administration. They imply directly that the Secretary General has a political role to play in the work of the organization. They have legitimized his concern with international developments in general, and particularly with matters affecting international peace. Each occupant of the office has in one way or another tested the outer limits of that role.

It is frequently said of Foreign Offices that they fare poorly in national politics because, unlike other cabinet departments, they have no constituency to plead on their behalf. This is even more true of the Secretary General. By quiet personal persuasion he can do more than is generally realized. But let him publicly take a position which is critical of a major power or bloc or one party to a conflict, and he risks losing the co-operation and support he needs to keep the organization functioning at its best.

The Secretary General is confronted with an unending series of dilemmas. Enjoying no sovereign authority and few material resources, he must do what he can to quell international tension. In situations where conflicting nations each affirm the righteousness of their cause, he must balance considerations of law, equity and the possibilities of practical adjustment in attempting to bring about political settlements. Sometimes he is the only objective actor who can do so. In other cases, it may be the better course of wisdom to stand aside. When he can move at all he must, like the classical mariner, steer between Scylla and Charybdis, always in quest of the narrow passage leading to possible agreement. And if, as is sometimes the case, the various United Nations organs saddle the Secretary General with impossible tasks when they cannot themselves reach agreements, that is simply a cross he must bear.

I always regarded it as my foremost task to work behind the scenes to harmonize the actions of nations, a purpose explicitly laid down in the Charter. With this in mind, I maintained frequent contact with more heads of state or government and more prime ministers than, I imagine, anyone else in the world. I met them as they came to the United Nations for the regular annual session of the General Assembly or at other times; and I visited every major region of the globe to facilitate progress in one or another aspect of the UN's work.

Success often eluded me, but on other occasions it arrived in quite unexpected ways. There are times when the Secretary General can use his contacts to help settle otherwise apparently insoluble problems of procedure. One such occasion arose in June 1981 when the Israeli Air Force carried out a raid against the Osirak nuclear reactor in Iraq in order to interrupt what the Israelis regarded as preparations for the manufacture of nuclear weapons. Whatever the merits of that contention, the Iraqis and others reacted sharply to this violation of their territory and called on the Security Council for sanctions against Israel. The United States and some other Western powers objected to sanctions and negotiations began on the terms of a resolution that could pass in the Council. What was required was a text that would condemn Israel in terms at least minimally satisfactory to the non-aligned group, including the Arab states, and also to the Western states concerned at the possible consequences for Israel.

There was an obstacle to negotiations: the United States had no diplomatic relations with Iraq. I happened to meet Ambassador Jeane Kirkpatrick in the delegates' lounge and asked her how things were going. 'My problem,' she said, 'is that I do not know the Iraqi Foreign Minister, Saadoun Hammadi. Because we have no relations with Iraq, I cannot contact him personally. Do you know him?' I did. I had met him in Iraq and at his annual visits to the General Assembly. Moreover, I had seen him strolling in the corridors a few minutes before.

I asked Brian Urquhart to seek out the Foreign Minister and tell him that Ambassador Kirkpatrick would like to talk to him in the little office I had just outside the Security Council chamber. Urquhart returned quickly with the reply, 'As long as it's in your office and in your presence, fine; otherwise, there would be difficulties, since they have no diplomatic relations. But if you invite him and Ambassador Kirkpatrick is there he will come.'

They met in my office in a series of negotiations running over a period of several days. Responding to the desire of both diplomats, I was present throughout, but I did not interfere except to give advice on purely technical points. The negotiations were tough, but finally Mrs Kirkpatrick proposed some American concessions on a particular point at issue. The Foreign Minister asked her if this was her bottom line. 'Yes,' she said, 'it is. I have been in Washington and have discussed it with the President and the Secretary of State.'

I had expected that the Foreign Minister would make a counter-proposal or even reject the American draft. Instead, he said, 'Okay, let's drop the whole paragraph in question.' This was the open sesame to final agreement. Though the non-aligned states wanted a stronger text, they could hardly object if the Iraqi representative accepted the compromise.

The upshot was a unanimous vote in the Security Council. Essentially, the resolution condemned the violation of Iraq's territory; recognized Iraq's right to redress for the destruction it had suffered; and demanded that Israel put its own nuclear facilities under the supervision of the International Atomic Energy Agency, as Iraq had long since done. In effect, this brought the matter to a close.

This is but one of many instances in which I was able to facilitate agreement between contending parties. No two cases are identical, and the action the Secretary General can take must be carefully modulated according to circumstances. It requires diplomatic subtlety and skill and a sure sense of timing, rather than charismatic or daring leadership. He cannot be regarded as the spokesman of any of the organization's regional or political blocs, nor can he be seen to lean towards one or another of the major powers. He must demonstrate an understanding of the basic political, economic and social forces that shape the thinking of widely differing national groups in every part of the world. His Secretariat, drawn from all its member states, can assist him. But the responsibility is ultimately his alone. As President Harry Truman rightly said, 'The buck stops here.'

As long as the United Nations responds mainly to political forces, it is the Secretary General's fate to be caught in their cross-currents. He simply cannot avoid them. But in no area is he more cruelly beset than in his responsibility for the budget.

Exerting pressure on one side is the Third World voting majority in the General Assembly – overwhelming in numbers, lacking in hard currency resources, favoured in the contributions scale, and clamorous for all the services the organization can provide to meet domestic needs. That majority is all too willing to support higher levels of expenditure. The cost, after all, is met predominantly by others.

Arrayed against this group are the major contributors, the Western industrialized countries and Japan, together with the USSR. This is one area in which ideological disputes and Cold War tensions are muted. These states act out of a common concern. The ten largest contributors to the United Nations budget pay 75% of the total figure. Seventy others pay only .01% each. Eighty-nine states together contribute just one per cent of the total assessment. Those who carry the financial burden lack the voting power to reduce it. But they can and do exert their influence on the Secretary General at every opportunity to hold the budget estimates down.

Somehow he has to respond to these conflicting pressures. He is asked simultaneously to add new programmes to deal with new problems as they are perceived; to expand one programme at the expense of others; to cut down waste and to eliminate obsolete programmes which governments in earlier years insisted on establishing. He has to make these decisions largely on his own. On wider issues of policies, he can rely on inter-governmental organs such as the Security Council and the Economic and Social Council to give him guidance and direction. But there is no counterpart in internal matters. The only review body is the General Assembly, acting through its Advisory Committee on Administrative and Budgetary Questions. It is a committee of the whole, meeting only while the Assembly is in session; and it is not at all suited to providing the Secretary General with the kind of guidance and assistance he should have in dealing with his day-to-day administrative problems.

What is more, the Secretary General's hands are increasingly tied by the General Assembly's tendency to create new, quasi-autonomous agencies – each depending on the Assembly's budget to provide the wherewithal to carry out the programmes they approve. Examples of such agencies are the United Nations Conference on Trade and Development (UNCTAD), the various regional economic commissions, the United Nations Environment Programme, and the Office of the United Nations High Commissioner for Refugees. The executive head of each of them comes to the Secretary General with a programme for which he has obtained approval from his organization's inter-governmental committee or council. These governing bodies are composed of only a minority of the members of the United Nations, seldom more than one third of the total membership. Yet in each case the executive head of the autonomous body can, and sometimes does, contend that, since his council has approved the programme he has proposed, the Secretary General has no alternative but to include the full amount required in his budget.

In a typical example, the United Nations Conference on Trade and Development, held in Nairobi in 1976, endorsed an extraordinary programme enlargement for the ensuing four-year period. Shortly after-wards I was approached in New York by a succession of ambassadors from most of the major contributing countries. They urged me in strong terms to 'hold the line', and even to aim at no growth at all in my preparation of the next biennial budget. Some presented me with written communications stressing the need to curb the steadily escalating budget increases. In response, I asked each ambassador whether his government's represen-tative on this or that body had voted in favour of new programmes or not. The answer was usually that they had indeed voted in favour.

These replies provided a textbook case of the ambivalence of many governments which approve proposals discussed without regard to their budgetary implications and then expect the Secretary General to step into the breach to provide their financing. I had hoped that my questions might have had some effect on the ambassadors and their governments. Four years later, in 1980, I was again the recipient of a collective brief presented by essentially the same governments and expressing the self-same concerns. Once more, it was left largely to me to be Horatio at the bridge at the final show-down.

I found it extremely difficult to find any means of establishing priorities among programmes and activities approved by the General Assembly. I would try vigorously to weed out items I considered outmoded or ineffective, usually with little success. There was almost always some state or regional group ready to weigh in with an opposing voice, because it had a vested interest in the programme.

It was equally difficult to restrain the Assembly's tendency to go to extremes in its support of activities dictated by strong political pressures. I recall my unhappiness with the measures adopted by the Assembly to advance the cause of the independence of Namibia. There was no question of the soundness of the political and legal basis of the Assembly's concern. It had been recorded, by overwhelming majorities, year after year. But I did not think it necessary for the Assembly to appoint both a Council of Namibia, consisting of some twenty-five members, and a Commissioner for Namibia – both acting in the same area but not always on the same wave-length. Nor did I think it necessary for the Council to travel around the world, holding meetings on Namibia. Too often their activities amounted to preaching to the converted. When I expressed my reservations on grounds of expense, I was reminded that the Assembly had directed that these activities should be financed from the budget. There was nothing I could do.

I had a somewhat similar experience when the United Nations Environment Programme was established. We had prepared its budget on the assumption that its headquarters would be set up at the United Nations' European headquarters in Geneva. Little additional expense would have been involved, since adequate facilities were available. But the Ambassador of Kenya lobbied heavily in the Assembly and obtained a political decision that the programme should be based in Nairobi. At one stroke that decision added $1 million to the budget.

All this goes to prove that if the Secretary General is to be expected to hold down the organization's expenditure, he must be given some additional tools to help him do so. He has no political constituency to help him withstand the inclinations of governments to spend United Nations funds. Currently, he can do little more than point out the financial implications of the resolutions adopted. In my view, that is simply not satisfactory.

Those are the hazards on the expenditure side. The revenue-raising process is similarly fraught. Under Article 1 of the Charter, member states bear the expenses of the organization as apportioned by the General Assembly. Determining the assessments to be levied upon members in accordance with wealth, population and other factors is a complex matter. But it is now well established that the United States, the largest contributor, will pay 25% of the total, and the Soviet Union somewhat less than half as much. Other members are assessed at lesser, even minimal, figures. Quite properly, in my view, the poorest and smallest bear the lightest load.

If a member state falls more than two years into arrears, it risks the not intolerable sanction of losing its voting power in the General Assembly – unless the failure to pay is judged to be due to conditions beyond its control. While there have been some close calls, I do not believe that any state has ever been subjected to this penalty. It is a rather remarkable record.

Yet it would be wrong to assume that the finances of the United Nations are in good shape. The Charter, as interpreted by the International Court of Justice, clearly establishes the principle that assessed contributions to the regular budget of the United Nations – unlike the voluntary contributions made for many special purposes – are a legal obligation of each member state. It is one of the Secretary General's managerial responsibilities to seek to collect what is due.

Unfortunately, the practice of arbitrarily withholding portions of assessed contributions has become increasingly prevalent among the membership. It began with the refusal of the Soviet bloc and several Arab states to pay their shares of the cost of the United Nations Emergency Force stationed in Egypt after the Suez crisis of 1956, and was enormously magnified when, in 1960, the Soviets and French refused to pay assessments to finance the largest-ever United Nations peace-keeping operation, in the Congo. In 1964, when the Soviets fell two years in arrears, they faced the prospect of losing their right to vote under Article 19 of the United Nations Charter. To avoid this contingency, the Assembly went through an entire session without a single formal vote. Eventually, the Article 19 provision was waived, and normal proceedings could resume.

But the practice of withholding for cause had thus been legitimized. More and more countries are resorting to it, including China for various purposes and the United States for activities involving Palestinian matters and expenses pertaining to the Law of the Sea Treaty. At least twenty-five governments are now retaining a portion of their assessments for political reasons, and the total deficiency involved exceeds $240 million. If this trend continues, it will eventually further undermine the already shaky United Nations' financial structure.

A variety of reasons have been given for refusing to pay for specific activities. It is sometimes argued that only the Security Council, and not the General Assembly, can authorize peace-keeping ventures. Or it is declared that whatever state the defaulter regards as an aggressor should pay the bill. Or it is claimed that a particular activity transcends the proper purposes of the organization. Whatever the justification, the practice clearly holds within it the seeds of disruption for the United Nations. Defaults obviously increase the difficulties faced by the Secretary General in managing the financial affairs of the organization.

The limited liquidity of the organization also poses problems. Because of delays in paying assessed contributions, the United Nations lives from hand to mouth. Under the General Assembly's financial regulations, member states are required to make such payments within thirty days of being notified of the amounts due, that is by the end of February of each year. This obligation is regularly ignored by the vast majority of member states. Over the last few years, the United States, for example, has delayed its assessed payment for the regular United Nations budget until the last quarter of the year.

The Secretary General is not authorized to borrow money to meet the running expenses of the organization. To keep it solvent, he is compelled, therefore, to draw on the emergency resource contained in its working capital fund. I had to fight hard to persuade delegations to enlarge the fund from $40 million to $100 million, so that I could meet current obligations. Even at that level, the fund is sufficient to carry the organization for only seven weeks while waiting for member states to pay.

In 1980, twenty nations, which contributed 85 per cent of the United Nations budget, voted against the revised budget for 1981. This is an unhealthy situation. If not remedied, it portends an eventual major budget revolt. The large contributors may some day join in an agreement to refuse to accept the increasing expenditure voted by the Assembly's majorities. They might limit their contributions to a ceiling they themselves establish. If they did so, a serious confrontation could result.

In recent years, the response to the problems I have discussed has been one of drift and uncertainty. I do not condemn anyone on this account: the situation is truly baffling. It can only be solved by action of the member states. To the extent that they are suffering from domestic financial stress, and are disenchanted about the actions or effectiveness of the United Nations, they are unlikely to give high priority to the matter. Yet unless something is done within a few years, the organization will find itself in a financial crisis. I do not believe we can expect the wealthier United Nations members who pay the bills indefinitely to allow the majority who do not to continue raising programme levels. Sooner or later, what the affluent regard as 'the tyranny of the majority' must be squarely faced.

The way out, it seems to me, must be some sort of negotiated understanding between the two groups. Each side would have to make its contribution. A beginning could be made by reviving the effort, begun after the costly Congo peace-keeping operation, to raise the funds needed to wipe out the existing United Nations deficit through voluntary contributions from the wealthier members. At that time Japan, then a new member, offered $10 million for that purpose. Other powers failed to carry the idea much further. Now it is time to try again.

In return, the larger contributors have the right to expect that specific budget ceilings will be adopted each year, with their agreement. The General Assembly majority will have to renounce its practice of repeatedly forcing the Secretary General's hand through approval of new projects which must then be financed through higher budgets. If growth in expenditure should exceed agreed levels, a mechanism must exist to bring about compensatory reductions. The Secretary General cannot do it alone.

The role of the Secretary General, whose limitation and potential I have described at length in this book, will, of course, largely depend on what happens to the organization as a whole. But even while recognizing that change comes slowly in these matters, I believe that some steps can be taken to utilize the Secretary General's capabilities more fully. Let me mention just a few examples:

The Secretary General needs more authority to co-ordinate the activities of the many loosely articulated parts of the United Nations system.

He should be given specific authority to cut through procedural complexities by convening high-level meetings to defuse threatening international problems through negotiation.

He should be invited to chair multilateral conferences when it is important to prevent procedural obstructionism and facilitate agreement.

His authority over the staff of the Secretariat should be strengthened against encroachment by patronage-hungry groups of members.

As a counterpart to his authority to propose items for consideration by United Nations organs, he should likewise receive authority to propose clearing the agenda of those organs of subjects that are endlessly debated year after year with no prospect of progress.

Where it would help to facilitate compromise, he should be permitted to introduce resolutions in United Nations organs in his own name.

Changes of this sort would not make the Secretary General much more of an executive agent than he is today. But they would give him an opportunity to exercise more effectively the talents he has, and the imagination he should have, to prod members along the path of international agreement and peaceful change.

These procedural prerogatives have a corollary. In this widening of his obligations and responsibilities, the Secretary General needs additional administrative assistance and services. He should have a Deputy, to serve as his *alter ego*. I know of no large bureaucratic organization or corporation which does not have a second-in-command. Someone should be available to act for the Secretary General when the latter is burdened with other matters or is absent from the headquarters on business or leave.

The situation today is a bureaucratic nightmare. Because of the lack of a proper hierarchical structure, no less than seventy Under Secretaries General, Assistant Secretaries General, and other officials of comparable rank, in New York and around the world, reported directly to me. This is an impossible span of managerial control. Moreover, whenever I left New York, no matter how pressing my business, I was constantly pursued by telephone and cable to make decisions that no one else was empowered to handle.

The common objection to proposals for a Deputy Secretary General is that his selection would pose an insuperable political problem. Presumably he would be chosen by the General Assembly. Given the political atmosphere in which that body works the Deputy would have to be drawn from a political group different from the Secretary General's. In the bureaucratic interplay in the Secretariat, he would be used as a counterbalance to his chief. This arouses memories of Nikita Khrushchev's 1960 'troika' proposal for a group of three, from the West, East and the Third World, to manage the Secretariat by consensus. The General Assembly has already decided to create the post of Director-General for Development and International Economic Cooperation, whose name appears directly under the Secretary General's on the organization charts. But he is not a deputy, and his responsibilities are limited to his own sphere, i.e. economic and development matters.

There is no denying the cogency of these objections. But I would point out that in the specialized agencies of the United Nations there are deputies, and they are selected by a political process. If no other satisfactory way can be found to choose a United Nations Deputy Secretary General, why should the choice not be left to the Secretary General, in the same way as the candidates for President of the United States and Prime Minister of many other countries in effect choose their own deputies?

As a second protective measure for the holder of the office, I would suggest the creation of a body, composed of a limited number of government representatives, to give him policy guidance and support. In substantive fields, he already works with the Security Council and the Economic and Social Council. It is a fruitful relationship, but it does not extend to administrative matters. Only the General Assembly is concerned with these. The Assembly and its Fifth Committee are too large to be effective for this purpose, and they normally meet only in the autumn. For the remainder of the time, except for ACABQ (Advisory Committee on Administrative and Budgetary Questions), which advises the General Assembly rather than the Secretary General, the latter has no shield to screen him from the demands or importunities of individual delegations and regional groups.

In the specialized agencies, the Directors General are more fortunate. Each of them works with an executive board, council or governing body for the discussion of policy matters. The Directors of the quasi-autonomous subordinate agencies of the United Nations, such as UNCTAD, the Environment Programme and the Office of the High Commissioner for Refugees, have the same arrangement. The chief executive officer of a typical corporation has his board of directors. Why not the Secretary General? Why should he work in an administrative vacuum?

Again, there are weighty practical objections. The creation of a major new inter-governmental organ of the United Nations would require an amendment of the Charter. There would be endless discussion of the competence, size, geographic distribution and other attributes of the new body. It might interfere with the Secretary General's prerogatives and rob him of what independence he currently has. It will increase costs. For my part I can only say that I should have been happy to have the support of such a board when I was subjected to pressures for higher budget expenditures, job preferment or other similar favours.

My third proposal for organizational improvement ranges beyond the field of administration. The Secretary General is an important diplomatic figure. It is his duty to follow closely a wide variety of political and other problems which either are, or may arrive, on the agenda of the deliberative organs of the United Nations. He raises matters for consideration by the Security Council, and his reports to the organization help to shape its subsequent actions. Responsibility for continuing peace-keeping operations is centralized in his office. Yet he has very limited resources of his own on which to base his findings and recommendations.

The United Nations sends representatives of various types to perhaps 600 points around the globe for various specialized purposes. The United Nations Development Programme, for example, and the Children's Fund (UNICEF) maintain their personnel in scores of countries. The major specialized agencies do the same. But these are experts in specific operational fields – foreign aid, child nutrition, refugee relief, agricultural improvement, or similar matters. They are not experienced diplomats who can represent the United Nations' political and general interests, or report in broad terms on developments affecting these interests. When I recall my experience as Austrian Foreign Minister, with a limited but professional diplomatic service in foreign countries supporting our efforts abroad, I am impressed with how serious an omission this can be.

Lacking other resources, the Secretary General is often compelled to rely on public information, which is partial and often unverified, and on what the permanent representatives in New York tell him – which is usually what their governments want him to hear. Both are valuable as far as they go, but both must be discounted. The Secretary General should have his own diplomatic representatives in the field.

When I visited a country on official business, an instructive tableau would present itself as I stepped off my plane on arrival. In strict order of rank, I would be greeted by the officials of the host country, and then by the Resident Representative of the United Nations Development Programme and the representatives of all the specialized agencies working in the country. All these international staff members would rank in the higher bureaucratic levels of their respective organizations. Far down at the end of the line, there would sometimes be standing the low-level official who ran the local United Nations Information Office. I have often wondered why, if these agencies can afford to have their representatives in so many countries, the United Nations' own representation needs to be so restricted. The usual response is that the agencies are engaged in operational or technical activities. But I do not believe that invalidates the case I am making for a United Nations diplomatic service.

I do not underestimate the negative reaction this proposal will evoke. Some will say that it would add too much to the organization's expenses. Others will fear that an independent United Nations observer might challenge the government information presented through the currently operating official channels. No doubt there would be problems. But I would like to see a beginning made, perhaps through the selection of a few high-level representatives at large to reside in each of the several regions where the United Nations is active. The experiment, I am certain, would be well worth-while.

It is the Secretary General's duty to manage the Secretariat, whatever the difficulties. I am not complaining about them; they are a part of the job. As Harry Truman said of the American Presidency, 'If you can't stand the heat, stay out of the kitchen.' But after ten years in office I was convinced that changes of the kind I have mentioned are sorely needed.

Without them I fear that both the effectiveness and the financial solvency of the organization will be gravely jeopardized.

16

The Tarnished Image

In my last annual report to the United Nations, I tried to assess the organization's ability to measure up to the new challenges of our times. 'I have to say,' I concluded, 'that, for all our efforts and our undoubted sincerity, the organization has not yet managed to cut through the political habits and attitudes of earlier and less hurried centuries and to come to grips decisively with the new factors of our existence.'

Indeed it has not. As a human organization, the United Nations is certainly flawed. I would be the first to admit that its defects limit its capacity for effective action. But to say this is not to assert, as some do, that the United Nations is no longer a useful organization. Those who hold this view use the wrong standard of comparison. The truly meaningful issue regarding the United Nations is not whether it functions perfectly, or even rather poorly. It is whether humankind, taken as a whole, is better off with it or without it. As to that, it seems to me, there can be no doubt.

Disenchantment with the United Nations is certainly widespread. The organization's critics attack it on the following grounds:

It is endlessly wordy, and its words more often than not do not reflect reality or result in 'real world' changes.

It is ineffective in dealing with the problems it was intended to handle, especially those relating to war and peace; it ignores many current international problems, and when it does deal with them it is often itself ignored.

Because of its one-nation, one-vote system, decision-making rests in the hands of majorities that cannot exercise responsibility for action; this leads to demagogy and extremism.

Because of its domination by the Third World majority, it approaches all its problems with a constant bias. It applies a double standard, with one rule for Western interests and concepts and another for those of the Third World and the left.

Consideration of non-political and technical matters is hampered, and the results are distorted, by the injection of political issues.

The United Nations bureaucracy has lost its dedication to the service of the organization; it is overstaffed, often incompetent, and increasingly composed of individuals serving exclusively national ends.

I have to admit that the United Nations is hardly in a state of robust health. But to look only at the organization's shortcomings is, in my judgement, a profound mistake. It is to disregard the forest for the trees. To gain perspective, it is useful to step back a pace from the present and to consider for a moment why the organization was created and what it was originally intended to do.

Like our ancestors, we live in a world dominated by sovereign states exercising control over specific territories and engaging the loyalties of their inhabitants. Within each country, structures of law and social relationships have fostered the development of communities in which men could live together in some order, for their mutual benefit. But between and among states, no such structure of order has existed. There have been alliances of convenience formed in the ceaseless rivalry between nations; but the general pattern has been one of wary co-existence broken by recurrent wars and preparation for war.

The United Nations, let us remember, was not the first but the second modern world organization created primarily to prevent the outbreak of increasingly catastrophic wars. Its predecessor, the League of Nations, emerged from the wave of revulsion against the carnage of the First World War. Its basic instrument, the Covenant, envisaged an international society of states which would settle their disputes by peaceful means. If any member resorted to war in violation of its commitments, all other members were obliged to join in applying sanctions against the offender.

It was a noble conception, but an unrealistic one. Sovereign states, by and large, were all too prone to use force to achieve their ends, and vastly unwilling to co-operate in restraining offenders. The League therefore failed in its objective of organizing peace. World War II followed – an even more frightful paroxysm of violence and destruction. Then, once again, the leaders of the victorious powers, responding to widespread popular desires, sought to shape a new international system that would prevent yet another recurrence of global war. Today the task is recognized to be more important than ever. Because of nuclear weaponry, another war between the great powers would threaten to obliterate the human race.

In its scope, detail and complexity the United Nations Organization is to the League of Nations what a modern jet airliner is to piston aircraft of the 1930s. Its Charter recognizes that the roots of war lie not only in controversies between nations, but also in economic, social and human rights problems. The Charter sets up machinery to settle international disputes and threats to peace, and procedures for dealing with breaches of the peace or acts of aggression through collective international action, both non-military and military.

On paper the system is impressive. It has frequently helped to avoid or contain international violence. Yet in recent years it has seemed to cope less and less effectively with international conflicts of various kinds, and its capabilities in other areas of international co-operation have also seemed to dwindle.

Depending on one's point of view, there are many explanations for this state of affairs. To me, one factor is fundamental. The war syndrome is an inevitable outgrowth of the doctrine of state sovereignty. As long as states insist that they are the supreme arbiters of their destinies – that as sovereign entities their decisions are subject to no higher authority – international organizations will never be able to guarantee the maintenance of peace. I do not say, nor do I believe, that the United Nations can do nothing in this area; that would be palpably false. But in the last analysis, a peaceful world order will require a revolution in human thinking dwarfing the great national revolutions of our time. Such a world order would entail the subordination of the system of national states as we know it to some sort of superior authority. Just as the law of a nation copes with violence within the state, so must a world organization be equipped to deal with violence on an international scale.

The statesmen who put together the United Nations at the end of World War II were quite aware of the need for some sort of supranational authority for an organization designed to prevent wars. But for understandable reasons they were unable, and indeed even unwilling, to make the radical changes needed to design a system that could be guaranteed to work. Accordingly, while the first *purpose* of the United Nations, as expressed in Article 1, paragraph 1 of its Charter, is 'to maintain international peace and security . . .', the first *principle* of the organization, as stated in Article 2, paragraph 1, is '. . . the sovereign equality of all its Members'.

Limited by that constraint, the United Nations' founding fathers went as far as they could to establish a system that would deter international conflict while it encouraged friendly relations among nations and economic growth and social progress through international co-operation. Essentially, the organization they created works through persuasion of sovereign states, not through compulsion. No substantive action of the United Nations General Assembly binds any member against its will. To a limited extent, members do agree to accept certain decisions of the

Security Council. But the enforcement of such decisions by military means depends on a plan of collective military co-operation that has remained a dead letter. True, the Security Council has on occasion decided to apply partial economic sanctions, and an arms embargo, notably in southern Africa. But these moves have had very limited effect.

Moreover, the five permanent members of the Security Council – the major victors of World War II – were given the authority to block enforcement action by the right of veto. This was justified on the pragmatic basis that any attempt to carry out sanctions over the opposition of a great power might result in a major war, or at least a break-up of the organization. In 1945 that seemed an unacceptable risk; it still seems so today. At that time and since, many other member states have chafed at the double standard implicit in a veto which only the five major powers enjoy. With considerable justice they criticize the excessive way in which the major powers use the veto. In a sense it puts the remaining members in a second-class category – to which their response has been to seek strength in voting blocs. But it is doubtful whether many of the non-privileged members can or would provide the muscle needed to make a truly supranational organization work.

What all this demonstrates is that the United Nations enjoys strictly limited powers entirely disproportionate to the all-encompassing objectives it was created to seek. It is small wonder that many of these objectives remain beyond reach. It is because people do not know, or have forgotten, how little authority the United Nations actually has, that they expect so much from it. In this sense it has been, as the Americans are accustomed to say, 'oversold'.

To put it another way, the United Nations is the creature of its sovereign member states. It can do only what they agree it should do. Its words will not be translated into deeds unless they assent and actively co-operate. The United Nations is like a mirror. It faithfully reflects the wishes, moods and positions of its members. If the image displeases, the remedy does not lie in shattering the mirror.

Disillusionment with the United Nations is understandable. To many, it has been a disappointment. But I am arguing that the fault, in the main, lies with the member states themselves. Large and small, they seek to use the organization for their own narrow national advantage. What is increasingly lacking is any sense of a broader, altruistic awareness of the benefits of negotiation, accommodation of opposing views, and acceptance of disinterested third-party judgement in the settlement of contentious cases.

It is unfortunate that the window of opportunity that seemed to be opening up after each of the two world wars quickly slammed shut. The shock effect of those wars on world opinion produced a frame of mind receptive to the idea that nations really could co-operate to surrender a limited part of their sovereign egoism to a functioning international authority. Before it faded back into the sad patterns of the past, that vision produced the Charter of the United Nations – an operational blueprint rather too visionary, too idealistic, for the everyday world of international politics.

Perhaps those who created the United Nations are open to the criticism that they led their peoples to expect too much from it, so that their disappointment is correspondingly greater. This point may be particularly applicable to Americans. In a sense, the United Nations is their own creation. As in the case of the League of Nations, which they never joined, they provided the major impetus for its establishment. The words of the Charter are in large part derived from the terminology of American political idealism, with its firm assumption of the basic goodness of mankind.

Europeans, on the other hand, are less optimistic. Generally speaking, they have had too much experience of wars and misfortunes to have excessive expectations of human institutions. Most of their governments have tended to regard the world organization as only one of the available tools of international diplomacy and politics, to be used in serving their national interests and disregarded as much as possible on other occasions.

For many Europeans, the projection of the American dream into the international arena could be a dangerous doctrine. They remember Woodrow Wilson and the tide of emotional support for a new world order on which he arrived in Europe to make peace after the First World War. They recall that in his noble naivety he permitted himself to be used for the parochial interests so ably advanced by Lloyd George and Georges Clemenceau. While assuring the birth of the League of Nations, he became a party to an inequitable peace treaty which helped to pave the way for Adolf Hitler.

The Yalta Agreement of 1945, under which the Allied powers established the post-war order in Europe, is only one example proving, to my mind, that the super-powers have an underlying preference for settling their problems unilaterally, rather than through the United Nations. Inevitably, it appears, they tend towards a preference for a policy of areas of influence involving their allies on both sides. In this regard they simply carry on with past history: the powers of the day have always preferred deals made bi-laterally, rather than through the use of internationally available multi-lateral means.

No doubt this is a more direct, far more simple and more practical way for the great powers to do business. But these powers, under the Charter, have the principal responsibility for maintaining international peace and security, and the privileged voting position that goes with such a responsibility. When they set such an example, who can blame other countries for pursuing the same course?

Past practice and precedent are important factors in national policy choices. It is not surprising that if the United Nations is flouted or ignored in one instance after another, countries pay progressively less attention to its activities and are less and less prone to use it to help settle their problems. Thus the habit of unilateralism becomes even more thoroughly ingrained. In a typical situation of conflict, only the weaker of two contestants has recourse to the United Nations. It does so less in the hope of gaining adequate redress than in order to use the organization for the public presentation of its view – while the stronger party would rather go it alone, without international interference.

This paradigm is, of course, an oversimplification. The sequence of events in a complex world does not follow so straightforward a path. But the basic point remains valid. Unless nations are willing to risk the consequences of settling their disputes peacefully through collective action, they cannot fairly criticize the organization they themselves created for that purpose.

Having said all this, I must recognize that the United Nations as it exists today is something more than an aggregation of the individual states that belong to it. It has developed a corporate personality and style of its own. Like all other significant institutions, it has evolved with time. And some of the changes in its operations have been largely responsible for the decline of its image in the world community.

The fifty-one founding members of the United Nations consisted essentially of two groups: a preponderant bloc of Western-oriented states, and a tightly cohesive Communist minority bloc. The set-piece dramas that took place on the United Nations stage in the early years of its life typically arrayed the majority against the minority, in highly publicized debates over cold-war matters that could have only one voting outcome. In one way or another, United Nations deliberations were relevant to virtually every crisis between East and West – for instance, as regards Berlin, unrest in Eastern Europe, Korea, and the Cuban missile crisis.

Predictably, the organization ordinarily came down on the side of the West, not just because the West had the votes, but also because the Charter is necessarily weighted against efforts to change the status quo by threats or acts of violence. Within the Western group, the same standards were sometimes applied. The United Nations, with American support, did not shrink from condemning the British and French, together with Israel, when they resorted to arms in 1956 to attack Egypt after the nationalization of the Suez Canal.

What is more, the United Nations, in its earlier configuration, was able to carry out many important tasks. It presided over the process of moving the former Italian colonies to independence. It was the midwife for the creation of the state of Israel. It spearheaded many aspects of the process of economic development. It made the defence of human rights a matter of international concern. There were, to be sure, regrets over its failure to do more. But on balance, the accomplishments of the organization, limited though they were, were both recognized and considered as a basis for future progress.

From 1955 onwards, the membership of the United Nations began to grow rapidly. Sixteen countries joined the organization in that year alone. In 1960, no less than seventeen joined. There was hardly a year without a new member. In 1984 the total membership reached 159.

The new members consisted predominantly of new states, created through the process of decolonization – a movement the United Nations itself fostered, endorsed, and, through the admissions process, legitimized. The new arrivals were overwhelmingly non-white, non-Western, under-developed and unschooled in the practice of national and international governance. They brought to the corridors of the United Nations a burning sense of the injustice done them under their former colonial masters, an insistence that the West therefore owed them the wherewithal needed for economic growth, and a more or less conscious rejection of the tenets of Western liberal democracy. For them the principal targets of human rights policy were not repressive measures against individuals but racial discrimination and economic and social backwardness. They saw themselves as the have-nots of the world, striving for nothing less than a new international order.

These adherents of the Charter of Economic Rights and Duties of States no doubt viewed it as a step towards the rectification of age-old wrongs. It proclaimed the absolute sovereignty of states over their natural resources, and in effect their right to treat foreign investment as they chose. It represented an understandable reaction to past 'imperialist' practices involving the exploitation of the labour and natural resources of former colonial territories.

But this all-out attack on existing relationships between the North and the South ignored certain basic realities. Economic development requires capital and technical skills that simply do not exist in most of the new countries. These have to be provided from the North, either through bi-lateral arrangements with business or governments, or through multi-lateral mechanisms like the World Bank, the United Nations Development Programme, and similar regional organizations of the same kind.

Currently, no other source can provide them on anything like the required scale.

Assistance of this sort will not be forthcoming if foreign investment is subject to expropriation at will, or if a fair return on such investment cannot flow back to the source. If the countries of the South wish to improve their economic status, they must recognize that no state can be fully independent in economic matters.

Fortunately, in recent years the pendulum on this particular issue has begun to swing back towards the centre. The two sides have come to appreciate that it is possible to work out mutually advantageous arrangements that will help to sustain economic growth in the North as well as the South. Old suspicions and hesitations still exist, and doubtless will continue to do so. But the trend is running towards the sort of helpful accommodation that an international organization should foster.

What has contributed to the decline in the stature of the United Nations has been the constant emphasis on a few highly inflammatory political issues of world-wide concern. Most dominant over the years have been the fierce altercations about the Arab-Israeli conflict and South Africa's policies pertaining to apartheid and Namibia.

The intense preoccupation of the organization with a few specific problems of this character, although understandable, is not healthy. This is particularly true when these issues are injected into discussion on general economic, social or technical matters in organs which were never intended to cope with such matters. Such tactics focus attention more often on highly political controversy than on the problem for which the meeting in question was convened. Inadequate time may be left to consider the issues on the agenda. Discussion of non-political problems in permanent organs of the United Nations can be hampered and distorted in the same way.

This is what gives rise to the often-heard complaint that the United Nations has become too politicized to function effectively. As much as I understand the emotions which sometimes influence the attitudes of delegates, I do not consider that this relentless emphasis helps to solve the problem at hand, and I feel it does more harm than good to the prestige and the credibility of the United Nations.

Critics should take into account two points worth making in this connection. First, the agencies of the United Nations are in large part deliberative bodies. In the same way as national legislatures, they tend to be long on talk and cumbersome in action. As they function, a certain amount of repetition, even of hyperbole, is unavoidable. In well-disciplined parliaments, this can be controlled through political parties or other means. But since the members of United Nations organs are representatives of sovereign states, they are much more difficult to manage, particularly when organized in blocs directed by their more extreme members. Still, the organization must find better ways to reduce time-wasting and repetitious debate; the excessive proliferation of solutions; the injection of extraneous and controversial political issues into forums where they have no proper place.

A second point to keep in mind is that these faults may be ameliorated with greater experience. Today, a large number of members of the United Nations are states with little experience in international diplomacy. It is hardly surprising that their representatives sometimes practise a rather unrestrained type of parliamentary politics. I am reminded of the concern shown by the founding fathers of the American constitution, two hundred years ago, over the effects of factionalism, extremism and demagogy in the new federal Congress they were establishing. Despite their fears, the American system of government has turned out to be exceptionally long-lasting and effective. While an international organization is not a government, I believe that it too can be shaped, with experience, to improve its procedures. It will take unremitting effort, to be sure; but it will not do to throw up one's hands in frustration.

The fact has to be faced that the United Nations has fallen upon hard times. It goes through its paces in a workaday routine that is progressively ignored or condemned by, and that threatens to become increasingly irrelevant to, the real world. Its vitality is being sapped. To some, its future is at best obscure. It is moving into fields of operation in which opposing interests threaten to tear it apart.

Alternative channels of mediation do no better – if anything, they do worse. The hostilities in Afghanistan, the Persian Gulf and Kampuchea continue, but similar tragedies have occurred, and are still occurring, in other parts of the world, without any effective United Nations intervention. Some have been the concern of the appropriate regional groups. But the record of more recent events tends to prove that such groupings cannot match the peace-making and peace-keeping capabilities of the United Nations, when these are fully engaged. It is not right that resort to regional organizations, when they are ineffective, should be used to hold the United Nations at arm's length.

The hostilities between Libya and Chad in 1981 are a case in point. The African countries insisted that this was a regional problem, and that it should be handled by the Organization of African Unity. Settlement of regional disputes by regional agencies is provided for in the Charter. But when the African states decided to organize their own peace force to operate in Chad, they soon discovered that they did not have the organizing experience, or the financial resources, to make such an enterprise successful. At that stage, they came to me, seeking United Nations financial and technical support. I had to inform them that the Security Council was hardly likely to provide material assistance for an operation over which it did not have authority.

In my judgement, if the Africans had brought the problem to the Security Council in the first place the Council would probably have organized an effective peace-keeping operation. The Africans wished to have a purely African peace-keeping force to resolve this issue. This consideration would not have entailed undue difficulty. Peace-keeping forces are raised only with the consent of those involved; and there are African units experienced in and available for such duties, for instance in Nigeria, Ghana and Senegal, as well as capable military forces in other African countries. Because considerations of African solidarity were allowed to stand in the way of an appeal to the United Nations, the OAU effort proved abortive, and its peace force soon had to be withdrawn from Chad.

Even so, there are brighter elements in the picture. Forty years after its foundation, the United Nations is more than ever a unique and universal organization. Unlike the League of Nations, it has not lost membership through withdrawals or ceased to exist. Membership remains the badge of legitimacy for every newly independent country. The organization can fairly-take credit for having contributed in some crisis situations to the prevention of general war. When countries wish to use it, it can still serve as an instrument of peace – either as a safety valve for the venting of dangerous emotions or as a peace-making or peace-keeping instrument for the containment of national rivalries. It is a meeting place for leaders and a forum in which opposing conceptions of world order can be reconciled. The world would be the worse for its disappearance. And, as a practical matter, it is just not possible realistically to expect its replacement by a better alternative.

I have the strong impression that in the earlier years of the United Nations most statesmen took the organization more seriously than they do today. The commitments of the Charter were fresher in their minds. When problems of potential concern to the United Nations arose, they were less likely to brush it aside or to seek ways to limit its participation.

Today, the spirit of international co-operation is waning. In matters involving international security the trend is perfectly clear, but it is less evident in other fields. In large part this is because so much activity in the economic, social, human rights and technological fields continues without attracting much notice, in spite of its usefulness. But in these areas, too, the United Nations is now approaching zones of sensitivity that sharply pit members of different backgrounds against one another.

One such area consists of domains not yet fully exploited by man and hence regarded by the organization as the common heritage of mankind. How far the deep sea bed, Antarctica and outer space should be subjected to United Nations control is becoming a subject of real importance. Similar attention is being given to the field of modern communication. Here, the developing nations seek to establish a new international information order that would, among other things, assure better coverage of developments in their countries. The Western world, especially the United States, vehemently objects to such an effort. These countries oppose changes that in their opinion violate classical concepts of freedom of information.

I am fully sympathetic to the misgivings of the developing countries, but I am just as fully convinced that freedom of the press can only be achieved if individual liberty is guaranteed. Far too many countries still have a long way to go in this respect. I sincerely wish that the West would take more heed of Third World problems, and so obviate the necessity of introducing regulatory machinery that cannot produce the desired result in the long run.

This new agenda, as well as the ongoing debate over the new international economic order, raises complex problems of equity, ideology and conflicting interests. States enjoying a technological or an economic lead tend to view United Nations intervention with suspicion. The United States has rejected the Law of the Sea Treaty, laboriously crafted over a period of many years with the concurrence of United States delegations representing earlier American administrations. And the United States perception of the threat posed by the new international information order was in large part responsible for the American decision to withdraw from the United Nations Educational, Scientific and Cultural Organization. On the other side, the Soviet Union continued to abstain from multi-lateral co-operation in the field of economic development.

Obviously the tensions engendered in these areas have serious implications for the future of the United Nations system. If the organization becomes polarized on such issues, this development will regrettably intensify the crisis of confidence which it already faces in the field of collective security. In the last analysis, the future of the organization depends on the political will of its members. It will be shaped less by grand summit-level pronouncements than by hundreds of day-to-day decisions, where the issue is whether to use the organization and to play by its rules, or to go it alone through unilateral action, in the traditional way.

In the long run I believe the enlightened self-interest of the nations will impel them to move in the right direction. I believe that they will increasingly recognize the need for the single great world community – the interdependent world order – that is embodied in the Charter. They will learn to live together in a single global village, adjusting their differences and settling their common problems in a spirit of mutual accommodation.

17

Back to Vienna

In 1981 a major decision loomed ahead of me: should I stand for a third term in office – an unprecedented and possibly disputed step in the history of the United Nations and its Secretaries General. Trygve Lie had been obliged to retire after only seven years, Dag Hammerskjöld had met an untimely death in the Congo after nine years in office, and U Thant, heavily criticized for having withdrawn the UN troops from the Sinai before the Six-Day War in 1967, had not stood for re-election after two full terms.

I must confess to being daunted by the decision. The signals I received from without were confusing, and equally contradictory was my own frame of mind. Ten years at the head of the international organization had stripped me of any illusions I might have harboured about the power associated with the office. In retrospect those ten years stand out on occasion as an almost unbroken series of frustrations and bitter disappointments. I often ask myself about the hopes I cherished at the outset. Yet, on the other hand, I had to concede that, despite all the countervailing forces, the office represented a small but indispensable wheel of reason in the increasingly chaotic machinery of international relations. It had to be conceded that in all those years we had obviated crises, defused countless conflicts and initiated innumerable dialogues. Furthermore, the ten years in office equipped me pre-eminently to carry out the task that confronted a Secretary General. Throughout all the dramatic events it had been possible to retain the trust and confidence of almost all the member countries. Should I, nevertheless, refrain from exercising my wealth of experience and utilizing the breadth of contacts for a further five years?

Before making my final decision I was determined to sound out the international community and ascertain the wishes of the member states. In any event, I wished to spare the organization a situation in which my personal wishes would be seen to be running counter to those of the family of nations.

The Charter itself contains no provisions relating to the length of a Secretary General's tenure. However, I was only too well aware of the fact that the unorthodoxy of a third term in itself could fuel the flames of opposition – especially among those countries who had displayed particular interest in ensuring the rotation of the appointment among the major regional groups. There was no denying the fact that three out of the four Secretaries General in the first thirty-six years had been Europeans. All my friends and colleagues, including the French Ambassador to the United Nations and later his country's Minister for Foreign Affairs, Louis de Guiringaud, had pointed to the problems involved. 'Aren't ten years enough?' he asked in his blunt quizzical manner, when he visited me in September 1981.

It was his successor at the UN, Jacques Leprette, who first drew my attention to a possible nucleus of opposition. I was on a visit to Paris in July 1981, and he had been good enough to meet my plane and accompany me during the usual round of discussions. Leprette was distinguished for his very close ties with many African countries, particularly those which had obtained their independence from France. He told me that there had been a somewhat disturbing development at the summit meeting of the Organization of African Unity in Nairobi in the summer of 1981. The last meeting had continued until the early morning hours, when many of the heads of state and prime ministers had already left the scene. At the behest of President Julius Nyerere of Tanzania, a proposal had been tabled that the African countries should support the candidature of Salim Ahmed Salim, the Tanzanian Foreign Minister, as the next Secretary General. He had been his country's Ambassador to the United Nations for many years and the President of the General Assembly in 1979. He was an experienced diplomat and a highly respected leader of the Third World. It appeared that there had been little time for proper discussion of this proposal, but it was a valid decision and as such binding on the African delegations.

The situation was by no means clear-cut. Many of the countries which were former French colonies were not at all happy at the decision. The former British colonies were more united. There was also an undercurrent of realization that the time was not yet ripe for an African to assume the office and that their nominee would stand a better chance in a few years' time.

Nevertheless it was a factor I had to bear in mind. Prior to 1981 there had been little organized regional group backing for candidates to the office but now the bloc tactics which had begun to dominate the proceedings of the United Nations were coming into play. There was no problem with the Asians, and the representatives of the association of South-East Asian Nations (ASEAN) particularly urged me to make myself available. Carlos Romulo, the Philippine Foreign Minister, one of the founding fathers and most distinguished statesmen of the United Nations, even suggested in private consultations with members of the Security Council that the elections should be held at the very beginning of the General Assembly session in September, since he was Council President for that month and assumed that my re-election would be a pure formality.

I was coming under strong pressure from several quarters to run again. Most of the Europeans wanted me to stay on. So did a number of Africans, trying to convince me that the Nairobi decision was not much more than a formality. The attitude of the permanent members of the Security Council was, of course, a crucial factor in the situation. During my customary visits to their capitals during the course of the year I was assured of broad support.

The Russians made it clear that I would get their backing. As Ambassador Troyanovskiy put it: 'An old shoe fits better than a new one.' The Americans and British were similarly positive and assured me of their support. The French, while endorsing my candidacy, indicated that they would also support Mr Salim so as not to antagonize the Africans. A similar policy was apparently to be followed by Spain and some others. Since a ballot is held on each candidate, in alphabetical order, a representative can vote for more than one person, a rather strange and illogical procedure.

The Chinese attitude was more ambiguous, but at least, to my European mentality, it did not seem directly unfavourable. They praised my performance and co-operation with them during the preceding ten years and expressed the hope that this might continue in the future. I was familiar with their voting pattern in the past, which after all had made my election possible, and assumed, mistakenly as it happened, that they might again first opt for a Third World candidate and then, when it became clear that none would be successful, shift to supporting me.

When they started arriving in New York for the autumn General Assembly session, the African group, led by my old antagonist in the Iranian hostage crisis, Ambassador Bedjaoui of Algeria, reaffirmed the decision to support Salim. However, many of the African and Asian delegates approached me individually to express their misgivings. They still considered that an African candidacy was premature and would be divisive.

I thus faced a major personal decision at the onset of the autumn session. Sixty-three years old, I was in excellent health and had acquired a wealth of experience, in addition to which I was assured of the support of a large majority of member states. I thus announced my decision to make myself available for re-election. What followed presented an interesting microcosm of how the United Nations functions when it has to make up its collective mind. I expected the usual manoeuvring in the Security Council but assumed that it, and later the General Assembly, would agree to my re-appointment.

My position appeared to have been strengthened at the Cancun summit in October. I received renewed assurances from the permanent members. President Reagan advised me 'not to worry' about the American position, confirming what I had already been told by Vice-President Bush, Secretary of State Haig and UN Ambassador Jeane Kirkpatrick. The Chinese reiterated their delphic ambiguities, but their Prime Minister, Zhao Zi Yang, assured me at Cancun a few days before the election started in New York that they 'highly appreciated' my work and were 'looking forward to further fruitful co-operation'. It was only when their Foreign Minister, Huang Hua, passed through Washington on his way back to Peking from Cancun that a change in their attitude became apparent. George Bush and Al Haig told me that when they had raised the question of my candidacy with Huang Hua he had 'stone-walled'.

In the first few Security Council ballots, late in October 1981, both Salim and I obtained more than the necessary nine votes, but not the necessary assent of all the permanent members. Salim's initial good showing was due to the French, Spanish and Irish delegates voting for him as well as for me as a gesture towards the Third World.

By the third ballot, Salim's total fell to six while mine remained above nine. I was still blocked by China. At this juncture, on the recommendation of the Irish delegate, the Council decided to postpone further voting in order to give the members an opportunity to seek new instructions. There was a general feeling that, when it resumed, the Chinese would abandon their veto and thus make my re-election possible. This, however, did not happen, and thus the deadlock continued in subsequent ballots. In each case I received more than nine votes, but Salim failed to do so, in some ballots.

I do not want to mention by name all the leading officials from Africa who came to see me repeatedly during the election process, pleading with me not to withdraw my candidacy. They wanted to have someone at the head of the organization who, due to his long experience, could, as they argued, provide firm and steady leadership in the critical years to come. They also thought it likely that, if their own candidate did not make it, the obvious Third World choice would be a Latin American, since an Asian, U Thant, had already headed the Secretariat.

What finally disposed of Salim's candidacy was the unyielding opposition of the United States. The reason for this forms part of United Nations history. It will be recalled that for twenty years the Americans had fought tooth and nail to keep Taiwan seated in all the United Nations organs as the representative of China as a whole. This dam had been breached at the General Assembly session in 1971, shortly before I assumed office. The credentials of Communist China had been accepted and the representatives from Peking took their seats. It had been the first resounding victory of the non-Western, non-aligned new majority in the United Nations over what was seen as the entrenched power of the United States and its supporters.

It had been a highly dramatic occasion. When the results of the vote were announced there was an outburst of cheering from the delegations which had prevailed and Salim, at that time the permanent representative of Tanzania, who had been in the forefront of the fight, led a victory demonstration in the aisles of the Assembly Hall, to the great discomfiture of the American delegation headed by George Bush. Some of them never forgot the unnecessary humiliation of that day. I was reminded of Talleyrand's classic dictum for diplomats: 'Above all, not too much zeal.'

In the end I fared no better than Salim. When the balloting in the Security Council resumed, the Chinese Ambassador telephoned me and said he had received 'unexpectedly tough instructions' not to change the Chinese vote. I never did learn why they had become so rigid. It may have been because I appeared to them to be 'the American candidate' at a moment when Chinese-American relations were tense because of American plans for the shipment of arms to Taiwan, including fighter planes. It could have been because the Russians were supporting me, and Chinese-Soviet relations were anything but warm. It might even have been because the party leadership in Peking overruled its Foreign Office. My relations with Huang Hua had always been excellent, but I had felt a certain coolness in the attitude of Deng Xiaoping, who entertained excellent relations with President Nyerere of Tanzania.

When it became clear that, despite my strength in each ballot, the Chinese would not change their position, I decided early in December to remove my name from any further consideration. As a matter of courtesy, I informed the permament members of my decision and wrote formally to Ambassador Olara Otunnu of Uganda, the President of the Security Council for the month of December. Troyanovskiy's comment in a private conversation with me had been that, if I were to withdraw my candidacy, Moscow 'could not veto all other candidates', meaning that I should not expect the deadlock to continue. The Russians obviously were now prepared to vote for a compromise candidate.

There remained some tactical skirmishing. The Chinese indicated to me that they would accept a splitting of the forthcoming term of office between Salim and myself, each of us serving for two and a half years. This was not appealing and the idea was quickly discarded. As Ambassador Kirk-patrick put it: 'How can we accept Salim for two and a half years, since he is on no account acceptable to us for a full term? That would not be logical.' The Chinese assured me that there was nothing personal in their position, that they appreciated our past fruitful co-operation, but that after three Europeans had been Secretary General they believed it was now necessary for a representative of the Third World to assume the post.

After my withdrawal, Salim continued to lobby hard and induced the Organization of African Unity to make strong representations on his behalf in Washington, but the American administration made it clear that it was not ready to change its attitude and that any further intervention would be pointless. Throughout this complex manoeuvring, other Third World candidates had been waiting in the wings, including Ambassador Ortiz de Rosas of Argentina, Prince Sadruddin Aga Khan of Pakistan, and Shridath Ramphal, the Secretary General of the Commonwealth secretariat. Also waiting patiently was my trusted and respected former colleague in the Secretariat, Javier Pérez de Cuellar of Peru.

To avoid wearisome rounds of further balloting, Otunnu organized an unofficial straw vote among his fellow Council members, a procedure already envisaged by his predecessor, Ambassador Taeb Slim of Tunisia. Otunnu was an extremely intelligent, quite young man who had studied in the United States and had asserted himself as chairman with great courtesy and imposed a business-like atmosphere on the proceedings. As a result, Pérez de Cuellar was elected in the first renewed ballot. He was the only candidate not vetoed by a permanent member, although there had been one abstention: we never did find out who it was. He met the Chinese requirement for a representative from the Third World, the Russians had known him as Peruvian Ambassador to Moscow and as my special representative for Afghanistan and evidently found him acceptable.

His personal qualifications were excellent. As a Latin American, he was accepted by everybody. As a former senior official of the UN secretariat he was familiar with its workings and had distinguished himself as a careful negotiator on several delicate diplomatic missions.

I trust it will not sound ungenerous or cold-blooded if I say, with the benefit of hindsight, that I did not regret the outcome of the election. Throughout the balloting I had received broader support than any other candidate. This alone was a heart-warming reward for my services. I had done all I could during ten long years to discharge my responsibilities as an international civil servant with all the resources at my command. I was too wise in the ways and cross-currents of the United Nations to be in any way affronted, and both my wife and I were looking forward to a period of calm and relaxation after the tense pressures of a whole decade. The General Assembly paid me the final compliment of a standing ovation before I left. Deeply moved, I expressed my thanks to the delegates and to my colleagues and staff for their loyalty and devotion.

Soon it turned out that the peace and tranquillity I had expected were not to be in store for me. Shortly afterwards, I was approached by a number of American universities as well as political research institutes to accept a position as a research professor or foreign policy analyst. It was Father Healey, President of the renowned Georgetown University in Washington, DC, who offered me a post as research professor for diplomacy and counsellor for the Landegger programme on business diplomacy. The Landegger family is a symbol of the many enormously successful Austrian families living in the United States. Having left his country during the inter-war period, Karl Landegger became one of the most prominent industrialists and philanthropists in the US. The friendship of the Landegger family ranks amongst the most pleasant memories of my stay in New York. My appointment did not call for regular lectures, but for directing special seminars on international affairs. The dynamic and popular Dean of the School of Foreign Service, Peter Krogh, also regularly asked me to be the key-note speaker on a number of important occasions, for instance in connection with visits of foreign dignitaries.

I welcomed this opportunity to enter into the world of the young, which extended far beyond Georgetown to similar activities at Florida State University and Chapel Hill University in North Carolina. My stay at Georgetown University permitted me to check through my voluminous personal archives, which I had taken with me from New York after my ten years at the United Nations. I also started to write my memoirs with the help of a very small but able research team. Finally, after having spent altogether more than seventeen years in the United States, I returned home.

On my return to Austria I was impressed by the change that had taken place in Vienna during my absence. The old metropolis on the fringe of world politics had become a centre of international activity. The government of Chancellor Josef Klaus, in which I had served as Foreign Minister, had decided in the late 1960s to build a United Nations centre on the banks of the Danube as a symbol of the policy of active neutrality that my country had embraced. A whole series of international organizations had moved to Vienna, including the International Atomic Energy Agency (IAEA), the United Nations Industrial Development Organization (UNIDO), the Centre for Social Development and Humanitarian Affairs (CSDHA), the United Nations Fund for Drug Abuse Control (UNFDAC) and the International Narcotics Control Board. One of my own last acts as

Secretary General was the transfer of the United Nations Relief and Works Agency for Palestine Refugees in the Near East (UNRWA) from Beirut to Vienna. This was essential because of the increased fighting and the constraints it imposed on the agency's work.

Parallel to the settlement of international organizations in Vienna, the Austrian government, under Chancellor Bruno Kreisky, who had succeeded Klaus, had taken an ever more pronounced stance in international questions, with regard both to East-West relations and to the North-South dialogue, as well as in the Middle East conflict.

It was a proud and happy hour for me when the Austrian federal government handed over to an Austrian Secretary General the vast complex of the Vienna International Centre, against a symbolic annual rent of one Austrian schilling, the equivalent of five US cents. A silver coin is kept in the safe at the United Nations New York headquarters as a gesture by the then Mayor of Vienna, Leopold Gratz, to cover the rent for the next thousand years. Soon after my return it became clear to me that Vienna is, of course, an ideal place to use my international experience for further international activities.

It was Bradford Morse, the Administrator of the United Nations Development Programme (UNDP), who approached me in 1983, during a brief stopover in New York on my way from Washington to Vienna, with the idea of setting up an international commission of former heads of state – soon to be nicknamed 'the council of wisdom'. Freed from the burden of office, this group of elder statesmen endeavoured to place their extensive experience at the disposal of the appropriate governments. Morse had already attracted the interest of Takeo Fukuda, the Prime Minister of Japan during the second half of the seventies, and now wanted to bring me in to assist in organizing the founding committee and the main council. We tried to cast our net as widely and even-handedly as possible and were able to attract the support of Helmut Schmidt, the former Federal German Chancellor, Misael Pastrana Borrero, the former President of Colombia, Manéa Manescu, who had been Chairman of the Council of Ministers in Romania, and Léopold Senghor, the former President of Senegal.

With their help we quickly attracted the participation of a total of thirty elder statesmen, including Guilio Andreotti of Italy, James Callaghan of the United Kingdom, Jacques Chaban-Delmas of France, Jenö Fock of Hungary, Pierre Elliott Trudeau of Canada, Malcolm Fraser of Australia, Ahmed Osman of Morocco, Michael Manley of Jamaica, General Obasanjo of Nigeria and Carlos Andrés Pérez, the former President of Venezuela. At our inaugural meeting in Vienna in November 1983, I was elected chairman of the Interaction Council.

What we had in mind was a completely new approach to advising governments – not through written reports, which we knew, based on past experience of other commissions, usually end up in the archives. Our method is to establish an on-going process of consultation with the governments in power. Our advantages are clear – long experience, informality, personal relations, independence and international prestige. Our aim is to develop proposals for action on the three great issues of our time: peace, security and disarmament; the revitalization of the world economy; and development, with special emphasis on the question of Third World debts. In practical terms the Council acts by sending small missions of two to three members, former heads of state or government, to key capitals in different parts of the world to discuss our proposals with the leaders of these countries. It was only natural that an international Council with such a distinguished membership, composed on a supra-national basis, should set up its headquarters on neutral ground. Vienna was, therefore, a natural choice, as the capital of a country which, thanks to its internal stability, its economic prosperity, its geo-political location, its cultural heritage, reaching far beyond the frontiers of East-West ideology, and its active neutrality, obviously offers itself as an ideal place for such an international venture. As the German playwright Friedrich Hebbel once wrote: '*Osterreich ist eine kleine Welt, in der die Große ihre Probe hält*' (Austria is a small world, but it is the testing ground for the great world).

18

Power Politics

On a cold winter's day, a pack of porcupines huddled close together seeking warmth and refuge from the frost. Very soon, however, they had to move apart again, as their quills struck home. Whenever the need for warmth drew them together, they soon found themselves being repelled by stabs of pain. Thus, they shifted from one extreme to the other until they kept their proper distance. In his fable, Schopenhauer, the German philosopher, describes, albeit unintentionally, the relationship between the two super-powers: an unending shuffling back and forth between mutual antagonism and *rapprochement*. Rarely – and definitely not during my ten years as Secretary General of the United Nations – have the United States of America and the Soviet Union ever established that proper distance where they could tolerate each other for a period of peaceful collaboration.

In 1971, the year of my election, the United States had just launched their 'ping-pong' diplomacy with China and, at the same time, one of their largest sea and air offensives in Indo-China. Willy Brandt's *Grundvertrag* between the two German states had stirred parliamentary emotions in Bonn, while the UN Security Council was unable to adopt resolutions on the Indo-Pakistani war, stymied by Soviet vetoes.

The years thereafter were marked by a complete change. The period of *détente* set in train a whole series of developments: talks on strategic arms control (SALT); the Helsinki process leading to the final act, the setting up of the Conference on Security and Co-operation in Europe; the Federal Republic of Germany's *Ostpolitik*; the American-Soviet understanding of a need for a comprehensive peace in the Middle East; and the Nixon-Kissinger approach to the management of relationships with adversaries.

By the time I left office in 1982, the pendulum had swung back again. Relations between Washington and Moscow had dramatically cooled brought on by a complete misunderstanding on both sides of what *détente* really meant, and by developments in Afghanistan, Poland and elsewhere: all of this against the backdrop of a new and even more frightening arms race. I cannot recall any other time in the post-war period when world politics had become such a playground of semantics. Never before had there been so much talk of war in US-Soviet relations. There was open discussion of the possibility of limited nuclear war and of a 40% probability of nuclear conflict. The best deterrent was seen to be preparation for a nuclear war that could be won. In answer to a question raised in the Senate about the possibility of a country surviving a nuclear onslaught, Eugene Rostow, Head of the American Arms Control Authority, replied that Japan had, 'after all, not only survived but flourished after the nuclear attack'.

Why was there this sudden upsurge of distrust and ill-feeling between the super-powers, who only a few years earlier had found it quite possible to agree on certain confidence-building measures? Contrary to repeated statements in both capitals, I am convinced that in the final analysis the reason has little to do with different ideologies. The two major powers have always subscribed to different ideologies, regardless of the relationship prevailing at any one time. The real difficulty seems to lie in a clash of perceptions adopted by the leaders in Washington and Moscow. Some historians, I know, believe that the course of world events is governed exclusively by political, economic and social forces. To some degree this is certainly true. At the same time, history is made by people: the personalities of top politicians and their perceptions. Having spent the best part of forty years travelling the world, I have had ample opportunity to meet literally hundreds of world leaders; this experience has convinced me that personalities clearly determine the fateful choices made by nations.

Under President Ronald Reagan, the Soviet Union is blamed for everything that is wrong and dangerous. Everything is reduced to a battle against the realm of darkness, to a confrontation between right and wrong, good and evil. Bound by the Marxist-Leninist principles of world revolution, the Soviet Union reciprocates by arguing along similar lines. To the Soviet mind, capitalism remains the root of all evil in the world. Exploitation, alienation, imperialism and war – all are engendered by capitalism. Both come to the same conclusion: were it not for the other, the world would be a glorious place and everybody could live in peace.

The strength of these perceptions lies in their simplicity and ease of comprehension. There is a concrete enemy who is the source of all evil. It is quite clear that this enemy must be fought with all available means. Furthermore, well-established and adequately tested methods exist for such a fight. Within the framework of these perceptions it is a simple task to stir emotions deeply rooted in the psychology of many peoples – the feeling of national superiority and of suspicion and hostility towards everything unusual or strange. These perceptions also tend to shape specific norms of political behaviour, identifying political courage with 'toughness' and intolerance with political wisdom.

By contrast, the philosophy of *détente* and peaceful co-existence is much more sophisticated. It deals with mutual survival, with establishing good relations and co-operation between states that are truly different in terms of social systems, political institutions, values, sympathies and anti-pathies. This is not easy; and it is even more difficult to understand that the source of trouble might be not only in the actions of the other side, but also in miscalculations and mistakes in one's own policies, to say nothing of objective processes taking place in the world.

When Henry Kissinger devised his policy of *détente* in the early seventies, he wanted to put an end to the continual changes of mood in US foreign policy. From the very outset, American awareness of history had been determined by two diametrically opposed factors – a messianic sense of mission (Thomas Paine: 'It is within our power to begin the world anew') and isolationism (George Washington: 'As little political connection as possible with foreign nations'). Kissinger felt that the relationship between the two super-powers was of such importance to the future of the world that it could not be left to a simple ringing of the changes between containment and Cold War, between pragmatism and ideological fervour. He was intent upon establishing a new sense of balance based on mutual respect for the interests of both states and systems. A new order should come about, oriented not towards the two nations' differences but towards their similarities of interest. He admitted that treaties would not deter nations from waging war if their hearts were set upon it. However, as he pointed out, everything should be done to create conditions under which they would no longer seek war. It was this emphasis on the commonalty of interest – the need for security and stability as well as financial considerations – rather than on ideological variance that paved the way for *détente*. As a result agreements were reached between the two nations and the Helsinki Conference was held. Seen in the abstract, *détente* was a competition between different ideas and different socio-political systems; and whilst it did not put an end to the struggle between the two conflicting systems, it certainly stabilized their degree of antagonism.

The crisis that eventually came was not caused by the lack of success or usefulness of *détente*; it stemmed rather from the degree of misplaced expectations. Today, it is tragically clear that both East and West in fact regarded *détente* as another offensive weapon, designed to bring about changes in the other's political system and undermine the other's structures with their own set of values. To put it more simply: the East saw *détente* as a means of establishing the inviolability of the borders drawn up in 1945 and of securing to themselves the right to intervene in the Warsaw Pact countries whenever riots occurred or opposition increased (the Brezhnev doctrine); and also as a way of improving economic and techno-scientific co-operation with the West to the benefit of its own industry. Furthermore, *détente* would make it possible to continue the ideological struggle and support visible 'progressive forces' such as peace movements in the West. Needless to say, *détente* was limited to Europe and was 'divisible'.

For its part, the West expected human contacts to improve with the exchange of information and with open frontiers, with the same respect being shown for individual human rights as in the West. The Carter administration used a policy of *détente* more and more openly as a means of changing the political system in Eastern Europe and weakening the Warsaw Pact. The main vehicle was Carter's human-rights policy, which emerged as a counter to the Kremlin's behaviour in Afghanistan and Poland, where Moscow's actions had precisely confirmed the image which the West had of it.

Ronald Reagan's election was a clear rejection on the part of the American electorate of the concept of *détente*, which they felt to be counter-productive; it was also a demonstration of their disappointment in President Carter himself, whom they considered to be a weak man. They wanted a strong man, a self-assured and assertive leader, to save the country from the humiliations they felt it had suffered through a number of Carter's actions, particularly his unfortunate handling of the hostage crisis in Iran. Reagan conjured up this image and was able to put his acting skills to convincingly good effect. His landslide re-election shows that his countrymen have even forgiven him his mistakes and other lapses, such as the occasional ill-calculated public statement. He is, of course, fervently anti-Communist. He dislikes Marxists and, by the same token, the Soviet leadership; he considers the Soviet Union to be the root of most evil in the world. He feels that tough attitudes adopted in Washington will force the Russians to yield. Furthermore, he has apparently convinced himself that the Soviets only respect power, so he will only negotiate with them on the basis of strength. It must be recognized, however, that he is a nationalist, not an internationalist. He is a strong believer in national interests and politics: he holds firmly to the belief that by creating a strong America he is helping the Western world in its struggle against the devil. He is intent on giving the United States superiority in the balance of power.

In matters of security, he was clearly convinced from his very first day in office that deterrence through nuclear strength was the only course open to the United States. Consequently, he felt that international organizations were unable to solve the problem of disarmament. During my time at the United Nations, this determined approach did not make our role any easier. Even so, I have to recognize that the President is a highly pragmatic political leader. In actions taken after my term in office, the Reagan administration has been compelled to move more towards the political centre, kicking and screaming though it may be, in a number of foreign policy areas. This has been particularly evident in his pursuit of arms control negotiations and in his administration's leadership in dealing with the persistent international debt crisis. How deep these apparent changes go will only be revealed by future developments.

Reagan also introduced a new policy towards the Third World. He adopts a simple formula: those countries which co-operate with America will get aid, but those which play what he calls a double game, demanding assistance and then voting against the United States in the international organizations, will go empty-handed. When I left office it was obvious that the US government placed no trust in the United Nations, which compelled them to sit down at the same table as Communists and 'traitors'. Within the new US administration there is a pronounced school of thought that sees the United Nations merely as a constraint upon American freedom of action. The decision to withdraw from UNESCO was a clear indication of US thinking and feelings. Whereas it may be true that the agency was having administrative problems, the real reasons for the American defection lie elsewhere.

In a democratic society such as the United States, perceptions can easily become the basis of policy; in America's relations with the other super-power it is, therefore, essential that the majority of Americans perceive the Soviet Union, its people and its leaders exactly as they are, not as they believe them to be. Politics should be based on facts, not on myths. Myths grow like weeds; unlike facts, they need nurturing. Soviet Russia has – in the words of Princeton Professor Stephen F. Cohen – 'been on our minds as a virtual obsession for more than sixty years. During these years far more has changed in the Soviet Union and in the world than in our perceptions and ideas.'

One of the reasons may be the regrettable lack of basic studies on the Soviet Union in the USA. It was Averell Harriman, the grand old man of American diplomacy and politics – his last official assignment was as US chief negotiator at the Vietnam negotiations in Paris, which I formally opened in 1973 – who wrote in his book on the Soviet Union that, like many other visitors to that country, his first and lasting impression had been the yearning for peace demonstrated by every Soviet citizen. This, he stated, has been accompanied by a demand for friendly relations with the United

States – and no American could escape the impression of a general desire for peace. I am unable to judge whether Harriman's impression can stand critical scrutiny, but I doubt whether a similar statement could be found today in an American book about the Soviet Union, given the current mood of the country.

George Kennan, like Harriman a long-serving Ambassador to Moscow, stated a few years ago that new data on the Soviet Union had scarcely been digested by American scholars, much less by the policy-makers, the critics and the old-timers. Kennan went on to say: 'Because of this long preoccupation with the subject – not despite it – it is time that our ideas on the USSR were taken thoroughly apart and put together again with relation, this time, to the present scene.'

One minor incident, which the Soviet Ambassador in Washington, Anatoly Dobrynin, told me during a meeting in 1984, serves as a useful illustration of this rather dangerous degree of misunderstanding and lack of knowledge of the Soviet hierarchy. Ignoring all customary diplomatic channels, the US disarmament specialist, General Scowcraft, leading an American study group on a private visit to Moscow, tried to deliver a personal letter from President Reagan to Soviet General Secretary Yuri Andropov, by-passing Foreign Minister Andrey Gromyko on the way. Since the necessary careful preparations had not been made through the Soviet Embassy in Washington, General Scowcraft soon came unstuck and saw no one in Moscow, whereupon the State Department spent that weekend searching high and low for Ambassador Dobrynin in an attempt to solicit his help in arranging a meeting with the Kremlin leader. It proved impossible to obtain an appointment and Scowcraft left Moscow – his letter undelivered. Anyone with any understanding of the governmental machinery in Moscow must have found this political naivety on the part of the Americans somewhat frightening.

John Kenneth Galbraith once wrote: 'Two great fears have pervaded political life in the United States: one is the fear of Communism, the other is the fear of being thought soft on Communism. With those fears endemic to the man in the street, the members of Congress and the man in the White House, a well-conceived, consistent foreign policy towards the Soviet Union is difficult if not impossible.' This is especially dangerous because deep down every American politician knows that the important issue confronting his country during the next decade will concern relations between the US and the USSR. That relationship will dwarf all others. Many US citizens feel that, because of the danger of mutual destruction, it is imperative to examine how to bring reason rather than emotion to bear on the formation and conduct of policies towards the Soviet Union.

Without wishing to set myself up as a psychiatrist, I am convinced that one of the strongest currents undermining the possibility of a more rational co-existence is a subconscious feeling of discomfort and insecurity. Over the centuries, the almost insurmountable barriers of two oceans have led to a firm belief in the overwhelming supremacy of the United States – a confidence that remained unshattered in the early post-war years. Today, however, the situation has changed: America finds itself not only roughly on a par with the Soviet Union in military terms, but also absolutely equal with other countries in terms of its own vulnerability to a nuclear holocaust. For the Americans this is a completely new situation, to which they find it difficult to get accustomed. It not only nurtures a climate of panic about the Soviet threat, but it also offers permanent temptation to follow those who promise a magic solution – a return to former invulnerability if only sufficient dollars are allocated and an adequate number of weapon systems produced.

It is precisely this subconscious American conviction which has given rise to fundamental differences of opinion within the Western alliance – that is, between the USA and its allies in Western Europe. For the Americans the Soviet Union stands as the global enemy in the irreconcilable struggle for power and in the battle for minds – an opponent who, wherever he appears, presents a threat in a conflict in which there is no room for neutrality. For many Europeans, however, the Russian empire is an unpleasant, disturbing neighbour with whom – despite all the differences – one must come to some sort of arrangement for pragmatic reasons, since – when all is said and done – Russia has been part of the European political system for centuries. It has been claimed – and I fully believe it – that the policy of *détente* looked, and looks, different to people in Western Europe than it did or does to those in California or Texas. To the latter it may appear as a policy of appeasement; to the Europeans it is unadulterated reality. I do not share the contention of some that current trends in Europe may lead to a gradual 'Balkanization' of Europe with each country trying to find a solution to its own national security interests: Germany emerging as the leader of non-nuclear Europe, Britain standing on the sidelines and France retaining its own vision of Europe. There is no doubt, however, that the demise of *détente* has profoundly shaken the basic tenets of the North Atlantic security system.

It was Margaret Thatcher, the British Prime Minister, herself a staunch Conservative and ardent believer in the NATO alliance, who impressed me in a conversation – a relaxed and informal chat during a holiday in a hunting lodge near Salzburg – with her very sensible and realistic attitude towards the Russians. She recognizes that there is no point in hammering the Russians the moment one sits down with them about their human rights violations; this only destroys the climate for constructive negotiations before they start. Once talks are under way the human rights issue can be brought up in due course. She told me that she had impressed this point on President Reagan; I would like to think that her cool recommendations have had some effect.

She is a great advocate of talks with the Soviet Union, for as long and with as wide an agenda as possible. I was greatly taken by her level-headed views. 'We should not believe that the Communist system in the Soviet Union will change,' she said. 'It will stay as it is.' There might be minor changes or nuances but its existence is a fact of life whether the Western world likes it or not, and to wait for a change in the circumstances before beginning negotiations would be wrong. 'It is no good waiting for the younger generation to take over,' she told me, 'that would take too long. We have to talk to the people who are there; that is the only way to get out of the present stalemate.'

Contrary to the general opinion that Margaret Thatcher is a tough, inflexible politician, I found her responsive enough to accept other opinions if they made sense. This was quite apparent in my talks with her on the problems of the Third World and its so-called automatic majority in the United Nations. Despite her full support for Reagan's policy, she demonstrated a clear understanding of the problems facing the developing countries – underscoring the close relations with Africa and Asia that date back to the days of the British Empire.

Although the German Chancellor, Helmut Kohl, only took up office after I had left the United Nations, I had known him for a long time, as we had been neighbours of sorts on many summer holidays in the lake district of Austria, the Salzkammergut. In my opinion, Kohl is a convincing blend of independent European, with a profound knowledge of history, one of the mainstays of the European Economic Community, and a strong supporter of positive co-operation with the United States, which he regards as a main pillar of his foreign policy. His firmness in dealing with the Soviet Union is matched by a sincere wish to contribute to a relaxation of East-West tension. Although the initial decision to deploy cruise and Pershing missiles was taken by the Social Democratic government in Bonn, the country maintains a balanced view of the military threat posed by the Soviet Union. With Berlin acting as a kind of barometer of East-West relations, Kohl's Christian Democratic government tries to retrieve as much as possible from *détente* and its *Ostpolitik*. Furthermore, since they will be in the forefront of any future military confrontation in Europe, the Germans are anxious to see the super-powers make renewed moves towards *rapprochement* and, despite its poor showing over the last decade, they still see arms control as a means of enhancing their security.

During my first term of office, in 1973, an unnatural situation was corrected with the admission of the two German states to the United Nations. This was certainly more than a mere increase in membership: it symbolized a new era in international relations, the policy of *détente*. For the first time, two countries from a divided nation had their own representatives, who sit next to each other in the General Assembly. Although the other members were somewhat uneasy about the danger of getting involved in quarrels between two Germans, this preoccupation soon turned out to be unfounded. I can gladly attest to the fact that the governments of both German states carefully avoided any bi-lateral confrontation within the United Nations. Both delegations expressed publicly their satisfaction that it was a German-speaking Secretary General who had helped them find their way around the complicated premises of the world organization during the initial phase of their membership.

Each of the West German chancellors with whom I dealt during my stay in New York contributed in his own specific way to the work of the United Nations. Willy Brandt drew up his dramatic report on North-South relations, which he entitled 'a programme for survival', and launched an historic endeavour to stabilize East-West relations – his famous *Ostpolitik*. Helmut Schmidt, whom I had first met in his capacity as Minister of Finance at the UNCTAD meeting in Chile in April 1972, maintained his special interest in the economic and social progress of the Third World. An acknowledged financial expert, he seized the opportunity during my first official visit to Bonn in 1975 to criticize the efficiency of the world organization and the stagnating North-South dialogue. He was unhappy to see the developing countries repeatedly presenting the same list of demands, knowing full well that the North was unable and unwilling to fulfil those wishes. 'Why,' he exclaimed, 'don't they state their priorities and concentrate on specific issues, which we could then discuss and, I trust, settle?' Schmidt was highly respected for his competence, but his image suffered on account of his pronounced ego.

Although the Christian Democrats under Helmut Kohl took over from the Social Democrats in 1982, German foreign policy underwent no fundamental change – due in part to Foreign Minister Hans-Dietrich Genscher. In close co-operation with Helmut Kohl, he kept as much of the *Ostpolitik* and *détente* alive as possible, and his personal background may have provided an appropriate incentive. Whereas the East German Honecker's original home was to be found in West Germany, Genscher had grown up on the banks of the Saale in East Germany.

In the course of conversations and negotiations, I came to appreciate the West German Foreign Minister as a trustworthy and accommodating partner. Within an incredibly short space of time, he managed to overcome his initial difficulties – his unfamiliarity with diplomatic practice and lack of languages – and soon became a highly esteemed international figure with a singular blend of cleverness, power of persuasion and common sense. Compared with other Western politicians, his commitment to the United Nations was well above average: a trait that he also put to good effect when promoting the international image of the Federal Republic. Genscher launched several initiatives, such as the resolution on hijacking which was adopted unanimously by the General Assembly. At the same time, the Conservative Kohl, together with the French Socialist François Mitterrand, continues along the path that the Social Democrat Helmut Schmidt had so successfully laid with the Conservative Francois Giscard d'Estaing before them – a firm friendship between the two great neighbours in Western Europe.

Despite their ideological differences, Kohl and Mitterrand share a common attitude towards the Soviet Union. Although the French President has publicly stated that he favours a 'renegotiation' of the alliance so as to put an immediate end to the 'chaos in Western strategy', he has long since stilled any doubts about the position that a French Socialist government might adopt with respect to the alliance.

Mitterrand came to power during my last year in office. He shares a certain sympathy for the 'glory' of France in international affairs with his predecessor, Giscard d'Estaing, for whom I have the highest regard as a competent leader with a profound knowledge of economic and financial problems. Both like prestige, the finer points of protocol, the trappings of power and the aura of publicity. On one of my visits to the Elysée, however, even the renowned French protocol failed at a luncheon given for African heads of state at the conference on sanctions against South Africa in May 1981 – but, as always, the United Nations lent a helping hand. In the course of the luncheon it transpired that some of the African leaders did not speak French, Mitterrand did not speak English and no interpreters were present, whereupon the French President – after a long silence – leant across the table and asked me whether I would be good enough to act as interpreter. I did so gladly, although I left the table rather hungry.

Most European leaders I have met over the years have experienced difficulty – of course to a varying degree – when endeavouring to attribute the wide swings in East-West relations mainly to changing Soviet attitudes towards the United States. Given the length in service of the Soviet Foreign Minister Andrey Gromyko and Ambassador Dobrynin, and the consistency with which Soviet policy statements have focused on what is termed peaceful co-existence, Western Europeans feel that the shifts in policy are mainly ascribable to Washington's lack of consistency.

Ever since the war, the Soviet Union has relied primarily on one man, Andrey Gromyko, to present its external policy. By the mid-1980s, after more than forty-five years in diplomatic service and almost thirty years as Soviet Foreign Minister, Gromyko had reached the peak of his power and influence before making his surprise move, at the behest of the new Kremlin chief, Mikhail Gorbachev, to the office of Soviet President in the summer of 1985. He had become the 'lead horse' or – to quote the former us Foreign Minister Henry Kissinger – 'the indispensable drive wheel of the Soviet Union's international conduct'. I consider him the shrewdest diplomat I have ever met. Hardened by many a crisis and tempered by countless conferences, with an intimate knowledge of all conflicts and their historic origins, he has become an expert of unparalleled skill – in East and West alike.

By 1981, towards the end of my term at the United Nations, it was clear that Gromyko had become the maker of policy rather than its mere purveyor. Although he has been a member of the Politburo since 1973 and is the nominated First Deputy Prime Minister, experts agree that his strength stems partly from the fact that he has never run for the top job – General Secretary of the Soviet Communist Party – and thus he is not continually suspected of being over-ambitious.

I obviously knew him best during my time at the United Nations. He is not an easy man to deal with. Rigid in his defence of Soviet interests, he was not usually disposed to seeking the compromises out of which UN resolutions are so often fashioned. However, in my dealings with Gromyko I always found him reliable. His manner is imperturbable, his skill in negotiation of a high order. Whatever his motives may have been, he always sought to maintain good relations with the organization and with me personally. But, despite the friendly atmosphere in his many conversations with me, Gromyko never entered into a substantive discussion. Whenever he came to a General Assembly session he would ask to see me shortly before the beginning of the meeting at which he was to deliver his annual statement. These cursory discussions invariably focused upon disarmament, but rarely on other issues of crucial importance. This was in marked contrast to the extensive and very substantive meetings I had with his American counterparts, whether they were Kissinger, Cyrus Vance, Edmund Muskie or Alexander Haig. Soon I realized that for Gromyko only one thing counted: power. That explained why he attached so much importance to Moscow's relations with the Americans. While painstakingly maintaining the utmost courtesy, he brought it home to me that power was exactly what both the United Nations and I myself lacked. If I had needed any proof of my impressions, it came years later in a book written by my former Soviet Under Secretary and most prominent Soviet defector, Arkady Shevchenko, entitled *Breaking with Moscow*. In the account of his talks with Gromyko, he recalled one significant remark by the Soviet Foreign Minister: 'As preparations for my new posting continued, I suggested that it might be a good idea for me to develop good working relations with the Secretary General of the UN, Kurt Waldheim. Gromyko frowned. "What important questions can you talk about with Waldheim? Neither he nor the UN as a whole is a great power. Never forget, Shevchenko, you're a Soviet Ambassador first, not an international bureaucrat. Don't hesitate to meet with anybody, even representatives of those countries we publicly attack." '

In formal negotiaton, Gromyko always speaks Russian. Privately he speaks English with some fluency, which he often did with me on informal occasions because he knows I have no Russian. He has a dry if rather heavy sense of humour, which he would draw on when he wanted to divert discussion away from some inconvenient point of policy. I recall a luncheon I gave for him and a few other diplomats at my residence in New York on an absolutely beautiful day. The view overlooking the garden and the East River was sparkling. The guests were no doubt expecting some intervention of substance from Gromyko in reply to my welcoming remarks, but all they received was the comment: 'I wish the climate in international affairs was as fine as the climate outside this room, but unfortunately it is not so.'

He is a man of immense self-discipline. On one occasion he almost collapsed on the rostrum while delivering a speech to the General Assembly. Two guards helped him to my office behind the rostrum and laid him down on a sofa. Fortunately, it was only a passing weakness, which he attributed to the heat and brightness of the television lights shining directly in his face. After a few minutes he insisted, despite my objections, on returning to the platform to conclude his remarks and thus dispel any doubts at home or abroad about his ability to carry on.

It is often speculated whether the high degree of continuity or consistency in the upper echelons of the Soviet power structure should be considered a major strength or weakness. Countless discussions have centred upon the question whether collective leadership saved the Soviet Union from disarray following the deaths, in rapid succession, of Leonid Brezhnev, Yuri Andropov and Konstantin Chernenko.

I have no wish to join the ranks of professional Kremlinologists. However, I do not subscribe to the growing body of Western opinion that the Communist system and ideology are so moribund that changes in the internal regime are inevitable. Communism has been the established ideology for more than sixty-five years and the people have become accustomed to it. They are unhappy about food shortages and they resent having to wait in long queues, but they accept them as facts of life and there is no real opposition to the regime. Two new generations have grown up not knowing anything else. The limited number of defectors are mostly artists and diplomats who have had occasion, during tours and residence abroad, to appreciate the values of Western democracy. The great mass of the population has not shared this experience. Although ideological enthusiasms may have faded, the system has certainly taken over.

Wheareas some shifts in emphasis may emerge when the younger generation reaches the top, no radical changes are to be expected. The younger generation occasionally creates the impression of being more open-minded. A cult of Western products such as blue jeans, ball-point pens and pop music has developed, and this leads to mounting pressure for a better consumer society – but, as far as we can see, always within the present framework.

Moreover, I do not believe for one single moment the speculation voiced from time to time that the party bureaucracy has become so hidebound and introspective that the Soviet army might exert its undoubted strength and take over. It may be true that, given the economic difficulties and the poor state of East-West relations, differences between political and military circles in the Soviet Union are likely to continue in the foreseeable future. But history tends to suggest that the commanders of the armed forces, themselves septuagenarians, do not aspire to political decision-making at the expense of the Party. Throughout its history and notwithstanding the many provocations it has endured, the military has never made any attempt to seize power, effect a *coup d'état*, or even acquire a decisive influence in the institutions through which the country is ruled. The most that can be said is that, in recent years, the military's role as adviser to the Politburo has undoubtedly been strengthened, as has its role in the execution and public justification of Soviet policy.

One other Western argument inevitably raises its head whenever East-West relations are on the decline. It is claimed that, if the Soviet Union is forced to increase its military spending, its economy will eventually be ruined. This is completely erroneous. It is nonsensical to expect Moscow to abandon the race for fear that it may become economically inferior to the United States. It is utterly wrong to claim that they will give up simply because they might be economically weaker than the United States and cannot afford to compete with the Americans any more. The contrary may well be true: after looking at some figures, I am inclined to believe that the military-industrial complex in the Soviet Union is probably stronger than in the United States. Consequently, engaging Moscow in an arms race may well keep the Soviet economic machine moving still faster.

Of course, the Achilles heel of the Soviet system remains the state of its economy: it is without doubt much weaker than the American economy in particular and Western economy in general. The Soviets face continuous problems with food shortages, industrial output and the supply of consumer goods. The Eastern Europeans are confronted with similar difficulties. These factors above all else will determine the Russians' long-term relationship with the Western world. There has been one common theme in all my conversations with the Russians over the years. For all their threats and rhetoric, there is a genuine desire to establish good relations with the Western world, especially with the United States, if possible on a bilateral basis. They need access to Western technology for a mutually prosperous economy.

I only repeat these well-known facts because I think they contain an important political message which the West continuously overlooks: the Soviet Union is basically a country of contradiction, split between outward power and inner weakness. Outwardly, it is the largest and most powerful of the great multinational empires. Inwardly, it is a country rent by huge problems. Unfortunately, many people, especially in the United States, have never really decided which aspect they should take more seriously: the country's military strength or its internal weakness. For too long too many Americans have focused exclusively on the strength of the USSR. Consequently, they have demanded of one President after another that the US be prepared militarily to stand up to the Soviets. The Americans would be better advised to focus on both the strengths and weaknesses of the Soviet Union in order to obtain a more valid long-term picture of their counterparts.

A similar mood prevails in the East. For all their military achievements, the Soviets still have a deep-rooted and endemic fear of the West. Averell Harriman once wrote that since the revolution Soviet propaganda had always emphasized that the Soviet Union, the bastion of Communism, was threatened by the capitalist world. The potential aggressor was always changing – for a long time it was Japan, then Nazi Germany. At the time of writing, it was the United States. In Harriman's view, the whole campaign was designed to urge the Soviet people on to still greater achievements, to justify the sacrifices made in the name of heavy industry and armaments production, and to vindicate the Kremlin's claim to blind obedience and the loyalty of the people as a safety measure. I am unable to judge the validity of Harriman's assessment, but I feel strongly that Western democracies are at fault if they assume that the Soviet fear of the West is nothing but a propaganda barrage for international and domestic consumption. The Russians were invaded by Napoleon and then by Hitler; they suffered some 20 million casualties in World War II and they fear the Western alliance, led by the Americans, as well as total encirclement, with Europe, Japan and China siding with the United States. The military threat, as they see it, even outweighs the ideological differences between Communism and capitalism.

The West, on the other hand, claims that the Soviet Union poses the real threat to world peace and points to Afghanistan. I, too, deplored that military intervention, which has certainly harmed the Soviet reputation in the United Nations. Despite world-wide apprehensions, one can discern the thinking of the Soviet leaders. Ever since the Yalta Conference, Soviet foreign policy has been concerned with the creation of a *cordon sanitaire*, which has figured so largely in their history. Clearly Moscow discerned a weakening of its strategic interests along its southernmost borders – and acted to pre-empt it.

Probably the Kremlin underestimated the reaction to events in Afghanistan. However, the Soviets are undoubtedly aware of the levels of American political and military tolerance in this politically sensitive area so close to the oil centre on the Gulf. Moscow also knows full well that any further advances in that area could alert China, and the Soviet leadership can have no real wish for a Sino-American commonality of interests. Not only for these reasons do I believe that, despite their demonstrations of power in and around Afghanistan, the Soviets are seeking a way of defusing the present situation without loss of face.

Under the pressure of harsh international reaction even within the Eastern bloc, the Kremlin – according to Western observers – has demonstrated a change in behaviour towards eastern Europe. Moscow, it is claimed, is showing far greater tolerance towards liberal tendencies and cautious endeavours on the part of individual states in that region to achieve some measure of political manoeuvrability. This held particularly true for Poland, where the Solidarity trade union under Lech Walesa constituted a challenge not only to the government in Warsaw but also to Soviet policy. Even at the climax of the dramatic events in Poland Moscow remained consciously in the background: tough on general principles but remarkably flexible as to the tactics by which General Jaruzelski has succeeded in maintaining his administrative control. Poland was not the first. In the course of the seventies, a number of other countries within the Soviet alliance succeeded – to a certain extent – in developing a tangible measure of national identity and pursuing more independent foreign and economic policies. In so doing, they managed to exert some influence on the future course of East-West relations.

In terms of foreign policy, Ceauşescu's Romania is by far the most outspoken nonconformist country in the group. Yet, whereas it takes considerable liberties in the field of foreign affairs, at home it has one of the most rigid Communist systems in the whole Eastern bloc. As long as this remains the case, Moscow is prepared to tolerate independent attitudes abroad.

Ceauşescu has manoeuvred with some skill. He probably has better political relationships with Western countries than any other member of the Soviet bloc. He is the only Communist leader to maintain relations with both Israel and the Arabs, and he is sufficiently respected by both to have played an important role in Sadat's initiative to go to Jerusalem. I have seen him with some frequency over the years, listening regularly to his outspoken criticisms of the shortcomings of the world organization, which he wanted to be far more efficient and actively involved in international affairs. This was part of his political design to take a large measure of responsibility away from the super-powers. I usually left him with mixed feelings, riled by his constant insistence on UN weaknesses and yet pleased that one more leader was advocating a vigorous role for the United Nations. He attaches importance to good living and entertains on an elaborate scale, which makes him a rather remarkable host.

His Hungarian colleague, János Kadar, is completely different in character. He closely follows the Soviet line in foreign policy, but at the same time makes sure that his people have at least enough to eat. Kadar is a very shrewd politician and knows how to handle the Soviets. The Hungarians, together with the German Democratic Republic, enjoy the highest standard of living in the Eastern bloc. Hungary had always been the bread-basket of the Austro-Hungarian Empire and the fertility of its soil is its greatest asset. Consumer goods abound and the economy enjoys some of the benefits of a free enterprise system. Limited private property is permitted and the people are offered an incentive to work. Moscow tolerates all this and apparently feels that, as long as the Hungarians are not turning against them politically, there is no reason for them to interfere.

Having been responsible for the execution of his predecessor, Imre Nagy, Kadar came to power as a tough, rigid hard-liner after the Hungarian uprising. He has become more accommodating with the passage of time. Personally, he is quite an impressive man, stocky and with a jovial manner that makes for easy conversation. He is a practical politician and a realist who knows his people well and makes an effort to see that they get what they want: of all the East European leaders he would most probably top the popularity poll. Something of the Austro-Hungarian tradition still lives on in him. In my last talk with Kadar, in 1979, I got the distinct impression that he wanted to keep the bridges to his Western neighbour, Austria, as wide open as possible – using this relationship as a showcase of practical peaceful co-existence, even in times of increasing East-West tension. Thanks to the close contacts which he had with the late Yuri Andropov, erstwhile Soviet Ambassador to Budapest, he apparently had no problems with Moscow as regards his excellent relations with the Austrians, despite the fact that they have gone far beyond the customary East-West contacts.

For completely different reasons, neither the Czechs nor the Bulgarians present the Kremlin with foreign policy problems. With a nation still cowed by the aftermath of the short-lived Dubček era, a powerful group of party leaders and members of the security forces in Prague pursues a rigid policy line towards their Western neighbours which has repeatedly led to unfortunate confrontations with Austria. At the same time, another group of leading politicians is endeavouring to normalize relations with the West. I personally maintained very friendly relatons with Foreign Minister Bohuslav Chňoupek, an amiable and skilful diplomat, popular in international circles. On meeting his party leader, President Gustáv Husák, I was intrigued by the extent of his concern about the arms race and his fear of what he called Western militarism. Since his country would be in the front line of any future European conflict, he was especially sensitive to the nuclear build-up.

In my many talks with Bulgarian leaders and diplomats, it was quite obvious that the government in Sofia toes Moscow's line unreservedly. Although an atheist Marxist country, Bulgaria surprised us by donating a gift of particular religious value to the UN headquarters in New York – a beautiful replica of a mosaic from the famous Ryla Monastery depicting the Virgin Mary and child.

In the eyes of the Soviet Union, the German Democratic Republic plays a singularly important role in East-West relations: thus the determined political attitude of the East German Erich Honecker takes on particular significance. At first sight, Honecker seems to symbolize the dogged endeavours of his country to achieve international recognition. In personal discussions, however, the party chief tends to relax, abandoning party rhetoric in favour of a calm, introverted approach with an occasional sentimental touch of national pride. The Saarland, Honecker's homeland in West Germany, is still part of a larger German *Heimat*. I got the impression that the foreign policy of the German Democratic Republic is guided by three fundamentals: the need for security, which is met by the Soviet Union; the awareness of belonging to Central Europe, which, given present political realities, is basically restricted to pursuing a policy of *rapprochement* towards the neutral states of Europe; and finally the unique relationship with the Federal Republic of Germany.

Immediately after taking up office as Chairman of the State Council, Honecker, as partner and counterpart of Willy Brandt, contributed to the normalization of relations between the two Germanies by supporting the *Grundsatzvertrag* and the Berlin Agreement, thereby enhancing the international legitimacy of the German Democratic Republic. Unlike his predecessor Walter Ulbricht, Honecker appears to have developed over the years the image of a confident and self-assured East Germany, despite the persistence of the inner-German tragedy as symbolized by the Berlin Wall.

In our talks, Honecker re-affirmed over and over again the importance of East-West dialogue and expressed concern at the lack of progress in the disarmament talks. This concern is reported to have become even more apparent in the years since I left office. In tandem with Hungary and Romania, the German Democratic Republic is making unmistakable attempts – as far as this is possible – to encourage the Soviet Union to move towards *détente* again. I had ample opportunity to observe that this was a real concern and not merely a piece of tactical manoeuvring in his dealings with the Federal Republic of Germany and the West German peace movement. The degree of licence accorded to East Germany within the Soviet alliance derives from the country's high standard of living and its industrial performance as well as its people, who have acquired a special position within the eastern alliance by virtue of their being the linguistic and geographical neighbours of the Federal Republic. Radio and television have long transcended national and ideological borders. However, despite all attempts at normalization, it remains an incontrovertible fact that Honecker will not budge an inch from the politico-ideological status quo of the German Democratic Republic.

Summing up the present state of East-West relations, one could point to some tragic paradoxes: both super-powers are devoting all their energy, intelligence and research, not to speak of financial resources, which they and the Third World desperately need for more important tasks, to the development and production of arms. Although neither of them wants war, both are afraid of the other starting it. Meanwhile, the leaders in Washington and Moscow still tend to blame each other for the present East-West tensions, although they know that it is the relationship between them which will shape the world for generations to come. Since everybody realizes that even a limited nuclear war between the super-powers would probably be waged in Europe, the Europeans on both sides of the post-war frontiers are doing their utmost to avoid fuelling that confrontation! Governments and people in Western and Eastern Europe alike are increasingly rejecting the idea of accumulating the largest arsenal ever of nuclear and conventional weapons in a region where nobody wants, but everybody fears war and warfare.

Maybe the Europeans in Bonn and Paris, Budapest or Prague have already learnt a lesson which regrettably still does not ring true for everybody in Washington and Moscow. Knowing that another war can only unite all nations in death and destruction, one can no longer be obsessed by the idea of 'what is best for me', but one should also think a little about 'what is good and acceptable for others'. If we do that, we shall have a better chance of overcoming the present crisis and opening the door to a much healthier development in East-West relations.

19

The Race against Time

When the first atomic bomb fell on Hiroshima on 5 August 1945 and the second on Nagasaki three days later to end World War II, the United Nations was a mere six weeks old, and determined 'to save succeeding generations from the scourge of war'. The Charter of the United Nations was drawn up in the very last days of the pre-atomic age, when nobody knew or imagined how great the scourge of a nuclear war would be. However, at their first meeting in January 1946 the member states accorded top priority to ending the atomic threat to mankind. They adopted a unanimous resolution calling for the elimination of nuclear weapons, and set up a negotiating body to achieve that objective.

After nearly forty years of endeavour – and more than four hundred UN resolutions on disarmament – the world is no nearer that much desired goal than it was at the outset.

Day by day the stockpiles of nuclear – and conventional – weapons grow not only larger, but also more dangerous. Vertical proliferation – the expansion of the arms race to new areas such as outer space and new methods of nuclear assault – proceeds virtually unchecked. Horizontal proliferation – an increase in the number of countries possessing nuclear weapons – is an ever-present possibility.

The super-powers possess a combined total of at least 50,000 nuclear warheads. Their destructive power is equivalent to more than one million bombs of the size that destroyed Hiroshima; expressed in other terms, it would bring about the death of 100,000 million human beings, or the population of the world twenty-five times over.

During all these years no agreement has ever been reached on a ceiling for nuclear weapons, nor has the situation been 'stabilized', as people have suggested at various times. Figures speak for themselves: the two atomic bombs dropped on Japan soon grew to a figure of around 1,000 in 1950, to 20,000 in 1960, to 35,000 in 1970 – and to more than 50,000 today. For the last forty years the two super-powers have been producing the equivalent of one Hiroshima bomb every twenty minutes, day and night, seven days a week. That is the nuclear reality in which we live.

Over the past decades peace between the two most powerful nations of the world has hinged on two principles which have since proved fictitious: deterrence, and the nuclear balance of power, which they had hoped to maintain through continued negotiations on arms control and disarmament. The whole philosophy of deterrence embodied in the first principle has become a doctrine of paradox. In earlier times the principle *si vis pacem, para bellum* (if you desire to maintain peace, be prepared for war) held true because everybody knew that peace usually lasted only a few decades. The balance of power and its political mechanisms worked because power relationships were occasionally put to the test. Today, however, any new war will most probably end in global suicide; confrontation is no longer a feasible proposition. Progress into the unknown in the armaments sector does not offer increased security but poses a lethal threat.

Robert McNamara once tried to establish the amount of nuclear weaponry needed for the doctrine of deterrence. He came to the conclusion that four hundred warheads were enough: with four hundred warheads he calculated that the United States could kill one-third of the Soviet population, and destroy up to two-thirds of its industry. In the meantime, the number of warheads on each side has increased at least by sixty-fold.

The second principle, the balance of power, has emerged as a dangerous illusion. Nobody, not even the experts – none of whom can claim to be absolutely objective – is at present capable of assessing the enormous lengths to which the super-powers have gone in the armaments sector in order to maintain that balance. It is no longer a question of counting warheads and calculating explosive power. Advantages can now be claimed at numerous other levels of sophistication: increased accuracy, shorter flight times, multiple weapon carriers (bombers, land-based missiles, submarine-launched missiles) and the like. To my mind, the demand for 'parity' is a purely political, not a military demand. In fact, either super-power could undertake a significant amount of unilateral nuclear disarmament without jeopardizing its security in any way; however, such a step would presuppose a minimum of confidence, which does not exist today.

It is hard to escape the paradox that any armament acquired by one country to increase its security automatically gives rise to insecurity in the minds of its rival, whose response in turn heightens the feelings of insecurity in the first country. Left to themselves, nations are liable to fall into that vicious trap. Whereas the American Strategic Defense Initiative (SDI) – the so-called 'star wars' programme – is officially designed to stop the nuclear arms race once and for all, I have my doubts about this approach and its success. In all probability, each side will concentrate on developing anti-satellite weapons in an endeavour to shoot down the other side's satellites. If anything, they will increase the number of nuclear weapons in order to swamp each other's defence systems.

Nothing is to be gained by attempting to apportion the blame for the horrendous escalation of arms: while the United States sets the pace in terms of quality, the Soviet Union does the same in terms of quantity. In my opinion, both super-powers are driven by the same impulses: the perception of a threat posed by the other side; the exaggeration of the other side's potential; and the process of technological elaboration, a blind process in which the technologists do not ask what happens when the other side does the same. It has been said that the super-powers are like five-year-olds playing chess: they have to be told that when one side has made a move, it's the other side's turn. Finally, one must not ignore the pressure mounted by the enormous research establishments both in the United States and the Soviet Union which exist simply to improve weaponry. It was the US Secretary of State for Defence, Caspar Weinberger, who told the American unions that a $10 billion cut in the military budget would 'deprive' 350,000 Americans of their jobs. This despite the fact that all studies have demonstrated the futility of investing public funds in the military sector in order to create jobs. If it were true that weapon systems have to be developed in order to generate employment, then the economic systems in East and West alike would be inhuman and absurd.

At present, the United States is incurring an enormous deficit by developing new weapon systems, while the people in the Soviet Union have had to endure an extended period of austerity. And the two super-powers are not the only runners in the race. Dozens of countries, which have not yet crossed the nuclear threshold and can ill afford the expense, are allocating still larger portions of their budgets to military projects. It should not be forgotten that conventional weapons are also becoming increasingly sophisticated and deadly, and that – even without the use of nuclear weapons – more than 135 wars have been waged since 1945, with more than 23 million casualties and 12 million refugees. None the less, it is the nuclear arms race which – for the first time in history – poses a hideous threat to millions of human beings, and to life as we know it on this planet.

At the risk of oversimplification, I wish to set military expenditure in perspective. The United States defence budget (comparable Soviet figures are not available but it may be assumed that they are of a similar magnitude) amounted to some $300 billion in 1984. This is equivalent to the total world military expenditure in 1977. Whereas not every country has increased its military outlay at the same rate, global military expenditure in 1985 and thereafter will almost certainly exceed $1,000 billion annually.

By way of contrast, the World Health Organization has spent about $83 *million* over ten years to eradicate smallpox in the world. Its malaria programme, which would have cost $450 million, has faltered for want of funds. These figures are paltry in comparison with the cost of armaments. So, for that matter, is the estimate of official development aid (ODA) to developing countries from all sources: in 1983 it came to no more than $33,600 million, or 3% of global military expenditure.

Disarmament thus lies at the very heart of the problem weighing upon the international order. Unfortunately, since World War II the very modest achievements have been more in the nature of arms limitation than disarmament, regulating competition and proscribing certain particularly undesirable developments rather than substantially reducing major weapon systems. It is now becoming increasingly clear that such an approach is wholly inadequate to stemming the tide of competition, where technological ingenuity tends to outstrip the pace of negotiation. If we continue to restrict ourselves to regulating the arms build-up, merely playing for time and treating the symptoms rather than the underlying causes, we shall run an increasing risk of pointing ourselves into a corner – of oblivion.

I fully recognize the special role of the great military powers and their responsibilities towards peace. The major nuclear-weapon states should obviously take the first steps towards nuclear disarmament. It is imperative that definitive and substantial progress should be made towards reducing the vast number of nuclear weapons, as well as towards controlling the dangerous and destabilizing influence of new weapon systems. The success of the cautious resumption of the East-West dialogue in Geneva in 1985 is also crucial to the creation of an atmosphere of international confidence in which further disarmament efforts can flourish.

Having said that, I nevertheless want to caution against linking arms control too closely to *détente*. During the seventies, when East-West negotiations were intensified, neither super-power reduced its military budget. This is not meant to detract from the validity of *détente*, but merely to indicate its limitations. It may be true that from a certain stage onwards political *rapprochement* induces a change in military trends away from re-armament and finally to disarmament. That stage, however, has not yet been reached. The only achievement has been a limited degree of arms control. Negotiations, however, are not without their merits: they should be continued, but *détente* should not be made contingent upon negotiation.

One lesson can be learnt from the seventies: responsibility for nuclear disarmament should not rest solely with the United States and the Soviet Union. Given the potential threat of mass destruction posed by nuclear weapons, other members of the international community, in particular the non-nuclear states, have an equally important interest in reducing nuclear arsenals and preventing the development of new weapon systems and stockpiles. One of the most important things we can do is mobilize world opinion about disarmament. Public awareness and public pressure are extremely important. Governments all over the world want to be re-elected. They have to take into account opinions shared by their constituents. The United Nations is still the only place where the fears and anger of the nations can be voiced on an international plane.

This was clearly demonstrated in 1978 at the first special session of the United Nations General Assembly devoted to disarmament, the largest and most representative conference ever held on that subject, where the nations of the world achieved consensus on a programme of action. Of all the decisions ever taken by the United Nations on disarmament, none offers a broader conceptual basis than the final document adopted at that session. Member states agreed that they would take concrete steps to move away from the abyss by seeking security not in the further accumulation of arms but in disarmament 'through a gradual but effective process beginning with the reduction in the present level of armaments'. Observers throughout the world admitted that the special session marked a milestone in the history of the United Nations. That no part of that programme has since been realized is not the fault of the world organization, but reflects the outcome of a dramatic change in the international climate.

The present and potential effectiveness of the United Nations is best put to use in a climate of mutual confidence and co-operation, and every endeavour must be made to induce such a climate. With all due respect for the numerous disarmament resolutions adopted every year by the General Assembly, it seems to me highly desirable to strengthen the role of the Geneva Disarmament Committee. This limited group of less than fifty countries could and should serve as a negotiating body, playing a useful and urgently needed umbrella function for major power negotiations and agreements.

The world organization should also serve as a major source of information and ideas in support of disarmament. Effective participation in the negotiating process is predicated upon the availability of data, particularly in the case of the Third World countries which lack adequate national research capabilities. Furthermore, it would only be logical for the United Nations to supervise agreements on the limitation of arms and the reduction of forces. Just as the inspectors of the International Atomic

Energy Agency have been able to convince the world that the plants covered by the non-proliferation treaty are not being misused for military purposes, a similar supervisory function could be extended to controlling arms limitation and other disarmament processes.

Over the years I have heard so many claims that, on account of its structure, the United Nations is incapable of achieving what the founding fathers enshrined in the Charter in the first flush of victory in June 1945: the determination 'that armed force shall not be used, save in the common interest'. In 1953 America's John Foster Dulles publicly stated. 'The UN Charter is thus a pre-atomic age document. In this sense, it was obsolete before it actually came into force. If the delegates there had known that the mysterious and immeasurable power of the atomic bomb would be available as a means of mass destruction, the provisions of the Charter dealing with disarmament and the regulation of armaments would have been far more emphatic and realistic . . .' Many efforts have been made to amend the Charter, and a Charter Review Committee has been in existence for many years. Although it would be an easy task to secure a two-thirds majority in the General Assembly in favour of a new Charter, because nobody really likes the power of veto, one of the organization's most controversial provisions, it would be equally impossible to obtain the consent of all five permanent members of the Security Council. In fact, I am convinced that were a new Charter to be drawn up today, it would in fact be less effective than the charter of 1945, when the peoples and governments of the world, still reeling from the shock of World War II, were more prepared to yield up certain parts of their sovereignty in favour of an international organization.

I must make one thing quite clear. The lack of success in the disarmament process is not due to the occasionally cumbersome UN machinery or the often emotional and protracted debates in its fora. The United Nations is as good or as bad as its members permit it to be. The lack of success is due simply to the attitude of the main parties, which currently lack the political will to take advantage of the international machinery at their disposal for the disarmament process.

To my mind, the nations of the world must be prepared to take much greater risks in their search for peace. They cannot continue to insist on their own unilateral arms proposals, demand airtight verification arrangements before concluding any nuclear arms agreements or reject reasonable verification facilities on their own territories. Unless there is mutual accommodation on these points, the arms race will simply continue to accelerate, and the world will move ever closer to febrile insecurity.

The nuclear powers must agree on a comprehensive test ban. This has to be done regardless of who at any one moment enjoys a lead in the development of this or that particular weapon or refinement. Such a ban would effectively inhibit the development of new weapon systems, since modern methods can detect underground tests with a high degree of accuracy. This would be an effective means of checking nuclear insanity. Such a measure, combined with SALT- or START-type Soviet-American agreements on intercontinental and intermediate-range nuclear weapons, would revive the world's hope of averting a nuclear holocaust.

Moreover, it is essential that the nuclear arms race should be confined to its present environment. The international community has negotiated agreements to exclude weapons of mass destruction from the Antarctic, outer space, and the seabed. At the time of their conclusion, these agreements were relatively easy to draw up, since the technology for exploiting those environments had hardly been developed. Particularly as regards outer space, that era has now come to an end. Rather than unleash a new confrontation in outer space, the international community should seek agreement on the use of internationally operated satellite systems to observe and verify compliance with nuclear arms agreements on earth.

Furthermore, constraints on the acquisition of nuclear weapons by non-nuclear weapon states must be strengthened. The Treaty on the Non-Proliferation of Nuclear Weapons is a self-denying ordinance for those states that have accepted it – 119 by the end of 1983. However, it is too much to expect all of them to comply with its terms indefinitely, or to expect the important non-signatories to adhere, as long as the nuclear-weapon states fail to pursue, in the spirit as well as in the letter, their obligations 'to carry out negotiations in good faith on effective measures relating to the cessation of the nuclear arms race at an early date and to nuclear disarmament, and to a treaty on general and complete disarmament under strict and effective international control'. It would be tragic if the line held in recent years against horizontal nuclear proliferation were now to disintegrate.

At the same time steps should be taken to strengthen the safeguards applied by the International Atomic Energy Agency so as to ensure that nuclear materials are not diverted to the clandestine production of weapons. Greater efforts must be made to exercise effective control over the increasing quantity of spent nuclear-reactor fuel.

The adoption of a number of ancillary measures relating to the limitation of nuclear and conventional weapons should be considered. Nuclear-free zones modelled on the Inter-American Tlatelolco Treaty should be established, the concept being extended perhaps to include other weapons by adopting 'zones of peace'. I realize, of course, that – despite the successful precedent in Latin America – the chances of establishing similar nuclear-free zones in Europe and other theatres of

East-West confrontation may be rather remote at the moment. But coming from a country whose neutrality in the heart of Europe has proven a successful stabilizing factor between East and West, I do not wish to abandon the idea of a nuclear *cordon sanitaire* across the centre of Europe.

As much as I would like to encourage verifiable mutual freezes on the development of nuclear weapons, on a temporary if not a permanent basis, I fear that, under the present circumstances, international agreements restricting the use, or at least the first use, of nuclear weapons will hardly be respected when most needed. A radical change in the politico-military environment is needed before such pledges can be kept.

As I have already emphasized, arms control cannot be viewed as a matter for the major powers alone. Regional arms races among developing countries, and the introduction of sophisticated weaponry to virgin territories, threaten to spark off conflagrations that might spread uncontrollably. Such matters should be of concern to regional inter-governmental organizations or, if they are unable to manage, to the United Nations.

An international agreement should also be drawn up to curb abuse in the international arms trade. Although this is a difficult and largely unexplored problem, it would be in the long-term interests of all parties concerned to prevent the disruption of regional balances of power by massive injections of new weapons.

The whole development is reminiscent of a Greek tragedy. Everybody watches the wheel of Fate as it turns, apparently incapable of putting a spoke in. The engine of unchecked armament is awesomely powerful, driven as it is by the quest for power. Whereas the measures I have indicated would provide relief in the short term, my ten years in office lead me to believe that, as long as states continue to pursue national interests through the potential threat of force, there is no lasting chance of salvation. At the threshold to an age in which rapid population growth, dwindling natural resources and an arsenal of weapons beyond compare will induce serious international tension, the nations of the world have to recognize that peace, security and economic well-being depend on the rapid reduction of arms. The Charter of the United Nations specifically talks of 'people' and not of governments. If leaders are unable to draw the all-important political conclusions, it will have to be the people who do so. More clearly than ever before, the people – regardless of frontiers – will have to make it quite clear that they do not want preparations for war, but designs for peace. Where politicians fail, popular reason, compassion and interest in survival can be an effective spur to political and intellectual innovation.

Epilogue

In the late summer of 1945, on the outskirts of a small town to the south of Vienna, my wife, my infant daughter Liselotte and I stood before the gutted remains of my parents' house. The war was over at last and, after countless trials and tribulations, we refugees had found our way home from the Austrian Alps. Our quest, however, was not yet over: we sought not only our parents but also a roof over our heads.

The appearance of my parents' house dashed all our hopes: a ruin scorched by fire with the wind whistling at will through the broken window-panes. Utterly dejected and in silence we crept around the garden to the back, convinced that nobody could be living within the shattered walls – until suddenly we heard voices, and a door opened. Within seconds we were being embraced by my father and mother: both had survived the war.

Forty years have passed since that day, which, after years of dictatorship and military service, marked for me the start to a new life: a life that at the outset had been filled with insecurity and anxiety about our future – a life that had also been marked by tragic events and experiences that were to determine my future thoughts and actions.

Many years later, after I had been elected by the United Nations to the highest office that the international community can bestow, I was repeatedly asked: where – behind all the impartiality of the office – were my real roots? Which principles had governed my life and work? What had guided me along the lonely path through the undergrowth of ideologies and vested interests?

Like all essential questions, no simple answer can be given. In retrospect, however, I feel that certain decisive influences can be traced: the history of Europe, my continent, and Austria, my homeland; my bitter experience of war; my study of law and my diplomatic career; as well as my belief in democracy and the tenets of Christianity. Together they helped me to observe the claims of my conscience amidst all the different and often conflicting advice submitted by my international advisers.

It was the tragic involvement of Europe in two world wars that engendered in me, as in so many of its citizens, the hope that national power politics could be overcome, and gave birth to my dream of a supranational world government.

It was Austria's indefatigable will to recover, and its active policy of neutrality, which showed me and my countrymen what solidarity and hard work can achieve and how bridges can be built between neighbours, however different their ideological concepts might be.

It was the war, with its hecatombs of innocent victims and ravages of minds and material, that convinced me of just how much men and women all over the world cherish one common desire: peace and security for themselves and their children.

It was my study of law that brought home to me the degree to which a peaceful family of nations is dependent upon the existence and observance of mutually accepted norms as well as upon an international mechanism for solving conflict.

It was in my diplomatic career, through which I had always hoped to contribute in some small way to furthering understanding between peoples and nations, that I learnt to overcome distrust and scepticism through personal contacts and patient dialogue free of all emotion.

It was allegiance to democracy, tempered by the experience of fascism, which taught me that in the final analysis nothing is weaker than dictatorship. During my countless journeys around the globe the shortcomings of democracy have not escaped my notice, yet nowhere have I found another system with a comparable degree of success and respect for human dignity.

Finally, it was my Christian faith that led me to recognize and, wherever possible, alleviate the spiritual and material misery of others. At the same time, there is nothing more profoundly disturbing than the use of religious fanaticism for political ends, regardless of denomination.

Years of close association with international politics has undoubtedly dampened the initial idealism of my youth and shaken my belief in the inevitable victory of international solidarity. The folly of those in power has often proved stronger than the aspirations of the people.

Yet I am not without hope – and this hope grows, the more I have an opportunity, during my lectures, seminars and talks, to meet, not so much those who exercise power, but the citizens of this world, in particular the young. I am a firm believer in the emerging groundswell of the people and have confidence in their silent but intensive rejection of the politics of the past. None the less, world peace will not come about through marches, speeches and prayers alone, but rather through those in power recognizing where the people's interests really lie. Sooner or later, some measure of national sovereignty will have to be relinquished in the interests of a broader global community. The first steps were taken forty years ago with the founding of the United Nations; many more must follow.

Acronyms

United Nations organizations, in order of appearance

UNO   United Nations Organization

UNDP   Development Programme

UNTSO   Truce Supervision Organization in Palestine

UNEF   Emergency Force

UNDOF   Disengagement Observer Force (Golan Heights)

UNFICYP   Force in Cyprus

UNTAG   Transition Assistance Group

UNCTAD   Conference on Trade and Development

UNICEF   International Children's Fund

UNESCO   Educational, Scientific and Cultural Organization

UNIFIL   Interim Force in Lebanon

UNITAR   Institute for Training and Research

UNIDO   Industrial Development Organization

UNRWA   Relief and Works Agency for Palestine Refugees in the Near East

Index